THE BEAST

AND THE

END-TIME EVENTS

DR. ZOMAYA S. SOLOMON

Solomons Computer Design, LLC
Ellicott City, Maryland 21042
ISBN 0-9717783-0-2

2002

The Beast and the End-Time Events / Zomaya S. Solomon

Library of Congress Cataloging-in-Publication Data

ISBN 0-9717783-0-2

Cover Design: David W. Grimes (Brother-in-Law)

          : Cindy Solomon (Daughter-in-Law)

Printed in the United States of America.

Zomaya S. Solomon (©)

Solomons Computer Designs, LLC

To my wife.

For your fathomless love, for your unending support, for your daily concern about our family, and for your faithfulness to the Lord, I wholeheartedly dedicate this book to you, Nancy Jane Solomon.

ACKNOWLEDGMENT

The idea of composing this book: *The Beast And the End-Time Events*, came about from an invitation for teaching a Sunday School Class at Chapelgate Presbyterian Church, Marriottsville, Maryland. Invited to deliver a series of lectures on the Beast, I declared on one occasion to the class — partially in jest — to develop the work into a book. In an uproar, the class unanimously encouraged me to do so.

Many thanks are due to my wife, Nancy, who enabled me to complete the work on time. Twice, she assisted me in proofreading the entire manuscript and supported me in checking its final draft. To my daughter-in-law, Cindy Solomon at Solomons Computer Designs, LLC, for her placing the manuscript into PageMaker, making it camera-ready for print. Many thanks are likewise due to Mr. Helmut E. Schrank who read the manuscript twice and made some beneficial suggestions. Thanks also are due to David Grimes, my Brother-in-law, who assisted Cindy in the cover design.

I do trust, however, that this book, having presented a large number of new ideas and interpretations, will enlighten and edify every believer that reads it. To God be the glory!

Zomaya S. Solomon

THE WINGED BULL

Revelation 4:6,7

And before the throne there was a sea of glass like unto crystal: and in the midst of the throne, and round about the throne, were four beasts full of eyes before and behind. And the first beast was like a lion, and the second beast like a calf, and the third beast had a face as a man, and the fourth beast was like a flying eagle.

TABLE OF CONTENTS

MAPS

PREFACE

1. THE JUSTIFICATION FOR this book rests upon the fact that it embodies a large number of totally new interpretations. Many old and worn out illuminations, that have been hashed and rehashed in almost every book on prophecy, are now replaced by some new logical considerations which the author has elaborately provided. Great men of God, at least within the last century, have made ample attempts to produce reasonable explanations and suitable clarification for every item of prophecy; their diagnoses, however, could not have been altogether plausible, because many of these interpretations have not been based upon an ordinary and rational interpretation of the Word of God.

2. The new approach we have pursued in this book provides a new understanding of prophecy that will gladden the very heart of the believing reader. Many of these Bible scholars and interpreters of the prophetic message have been a great blessing to the heart of this author and, I believe, to the heart of many others; yet, a goodly number of their explanations were usually highly played out and reiterated over again by every writer who attempted to make, supposedly, his illustrations understandable. Some of the interpretations provided, in one book or another, were simply a product of extraordinary and exotic exaggerations, misunderstandings, and outright misinterpretations.

3. The Church of Jesus Christ is a vast and well-rooted Church, both corporeally and spiritually. While, admittedly, not all the many branches of Christendom, over the entire world today, are faithful to the Word of God, yet, many such bodies of believers are equally burdened for a proper interpretation of prophecy. These churches deserve ample praise for their works and, particularly, their interpretation of the prophetic message. Any prophetic passage that is not interpreted according to the Scriptures, is neither acceptable nor praiseworthy of the Church of our Saviour. (See Appendix B).

4. The subject matter dealt with here is not inherently simple, to be taken lightly, nor is it going to be demonstrated according to the usual norms of interpretation. The book of Daniel is basically interpreted by the book of Revelation; the book of Revelation contains the interpretations of the book of Daniel. Despite the different dispensations and circumstances of each writer, the two books complement one another considerably. It is a well-known fact that, by the same token, the Old Testament is interpreted by the New; and the New Testament is concealed in the Old. And the two Books — the book of Daniel and the book of Revelation — although both apocalyptic in nature, to some extent, are a good example for the rest of the Bible. The interpreter must, at all times, however, make every effort to take into account both Testaments when he is interpreting a prophetic passage.

5. It is interesting to observe that the entire Bible is embedded with passages of prophecy. Every book and almost every chapter of it are likewise hammered in with some sort of a prophetic passage or communication. In fact, one of the Bible's proof for its inerrancy is supported by the already fulfilled message of its prophecy. And the fact that its prophetic passages are many and are widely strewn over the two Testaments, makes the Bible's burden even greater in support of its inerrancy. It is this inerrancy — both verbal and plenary — that allows us to delve deeply into the Word of God seeking the hidden meanings of the Scriptures. And the Holy Spirit enables us to do just that.

6. In our study of prophecy, particularly for this work, we have convened a relatively large number of books on the subject (see Bibliography). While not every book mentioned is quoted from; most are, however, either fully read by the author or perused through to some extent to provide a first hand review and learned familiarity with the subject at hand. Fortunately, this author, since early age, had always studied prophecy, taught it in Sunday School Classes and, for several years in a row, taught it at the Arlington Bible Institute. While the author does not claim to be perfect in his knowledge about the subject, he is grateful to the Lord who has, indeed, enabled him to understand what is proper and what is necessary for writing this book that many others will be blessed by it. All in all, I am greatly indebted to all the authors of the books sited in the bibliography and in many other booklets and pamphlets that have not been mentioned.

7. Throughout this book, the King James Version of the Bible is employed. On one occasion only, a personal translation, based upon the Syriac *Peshitta* and on the Biblical Aramaic, is employed (Chapter 2, paragraph 27). Many other Bible translations are equally competent and valid and have been consulted occasionally. By and large, we have steadfastly adhered to the King James Version. Likewise, we have taken the authorship of both books — Daniel and Revelation — to be authentic, needing no argument or defense. By the same token, the entire Bible is believed, particularly by this author, to enjoy a verbatim and plenary inerrancy in its original.

8. As has my style always been in writing, I have composed this book in a rather simple, clear-cut and discernible English so that a large majority of readers may fully understand its contents. Moreover, time and again, I have repeated certain aspects of some subject matter, making sure that the reader will not find himself or herself lost in the thoughts presented in the book. The believing Christian must find the general content of this book very persuasive and factual. God's child must find the entire narration of this book understandable, and how every event in its content develops and leaves its impressions on the reader without much ado.

9. The entire book is presented in paragraphs that are almost equal in size, thus making the work quite different from the norm. These paragraphs are numbered through an emboldened digit. Most every paragraph is complete in itself; rarely a paragraph may be a continuation of the paragraph that preceded. The entire work is divided into 18 chapters; usually, each chapter is divided into a number of sub-topics. In addition to the introduction, there are four appendices attached to the end of the book. The first deals with the method of interpretation; the second appendix presents the unordinary interpretation of certain passages of the Scriptures; the third offers a list of some of the new interpretations that are different from those provided by any other book; the fourth appendix gives us a brief insight into the act of terrorism that struck September 11, 2001, the two World Trade Centers in New York. It would be advisable that the reader should first read these four appendices before starting to read this book.

Zomaya S. Solomon

THE BEAST

AND THE

END-TIME EVENTS

INTRODUCTION

I. The Beast

1. THE END-TIME BEAST is an enigma, to say the least. He is first mentioned in Daniel. He joins the ten horns of Daniel, Chapter 7, Verse 8, and the seven kings of Revelation, Chapter 17, Verse 11. It is apparent from the last reference that the "seven mountains, on which the woman sitteth" of Verse 9, are "the seven heads [leaders]," of the same verse. These seven heads are also synonymous with the "seven kings" of Verse 10, to whom of Verse 11, the Beast joins, from outside of the Revived Roman Empire, as king number eight. From Revelation, Chapter 17, Verse 12, we learn that just before the Beast appears, or comes to join in and to take over the European Empire, the ten horns, which are ten kings, are about ready to receive power, to rule, each of them "for one hour," or a specific term of time with the Beast.

2. At this juncture of affairs, something unusual happens; the ten kings, possibly under pressure from the Beast, the little horn of Daniel, unanimously agree to surrender their power to him. The first step the Beast takes, it appears, is to consolidate his power over the Revived Roman Empire. He, first, ousts three of the ten horns, or kings, from exercising power outside of the ten-nation European General Council, and then he forms a Presidium, or an Upper House. From Revelation, Chapter 17, Verses 10 and 11, we learn that five of the remaining seven kings "are fallen," that is, have already completed their terms of rule, of possibly "one hour" or one year each. "One [king, number six] is [incumbent, still in power]." "[T]he other [one, number seven,] is not yet come," that is, he has not as yet assumed power. And just as his term arrives and he takes power, he, along with the rest of the ten kings, will, for an unknown reason, expeditiously surrender that power to the Beast.

3. During the Tribulation Period, the Beast, who is the Antichrist, will play an important role in the affairs of mankind. He is a personage who will excel in his disposition and in his worldly character, over possibly all other secular men who ever lived on the face of the earth. Within this

Satanic Trinity, he exemplifies the Lord Jesus Christ, whom he will as closely as imaginable, imitate, and will attempt to deceive mankind to the very end. He will be the choicest among men and will accomplish a great deal for the depraved humanity. Alas, his end is sure — death in the pit of fire; for eternity will be his "unresting" place.

4. As to the identity of the Beast, no one can tell. Just prior to his introduction to the world, by none other than the Dragon himself (Rev. 13:3-5), he will live almost clandestinely among the ordinary children of men. He is just another world leader, another statesman. When the Dragon finally declares him to humanity and proclaims him to be the new savior of mankind, only then will the people of the world recognize him as who he is, the Beast. But, Alas for him; the Church of the Saviour is no longer on the earth; it is now already in the heavenly places, safe and sound with her Bridegroom, where this Wicked One will do no more harm to her.

5. In the King James Version of the Bible, the term "beast" is applied in three different ways: First, to signify ordinary animals; secondly, to describe the four personages which are constantly — day and night — at the throne of God. In some Bible translations, the word "beast" is often translated as the "creature," or "the living creature." Thirdly, it is used twice to describe the two evil personages: the Beast proper and the False Prophet. Specifically, the latter term "Beast" means that this personage is highly distinguished and magnanimous among the human race; he unusually surpasses in his personal apportionments any ordinary member of the human race.

6. In Biblical Aramaic of the Old Testament, the term used for the Beast is, **kheva** *beast*, and its plural, **khevan** *beasts*. In the New Testament Greek, the term is *therion*. Both terms mean one and the same. Some English translations have used the word "creature" to distinguish it from an animal. The Beast differs not in his humanistic inclinations, however, from an animal. God had made King Nebuchadnezzar a beast to taste the degradation of an animal, a beast. He made him become like an ox and live among the animals of the prairies for seven years.

II. Nimrod, the Mighty Hunter

The Gentile World Power did not begin with Nimrod nor with the Assyrian Empire. Nimrod has been vilified in prophecy for over a century and more. It is not known, although one could guess, how this man of God becomes willfully denigrated. Strangely enough, his name is associated with legendaries, myths and fictional events of which the Bible makes no mention whatsoever. Nimrod is depicted, in a western movie, as throwing an arrow towards the heaven for the purpose of shooting down the God of heaven. He is the one who supposedly led the people of the earth to rebel against God and to build a tower that would reach heaven thereby making a name for himself and his people.

8. Four times the name of Nimrod has been mentioned in the Scripture: twice in the book of Genesis, where it is said of him: "Even as Nimrod the mighty hunter before the Lord" (Gen. 10:9). Once, the proper name Nimrod is mentioned in the book of I Chronicles; here, a quotation from the book of Genesis is made about him: "And Cush begot Nimrod: he began to be mighty upon the earth" (I Chro. 1:10). Micah also makes a mention of Nimrod, where he equates "the land of Nimrod" with "the land of Assyria," saying: "and the land of Nimrod in the entrances thereof" (Mic. 5:6). Throughout the Bible, the very language about Nimrod is altogether positive and complimentary: *He began to be mighty upon the earth*; this could not be said about someone who opposes God.

9. Interestingly, in no place in the Scriptures, has Nimrod been mentioned as having an unholy disposition before the Lord. And the Hebrew preposition, **li-fné** *before*, signifies the good character this man had before the Lord. For if Nimrod had a bad character, the Hebrew preposition employed would have been **néged** *against*, or some other such negative and irreconcilable preposition. The Scripture quoted and transliterated here is: **'Al-ken ye'amar k-Nimrod gibbor s'ayyid li-fné Y(e)hvah** *"Wherefore it is said, [e]ven as Nimrod who was a mighty hunter before the Lord"* (Gen. 10:9). The fact that his proper name, Nimrod, implies *rebel*, has nothing to do with the man's own character. It should be remembered that he did not chose that name for himself; it was given to him upon his birth. Nevertheless, if he was a rebel, then his rebellion was against the wickedness of his day. "The voice of one crying in the wilderness, Prepare ye the way of the Lord, make his path straight" (Matt. 3:3^b).

III. The Assyrian Empire

10. Under no circumstance, can Assyria be counted among the nations of the Gentile World Power. There are many Scriptural reasons for this. To begin with, the Gentile World Power began with the extensive Empire of King Nebuchadnezzar, who had already conquered and incorporated the Assyrian Empire. The Babylonian Monarch had just made an image of gold and had it placed in the plain of Dura to be worshipped. Historically, this New Babylonian Empire, which God identified to be the beginning of the Gentile World Powers, superseded the Assyrian Empire. Scriptural references abound about the Assyrians; many of these verses often brought a condemnation upon the arrogant, vainglorious, and mighty warrior nation. But this "burden," in Hebrew **ha-Massa'** against Assyria was not different from those that were predicted by the same prophets against Israel, against Jerusalem, against Samaria, and against many other neighboring nations.

11. Approximately one hundred and fifty years after the Hebrew missionary's message was a stunning success in Nineveh, the great capital city of Assyria; Nahum, another Hebrew prophet, foretold the destruction of this very Assyrian Empire. Having delinquently abandoned the salvation the people of Nineveh had initially very fervently adopted through Jonah's preaching, the empire came to an end. As fiercely as Nahum could make his calamitous prophecies against Nineveh, almost that fast, the Assyrian nation had forgotten their glorious salvation and had almost vanished from the surface of the earth. Nor was Israel willing to send follow-up "missionaries" to the capital city of Nineveh, to establish the faith the Assyrians had exercised in Jehovah's message of deliverance. Accordingly, that great empire fell and the Assyrian nation, which had ruled over the Middle East for almost one thousand years, crumbled and almost disappeared from the picture immediately. So, Nahum says:

Woe to the bloody city [Nineveh]! It is all full of lies and robbery; the prey departeth not; [t]he noise of a whip, and the noise of the rattling of the wheels, and of the pransing horses, and of the jumping chariots. . . . Nineveh is laid waste: who will bemoan her? whence shall I seek comforters for thee? Thy shepherds slumber, O king of Assyria: thy nobles shall dwell the dust: thy people is scattered upon the mountains, and no man gathereth them (Nah. 3:1, 2, 7ᵇ, 18).

12. Despite what had happened to Assyria, the Assyrian people were the first nation to accept Christianity in the very early days of that Faith. Armenian claims notwithstanding, the Assyrian missionaries, often called Nestorians, were the first who converted the Armenians to Christ, created an alphabet for the Armenian language, and put that language in writing. Assyrian missionaries roamed all over the East; beginning with the Mesopotamian plains, going on to Persia, Afghanistan, Pakistan, India, Mongolia, China, Korea and Japan.[1] They also carried the Word of Life to the entire Arabian Peninsula. Until the time of Mohammed, about the year 630 A.D., there was a Christian kingdom in Hijaz, a province in today's Western Saudi Arabia.

13. For more than one millennia, the Assyrian Nestorian Church was, most probably, the largest church ever in the entire world. In China alone, some forty Bishoprics existed that covered the entire nation; the majority of these Bishops were native Chinese and only a few of the remaining were Assyrians. In India there still exists today the Assyrian Nestorian Church in Malabar, where Old Aramaic (Syriac) is still taught and in some ecclesiastical circles even spoken. Since the invention of the printing press, most Aramaic church books used in Mesopotamia were printed in India. Even today the church at Trichur, Malabar, is a Bishopric attached to the Assyrian Nestorian Church whose Patriarch resides today in the United States of America.

14. Quoting from an article written by Benjamin George Wilkinson, Ph.D., published in the Assyrian magazine *Nineveh*[2], the author says: "The remarkable fact is that in the face of titanic difficulties the Church of the East was able to maintain through [the] ages such wonderful unity of belief and soundness of Biblical living. '. . . the Nestorian church has always cherished a remarkable veneration for the Holy Scriptures. Their Rule of Faith has been, and is, the written [W]ord of God'. . . . Here is a list of the doctrines of the branch of the Assyrian Christians in India which is called the St. Thomas Christians.[3] Those believers —

1. Condemned the pope's supremacy,
2. Affirmed that the Roman Church had departed from the faith,
3. Denied transubstantiation,
4. Condemned the worship of images,
5. Made no use of oil,
6. Denied purgatory,
7. Would not admit of spiritual affinity,
8. Knew nothing of auricular confessions,
9. Never heard of extreme unction,
10. Permitted the clergy to marry,
11. Denied that matrimony and consecration were sacraments,
12. Celebrated with leavened bread and consecrated with prayer."

15. According to Isaiah's prophecy, Assyrians will yet be gathered together (Is. 11:16), and, along with Egypt and Israel (Is. 19:23-25), a triumvirate state covering also Assyria will be created by none other than the Lord God of heaven, Himself. The Almighty brings about this Tripartite Union for a purpose; to strengthen Israel through such an alliance and to make it more effective in its dealings with the people of the world during the Millennial Kingdom. Under the blessings of God Almighty, the threefold new nation will exercise great power and many exploits that will bring glory to God the Father. Assyria will never experience a final demise such as the one that Babylon experienced.

16. It is interesting to observe that the Bible scholars and prophecy interpreters today usually pay scant attention to the two important passages of prophecy recorded in Isaiah about Assyria. The first portion of the prophetic scripture is found in Isaiah, Chapter 11, Verse 16. Here, the prophet says that a "remnant of his people [Assyrians], which shall be left from Assyria" will be gathered together in preparation for the future Tri-partite Union. That this "remnant" is not a remnant of Israel, the grammatical comparative proposition that follows makes it amply clear. The second portion is found in Isaiah, Chapter 19, Verses 23-25, where the union is already established and God blesses that union individually.

IV. America in Prophecy

17. Many Bible scholars, who deal with the prophetic message of the Scripture, have raised this momentous question: "Does America figure in the prophetic message of the Bible, especially with respect to the Revived Roman Empire and to the end-time events?" With respect to this all important question, different propositions have been put forth, here and there, and in good faith. Gromacki rightfully states: "This means that he [the Beast] will be a European or possibly an American (since the United States is basically an extension of European ideas and peoples)."[4] However, no convincing answer has thus far been provided. For one thing, unless a prophetic proposition is, implicitly or explicitly, attested to by the Scriptures, it can not stand on its own feet. No one can be dogmatic about an interpretation, unless that interpretation is corroborated by the Scriptures.

18. America is still the mightiest country in the world and a good candidate to provide leadership to the people of the world. Right now, in these very days, our media is complaining, because of the world economic down turn, primarily in the far East, and that our merchant ships are returning to their bases usually empty. These ships sail full of cargo and return home mostly empty. This is primarily resulting, they say, from the stock market crash in the far-eastern countries, such as Japan, Indonesia, Korea, etc. We today conduct trade with almost every country on the globe. While we can forego such a trade with many countries worldwide, especially the smaller ones; these countries themselves, however, cannot afford to stop trading with us. Their trade with us is almost a matter of life and death to them.

19. America, being the only superpower left, has a unique opportunity to extend its hegemony over the entire world. Reading Revelation,

Chapter 18, one finds that no other nation in the world fits the description provided in that chapter about the political commercial Babylon. "Babylon the great is fallen, is fallen, and is become the habitation of devils, and the hold of every foul spirit, and a cage of every unclean and hateful bird" (Rev. 18:2). To think that this Babylon, which is mentioned in Chapter 18 of the book of Revelation, is the same as the Old Babylon — of which some prominent segments are now reconstructed — is as ridiculous as to expect the mystery Babylon of Chapter 17 of the same book, to be the same. The term Babylon is used symbolically in both chapters: in Chapter 17, Babylon stands for the Apostate Church and likewise for the Apostate City of Rome as the headquarter of that church; in Chapter 18, Babylon is employed symbolically for the political, commercial Babylon the worship of which, particularly during the last half of the Tribulation Period, centers around the person of the Beast and his image.

20. If there ever was a country so degenerate, so full of evil works, and so prone to engender and proliferate evil, America today is, unfortunately, that country. On the one hand, America is, indeed, blessed nowadays with a great deal of spiritual benefits. We still can lift up our eyes toward the heavens and thank God for His bountiful mercies upon us. Yet, this very America is slipping downward and fast, for which decline there appears to be hardly any remedy. When the people have lost their wholesome and positive conscience, any evil works can be perpetrated by them without any injured feelings. This is where America is now; the majority of its people, it appears, have lost their wholesome conscience.

21. The overthrow of this Babylon will be immediate and as quick as the lightening. "For in one hour so great riches is come to nought. And every shipmaster, and all the company in ships, and sailors, and as many as trade by sea, stood afar off, [a]nd cried when they saw the smoke of her burning, saying, 'What city is like unto this great city!'" (Rev. 18:17, 18). Alas, it is now all gone! It is gone, because it has martyred God's people, the precious believers whom the Almighty God had saved through the precious blood of His Son. Babylon had thought that it could persecute the people of God with impunity, that it would kill the saints of the Most High without retribution. God is mighty and is capable of inflicting severe judgment upon her for her evil. The heaven itself will rejoice over this Babylon's punishment.

> *Rejoice over her, thou heaven, and ye holy apostles and prophets; for God hath avenged you on her. And in her was found the blood of prophets, and of saints, and of all that were slain upon the earth (Rev. 18:20, 24).*

V. Reconstruction of Babylon

22. Some Bible scholars believe that, at the end time, the old Babylon will be resurrected once again, from where the Beast will direct his affairs. The reconstructed Babylon will become the seat of his headquarters. Yet, the Scriptures tell us plainly that when God had allowed Babylon to be destroyed, it was destroyed once and for all. The Bible predicts the destruction of a literal Babylon. "And Babylon, the glory of kingdoms, the beauty of the Chaldees' excellency, shall be as when God overthrew Sodom and Gomorrah" (Is. 13:19). Now Sodom and Gomorrah have not and will not be ever reconstructed; likewise, the literal city of Babylon will never be reconstructed, ever. The literal Babylon will never see the day light of God again.

23. It would be impossible to rebuild Babylon, especially because the city sings a different tune today from the tune that it sang in its heydays. As the first Gentile World Power, its glory, its supremacy, and its unending oppression are gone for ever. Its inhabitants today have changed from Chaldean Aramaeans to Arabs, who see no glory in the city's renewal save for the purpose of archeological justification and tourism. Therefore, Isaiah and Jeremiah prophesy:

> *Come down, and sit in the dust, O virgin daughter of Babylon, sit on the ground: there is no throne, O daughter of the Chaldeans: for thou shalt no more be called tender and delicate (Is. 47:1).*

> *How is the hammer of the whole earth cut asunder and broken! [H]ow is Babylon become a desolation among the*

*nations! I have laid a snare for thee, and thou art also taken,
O Babylon, and thou was not aware: thou art found, and also
caught, because thou hast striven against the Lord (Jer. 50:23,
24).*

VI. The State of the Jews in Exile

24. Many interpreters of the Bible prophecy and novice Sunday
School teachers believe that the Jews who were in Babylon were held
there captives. Such a view grossly falsifies the conditions of the Jewish in
that country. While, admittedly, they were taken captive to Babylon; but
once there, they were, however, released to live freely and to do whatever they wanted. They competed in everyday life and even in government positions and excelled. It should be remembered that the Jews were
not the only people taken captive to Babylon; people of many other nationalities were, likewise, carried to that country. King Nebuchadnezzar
of Babylon was not an ignoramus monarch to have recommended to his
servant to include among the students some of the Hebrew youngsters to
be trained to take over the affairs of the state. We read in Daniel the
following:

> *And the king spake unto Ashpenaz the master of his eu-
> nuchs, that he should bring certain of the children of Israel,
> and of the king's seed, and of the princes; [c]hildren in whom
> was no blemish, but well favoured, and skilful in all wisdom,
> and cunning in knowledge, and understanding science, and
> such as had ability in them to stand in the king's palace, and
> whom they might teach the learning and the tongue of the
> Chaldeans (Aramaic). . . . Now among these were of the chil-
> dren of Judah, Daniel, Hananiah, Mishael, and Azariah (Dan.
> 1:3, 4, 6).*

25. The biblical history tells us that Daniel and his companions, while
attending the Babyl0nian Royal Institute of Languages, had made great
strides in their learning the language of the Chaldeans and had achieved
prominence in government. Under Nebuchadnezzar, Daniel became the

president of the province of Babylon itself, the seat of the Empire. Likewise, for his three companions — Hananiah, Mishael, and Azariah — Daniel requested to be appointed under himself to serve "over the affairs of the province of Babylon." For we read in the book of Daniel the following:

> Then the king made Daniel a great man, and gave him
> many gifts, and made him ruler over the province of Babylon,
> and chief of the governors over all the wise men of Babylon.
> Then Daniel requested of the king, and he set Shadrach,
> Meshach, and Abed-nego, over the affairs of the province of
> Babylon: but Daniel sat in the gate of the king (Dan. 2:48,
> 49).

26. Secular history tells us that the Jews, of whom a large number stayed in Babylon after some of them returned to Jerusalem, soon became prosperous enjoying their riches in Mesopotamia. A very learned community of the Jewish people developed at Babylon establishing an independent Jewish culture and writings including the Babylonian Talmud with its two branches: Mishnah and Gemara, both of which presented the commentary of the biblical Hebrew in Aramaic, the language the Jews of Babylon spoke at this time. Thanks to these Jews of Mesopotamia, today we have the rudiments of the grammar of Babylonian Aramaic: An Aramaic completely presented and put to use; an Aramaic which we can hold in our hands and learn it.

27. For the writing of the Babylonian Aramaic, the learned Jews of Babylon borrowed, at the time, what they called **ktav merubba'** *the square writing*, or also **ktav Ashshuriy** *the Assyrian characters*,[5] because it was first used in Assyria for the Assyrian Aramaic. Unfortunately, we have nothing of substance preserved today of the writings of the Assyrian Aramaic language of that day. It is this Assyrian Aramaic that has not come down to us in writing; it is this Assyrian Aramaic that the present-day Assyrians, who are dispersed all over the world, speak today. Unaware of the fact that they today are still speaking the same Neo-Aramaic of Assyria, the language spoken by their forefathers and which is not an off-shoot of Syriac.

CHAPTER 1

THE BEAST'S BEGINNINGS

. . . to the intent that the living may know that the most High God ruleth in the kingdom of men, and giveth it to whomsoever he will, and setteth up over it the basest of men (Dan. 4:17^b).

I. The First Image

1. "NEBUCHADNEZZAR THE KING of Babylon made an image of gold, whose height was three score cubits, and the breadth thereof six cubits: he set it up in the plain of Dura, in the Province of Babylon" (Dan. 3:1). And the king commanded that all "peoples, nations and languages" fall down and worship the golden image. "And whoso falleth not down and worshippeth shall the same hour be cast into the midst of a burning fiery furnace" (Dan. 3:6). Such were the orders this mighty conqueror published throughout his Empire with respect to this image. Through the establishment of this idol, most likely unbeknown to the king, the Great Monarch, King Nebuchadnezzar, laid down the very first foundation of the Gentile World Empire.

2. In Daniel, Chapter 2, we read a very interesting story. King Nebuchadnezzar, the great king of Babylon, had a dream which troubled him considerably. Having forgotten the dream, he now urgently desired to know both the dream and the interpretation of it from the wise men of his kingdom. Not an easy matter, indeed! Having failed to make known to the king the dream and its interpretation, the wise men of Babylon were about to face destruction from the troubled monarch (Dan. 2:12). After much prayer and supplication with his three faithful companions — Hananiah, Mishael, and Azariah — to Daniel, God's servant, the dream was revealed and the secret of its interpretation.

3. According to Daniel, Nebuchadnezzar's dream was about a great and bright image that was, at the same time, extremely terrible. Daniel describes the image to Nebuchadnezzar as follows: "This image's head was of fine gold, his breast and his arms of silver, his belly and his thighs of brass, [h]is legs of iron, his feet part of iron and part of clay" (Dan. 2:32-33). By way of interpretation, Daniel said to the king of Babylon, "Thou [along with thy Empire] art this head of gold" (Dan. 2:38). He then provides, by way of description, the identity of the other three powers that would follow the Babylonian Empire, which were: the Medo-Persian, the Grecian, and the Roman Empires.

4. Through the erection of this image of gold in his far-flung dominion, as a new idol for universal worship and as a substitute for the worship of the God of heaven, the king of Babylon initiated the very first ungodly Gentile World Empire. Through the mouth of Daniel, God had on several occasions graciously warned Nebuchadnezzar of his folly, but to no avail. Despite God's unceasing efforts to reveal to this Monarch of Babylon who the real King *is*, and despite the king's own hollow confession that God's "kingdom is an everlasting kingdom, and his dominion is from generation to generation" (Dan. 4:3), Nebuchadnezzar, callously and carelessly spurned the oft repeated heavenly warning, "that the most High ruleth [and still rules] in the kingdom of men" (Dan. 4:17).

5 This bewildered "king of kings" — to whom "the God of heaven [had given] a kingdom, power, and strength, and glory" (Dan. 2:37) — heeded not the solemn warning. He blatantly refused to submit himself, his power, and his dominion to the true "KING OF KINGS AND LORD OF LORDS" (Rev. 19:16[b]). Through his foolhardy command that all "peoples, nations, and languages" worship the dumb idol, the beginning of an ungodly, yet highly organized Gentile World Power was, for the first time, established on the earth.

II. Nimrod and the Assyrian Empire

6. The seeds of this rebellious Gentile World Power did not start with Nimrod, as some would have you believe. On the contrary, Nimrod was a very courageous rebel — if rebel he was. His rebellion was only against the wickedness and ungodliness of his day. Because of his godly stand, he became known as a mighty hunter **li-fné** *before* the Lord. If we ignore the appropriate meaning of this Hebrew preposition, *before*, and attempt to translate it adversely, such as *against*; in that event, we must reverse the preposition's meaning in a limitless number of cases in the entire Old Testament, wherever it appears. Since we cannot have it both ways, then, at least with respect to Nimrod, it must be translated the way it signifies, *before*. We read in Genesis the following:

> *And Cush begot Nimrod: he began to be a mighty one in the earth. He was a mighty hunter before the Lord: wherefore it is said, [e]ven as Nimrod the mighty hunter before the Lord (Gen. 10:8, 9).*

> *And Cush begot Nimrod: he began to be mighty upon the earth (I Chro. 1:10).*

7. Nor did this Satan-inspired World Empire originate with the beginnings of the dreadful and now obsolete Assyrian Empire, as others have suggested.[1] Despite its past wickedness, Assyria has yet a vital and pre-ordained role to play during the Millennial Age (Isa. 11:16; 19:23-25; 27:13). God who called Assyria "the rod of mine anger" as He used it against His own people, Israel (Is. 10:5), and for whose repentance, deliverance, and salvation, the prophet Jonah was sent, He will yet, in that day, forgive this nation just as He will forgive and redeem the Jewish nation. As He did with the redeemed Israel — along with the first-smitten and then-healed Egypt (Is. 19:20) — God will forgive and restore Assyria to its greatness in order to make out of the three restored nations — restored physically and spiritually — a triumvirate of nations to become a blessing in the midst of the land, in the midst of the earth (Is. 19:23-25).

8. Of this future restoration of Assyria and its establishment as a third nation in a heavenly instituted alliance, this is what the prophet Isaiah says:

> *In that day shall there be a highway out of Egypt to Assyria, and the Assyrian shall come into Egypt, and the Egyptian into Assyria, and the Egyptians shall serve with the*

Assyrians. In that day shall Israel be the third with Egypt and with Assyria, even a blessing in the midst of the land (Isa. 19:23-25).

9. The restoration and revival of a remnant of Assyria, at the end times, although obliquely declared, is yet prophetically cited and reinforced by the prophet Isaiah. "And there shall be a highway for the remnant of his people, which shall be left from Assyria; like as it was to Israel in the day that he came up out of the land of Egypt" (Is. 11:16). Structurally, the comparison made in this verse is clearly between the two situations: "those left from Assyria," at the end time, and "those left from Israel," in the day that God brought him up out of the land of Egypt. The two terms, "His people" and "Israel" are the two components with their statements compared; they are compared in their situation and for the glory of their future.

10. Parenthetically, it would be interesting to observe how the Lord Jesus Christ made refrence to the acient Assyrians of Nineveh when He said to the unbelievable Jews: "The men of Nineveh shall rise in judgement with this generation, and shall condemn it: because they repented at the preaching of Jonas; and, behold, a greater than Jonas is here: (Matt. 12:41). Our blessed Lord spoke of these Ninevites as those who would judge the people of God and condemn them for their unbelieving in Jesus their King. The unbelieving Jews rejected the King and His kingdom; the day will soon come, however, when that kingdom will become a Triumvirate of three specally chosen nations: The believing remnants of Assyria, Egypt and Isreal whom the Lord God will bless indeed.

Whom the Lord of hosts shall bless, saying, Blessed be Egypt my people, and Assyria the work of my hand, and Isreal mine inheritance" (Is. 19:25).

III. Lucifer's Rebellion

11. In reality, the beginning of this ungodly Gentile World Power, the precursor of the wicked kingdom of the Antichrist, took place in heaven, in the very presence of the Almighty God, and is rooted in the rebellion of

Lucifer himself (Is. 14:12-14). It was later implanted among the children of men through the Serpent's triumphant beguiling of Adam and Eve in the Garden of Eden (Gen. 3:1-7).

12. One would think that after Adam's painful experience in the Garden and his expulsion from God's presence, man would have learned a valid lesson. Unfortunately, this has not been the case. And despite the fact that God has prepared an expedient way for reconciliation (Rom. 5:10), the majority of mankind has preferred to remain in darkness and to disregard the heavenly call. As though the teeming millions that have since blindly followed the Son of Perdition are not enough, the Antichrist fervently continues to snatch away from among the children of men as many souls as he can prevent them from entering the heavenly Kingdom.

13. As the counterfeit of Christ, who is the perfect and absolute embodiment of God's holiness and righteousness, the Beast, it should be pointed out, is likewise the absolute embodiment of Satan and his blasphemies. As the Father's will on the earth is accomplished through the incarnate Son, Satan's wicked works are likewise accomplished on the earth through the "incarnate" Beast and his human emissaries. Just as Jesus is Life Himself, so also is the Devil, the very Death itself. For we read in the book of Hebrews the following:

> *Forasmuch then as the children are partakers of flesh and blood, he also himself likewise took part of the same; that through death he might destroy him that had the power of death, that is, the devil; And deliver them who through fear of death were all their lifetime subject to bondage [of death] (Heb. 2:14-15).*

14. Satan, in order to frustrate and deprive Christ of His rightful position to re-establish the Davidic Kingdom on the earth and to reclaim His throne, is presently in utter frenzy and indignation against the Holy One of Israel. He must now hasten to establish his own humanistic kingdom and offer it to this wicked world gratis before Christ's descent to the Mount of Olives. Indeed, the Devil's ultimate struggle has not so much been against our inconsequential humanity, but against the God of heaven whom he despises and continually seeks to dethrone (II Thes. 2:4).

IV. The Character of The Beast

15. Since the fall of the Old Roman Empire, Satan has been once again extremely busy in an attempt to revive and re-establish a One World Empire for the sole purpose of thwarting off the establishment of the promised Millennial Kingdom by our Saviour. Despite the passing of almost two thousand years under the dispensation of grace, Satan has relentlessly endeavored to mislead the world. He is cognizant of his impending doom. Accordingly, he hastens to establish his own kingdom — ruled by a universal, possibly humanistic government — under the absolute rule of the Beast.

16. Satan has made his many attempts during the last several centuries to establish his dominion among men and to consolidate his power on the earth. Beginning with the Holy Roman Empire of Europe, to Napoleon's European Empire, to Hitler's One-Thousand-Year Reich, to the most recent, defunct Communist Soviet Empire, all have come to naught, most likely because they all came about in defiance of God's prophetic timetable. But now the opportune time is finally at hand for the Old Serpent to enact his evil program as forcefully and expeditiously as possible.

17. It should not be lost to the believing Christian that speedy and serious preparations for the establishment of this wicked kingdom on the remains of the Old Roman Empire are at this very moment taking place, even while the Holy Spirit and the Church are yet on the earth. Before Satan openly and ceremonially installs the Beast as the new ruler of the world, several major events must take place: (1) A political, socioeconomic and military ground-frame for the establishment of this One World Empire must first become a reality that is conducive to Satan's end-time program. (2) The Evil Trinity, composed of Satan, the Beast, and the False Prophet, as a counterfeit of the heavenly Trinity, must be ready and in position, before the introduction of the Beast by the Dragon to the entire world. (3) The Church, the Bride of Christ, along with the Holy

Spirit (II Thes. 2:3-9), must be raptured, caught up in the air, to be with the Bridegroom for eternity.

18. With respect to Satan's introduction of the Beast, the fraudulent pretender to Christ's dominion and throne on the earth, this is what the beloved disciple, John, writes:

> *And the beast which I saw was like unto a leopard, and his feet were as the feet of a bear, and his mouth as the mouth of a lion: and the dragon gave him his [the dragon's] power, and his [the dragon's] seat, and great authority. . . and all the world wondered after the beast [namely, marveled at the beast]. And they worshipped the dragon which gave power unto the beast, saying, Who is like unto the beast? [W]ho is able to make war with him? (Rev. 13:2-4).*

V. The Term "Beast"

19. We first encounter the term "beast," used in the prophetic Word of Daniel, Chapter 7, Verse 3. Daniel saw the Beast in a vision. For we read: "Daniel spake and said, I saw in my vision by night, and, behold, the four winds of the heaven strove upon the great sea. And four great beasts came up from the sea, diverse one from another" (Dan. 7:2, 3). From these two verses and from the description Daniel gives in the verses that follow, two important facts become instantly obvious: First, there is a succession of four Beasts, representing the four Gentile World Empires, each of which is diverse from its predecessor — diverse in power, in organization, and in its geography, size and shape; these four beasts came up from the sea, signifying their Gentile origin. Secondly, despite their arrogance against the God of heaven, each of the four Beasts is indeed indirectly fulfilling the will of God on the earth — a fact that no believer should ever forget.

20. With respect to God's dealings with human affairs, the Almighty God shifts the responsibility of using the chosen people, the Israelites, to do His will, as in the past, directly to the Gentile World Powers themselves as an unbelieving world. This is very likely, since the nation He had specially chosen for Himself to become a witness of Jehovah among the Gentiles, had miserably failed to accomplish her mission. God had to do something else. This change not only gave the Gentile World Powers their freedom to act according to their own ungodly desires as being led by Satan and his cohorts, but at the same time, God puts aside, though for a short season, His own people, especially as that nation formally rejected their hoped-for King, their Messiah, the Lord Jesus Christ. Of this fall Paul says:

> *According as it is written, God hath given them the spirit of slumber, eyes that they should not see, and ears that they should not hear; unto this day. . . . I say then, Have they stumbled that they should fall? God forbid: but rather through their fall salvation is come unto the Gentiles, for to provoke them to jealousy. Now if the fall of them be the riches of the world, and the diminishing of them the riches of the Gentiles; how much more their fullness (Rom. 11:8, 11-12).*

21. After the death of King Nebuchadnezzar, during the reign of a grandson, Belshazzar, Daniel apparently found himself, at least for a season, out of power and possibly also out of favor with the new king. From Daniel, Chapter 5, Verses 10 and 16, we learn that Belshazzar very likely had taken over the realm of his grandfather, King Nebuchadnezzar. During this period of Daniel's dormancy, the forgotten prophet had plenty of time to think and even to dream dreams. While Daniel was in this forgotten state, King Belshazzar "made a great feast to a thousand of his lords, and drank wine before the thousand" (Dan. 5:1).

22. King Belshazzar threw a great and wild party for his lords, "his princes, his wives, and his concubines," possibly on the first anniversary of his ascension to the throne of Babylon. During the celebration, they all made merriment and drank wine using the vessels of gold and silver which Nebuchadnezzar had taken out of the house of God at Jerusalem. It should be recalled that the Great Monarch, King Nebuchadnezzar, never desecrated these "holy vessels," knowing full well to whom they belonged.

The Bible says that while the people were all drunk, "[i]n the same hour came forth fingers of a man's hand, and wrote over against the candlestick upon the plaster of the wall of the king's palace: and the king saw the part of the hand that wrote" (Dan. 5:5).

23. Through the intermediacy of the Queen Mother, Daniel was brought back before the king and was told the anecdote. And the writing that was written on the wall was: "*mene, mene, tekel, upharsin*" (Dan. 5:25). By way of interpretation, Daniel translates the sketch as follows: God has *numbered* (**mne'**) thy kingdom, says Daniel, He has *weighed* it (**tqel**) and it falls short of His expectation; He has *separated* it from thee (**upharsin**) and has given it to someone else. Despite Belshazzar's recommendation to clothe "Daniel with scarlet, and put a chain of gold about his neck, and [make] a proclamation concerning him that he should be the third ruler in the kingdom" (Dan. 5:29), Daniel bluntly rejected the offer of the king's rewards. "In that night was Belshazzar the king of the Chaldeans slain" (Dan. 5:30). With this warning, God made it known to this feeble-minded king that his kingdom was taken away from him and was given to another king, to Darius the Median.

24, By way of explanation, the term "beast" signifies an unusual being, an unusual creature — unusual in his character, in his outlook on world matters, and in his actions. The word is used for both, the good and the evil. Two end-time personages are called by this name, "the beast." In Revelation, Chapter 13, Verses 1 and 2, it is used to imply the worst of evil that ever existed. While the first Beast is a mighty conqueror and shrewd politician; the second beast, in Verse 11, is described as a deceptive False Prophet. The two beasts will dominate both the political and the religious power during the end-time period. They are both empowered by the Dragon himself. Of the second beast, the Bible says, "he spake as a dragon," signifying that, like the first beast, his power and authority to exercise his will are received from the Dragon (Rev. 13:11, 12). Of the first beast, the Word of God declares: "and the dragon gave him his [the Dragon's] power, and his [the Dragon's] seat, and great authority" (Rev. 13:2^b).

25. By way of clarification, the term "beast," first, refers to the "Sovereign" who ruled over each of the first four Gentile World Powers: the Babylonian, the Medo-Persian, the Grecian, and the Roman Empires. At the same time, the term also applies collectively to each of the four preceding Empires, along with their ungodly systems of government and their leaders. Prophetically, each of the four successive beasts, along with the imperial system he governed, becomes a precursor, or a prototype, of the coming end-time Beast. From Daniel, Chapter 7, Verse 8, we learn that the "little horn," is the eleventh horn — which in Revelation, Chapter 17, Verse 12, is identified as being the eighth king; in Revelation, Chapter 17, Verses 11 and 13, he corresponds to the Beast of the end time and will become the Supreme Ruler over the Revived Roman Empire and over much of the rest of the world.

VI. The First Four Empires

26. The prophet Daniel began to describe each of the three last kingdoms, providing their specific actions, achievements and qualities. Daniel told Nebuchadnezzar that the king himself was the first of these kings: "the God of heaven hath given thee a kingdom, power, and strength, and glory" (Dan. 2:37^b). Daniel continues, "Thou art this head of gold" (Dan. 2:38^b). I am sure that King Nebuchadnezzar was listening very attentively. The Monarch wanted to know the meaning of the rest of his dream which had troubled him extremely. You can almost hear the King saying: "Keep on talking, Daniel! Don't stop!"

27. Then Daniel continued the interpretation of the king's dream. "And after thee shall arise another inferior [king] to these, and another third kingdom of brass, which shall bear rule over all the earth" (Dan. 2:39). Here, the prophet speaks first of the Medo-Persian World Empire and explains its exploits, and then about the Alexandrian World Empire and defines its expansion. About the Second World Empire, Daniel saw in his vision that "it raised up itself on one side," signifying that it was composed of two main powers -- two nations -- of which one was the stronger. Of the Third Empire, Daniel mentions that he saw in his dream that "the beast had also four heads," signifying that, after the death of

Alexander, the Empire would be divided into four parts ruled by one of his four generals.[2]

28. Interestingly, Daniel's vision of these four major World Empires does not differ much from King Nebuchadnezzar's dream. It is very likely that the prophet had his vision as a result of his contemplation about the King's dream. Be that as it may, Daniel delves more deeply into the interpretation of the Fourth World Empire, the Roman Empire. Daniel mentions that it is a strong power that subdues all things after breaking every resistance that arises. The prophet talks about the "ten toes" made up of clay and of iron to signify the dual nature of the kingdom: "partly strong, and partly broken" (Dan. 2:42[b]). Then Daniel provides another description of this Fourth Empire. The iron and clay, Daniel says, "shall not cleave one to another" (Dan. 2:43[b]). As the Revived Roman Empire begins to come together at the end time, which, it appears, it is taking place nowadays, it will not stick together wholeheartedly. It is made of weak material: "partly strong, and partly broken."

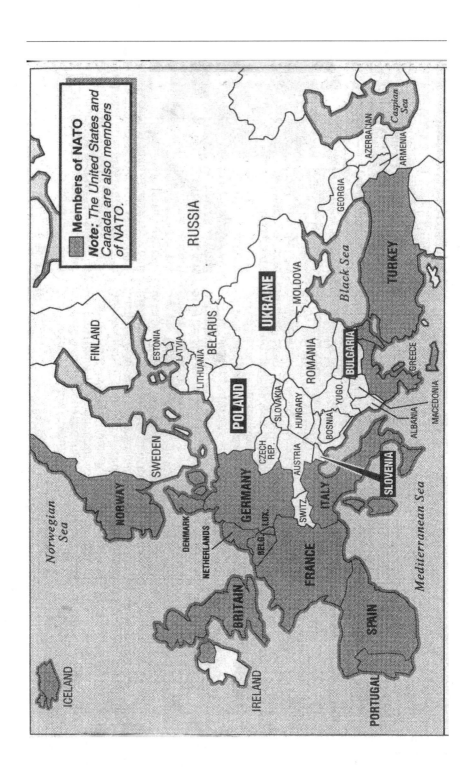

Members of NATO

Note: The United States and Canada are also members of NATO.

CHAPTER 2

DANIEL'S LITTLE HORN

And the ten horns out of this kingdom are ten kings that shall arise: and another [little horn] shall rise after them [the ten horns/kings]; and he shall be diverse from the first [beast, representing the Old Roman Empire], and he shall subdue three kings [or horns] (Dan. 7:24).

I. Daniel's Vision

1. IT SHOULD BE BORNE IN MIND that the vision Daniel saw is only a repetition, or a confirmation, of the prophetic message contained in King Nebuchadnezzar's vision. One of the most fascinating personages mentioned in the Book of Daniel is the "little horn." It is mentioned twice: once in Daniel, Chapter 7, Verse 8; another time in Daniel, Chapter 8, Verse 9. Bible commentators and prophecy interpreters have throughout centuries raised many questions concerning this "little horn," usually with respect to its identity and how it conforms historically and prophetically in the fulfillment of Daniel's prophecy. On one occasion, Daniel describes this self-willed "brat" as follows: "And he shall speak great words against the Most High, and shall wear out the saints of the Most High. . ." (Dan. 7:25).

2. While in the prophetic message there is some difference between the two "little horns," mentioned in Daniel: first, in Chapter 7, Verse 8; and, second, in Chapter 8, Verse 9; yet, they are one and the same in their signification. In Daniel, Chapter 8, Verse 9, the "little horn," it appears, signifies "a prophecy fulfilled in the person of Antiochus Epiphanes, B. C. 175, who profaned the temple and terribly persecuted the Jews."[1] In Daniel, Chapter 7, Verse 8, speaking of the Beast, we have the "little horn" the end-time Antichrist. Antiochus Epiphanes attempted to become the end-time Beast in his day; but, for the most part, he failed miserably.

3. In the very first vision Daniel had seen during King Belshazzar's reign over Babylon, the prophet saw four successive empires represented by the four beasts among which the fourth was excessively different. Daniel provides a brief description for each of the four beasts and their dominion. By interpretation, each of these four beasts represented a mighty Gentile World Power. The details of the fourth beast, however, were considerably perplexing to Daniel. Apparently, what perturbed Daniel the most was the ten horns to which he gives a great deal of consideration. Daniel says:

> *After this I saw in the night vision, and behold a fourth beast, dreadful and terrible, and strong exceedingly; and it had great iron teeth: it devoured and brake in pieces, and stamped the residue with the feet of it; and it was diverse from all the beasts that were before it; and it had ten horns (Dan. 7:7).*

4. To understand the interpretation of this first of Daniel's several visions, the word "horn," or "horns," or "little horn," places before us a great challenge, indeed. Daniel himself had to examine carefully the connotative meaning of the word. While contemplating the question of the ten horns[2] and deeply considering[3] what type of meaning or interpretation to attach to the word "horn," Daniel observes yet another little horn, an eleventh one, coming up to join the first ten.[4] For we read:

> *I considered the horns and, behold, there came up among them another little horn, before whom there were three of the first horns plucked up by the roots: and, behold, in this horn were eyes like the eyes of man, and a mouth speaking great things (Dan. 7:8).*

5. In this vision, which was Daniel's first concerning the end-time Beast, who is called here a "little horn," the prophet is carried away by the prophetic Spirit of God into the distant future, across a time span of more than twenty-five centuries as of now. Through the telescope of prophecy, Daniel is told about the Fourth Empire and about its greatness, its subsequent disintegration and fall, and about its end-time revival in a coalition of ten states as symbolized by the image's ten horns corresponding to the ten toes of the image which King Nebbuchadnezzar had seen in his own vision (Dan. 7:7).

6. Parenthetically, it should be stated here that, in order to understand the contents of Daniel's prophecy, especially those events that are to be fulfilled only during the end times which are closely related to the time when the Beast will make his debut and thereafter, the prophet is informed that, in no uncertain terms, the fulfillment of all such events is reserved to the end times. Notice God's following warnings:

> *Understand, O son of man: for at the time of the end shall be the vision [fulfilled] (Dan. 8:17^b).*
> *. . . for at the time appointed the end [for the fulfillment of this vision] shall be (Dan. 8:19^b).*
> *But thou, O Daniel, shut up the words [of this vision], and seal the book, even to the time of the end. . . . (Dan. 12:4).*
> *And he said, Go thy way, Daniel, for the words are closed up and sealed till the time of the end (Dan. 12:9).*

7. Daniel is exhorted that he should "shut up the words and seal the book" (Dan. 12:4). Since the book, in those days, was a scroll that would be opened and shut and even sealed, Daniel received such instructions from the mouth of God Almighty Himself. And once Daniel had fulfilled the commandment of God and had shut the book and had sealed it, he is now told to "Go thy way, Daniel, for the words are closed up and sealed till the time of the end" (Dan. 12:9).

II. Prophecies Fulfilled

8. It should be clearly stated here that, with but two conspicuous exceptions — the rise of the four Gentile World Empires and the vision of "the ram and the he-goat" (Dan. 8:1-27), both of which having already been fulfilled — almost all other prophecies of Daniel, as stated in the above-quoted verses, have been reserved for their end-time fulfillment. It is very interesting to know that God somehow considers it necessary for Daniel, and likewise for us today, to be informed of this matter, namely, the delaying of these prophecies' fulfillment to the time of the Beast.

9. It has already been mentioned that the "little horn" of Daniel, Chapter 8, Verse 9, as an approximation, has been partially fulfilled by the exploits of the Grecian General Antiochus Epiphanes. This Seleucid ruler of the colonized Syria, a Grecian sovereign — who himself was a precursor of the Beast, the "little horn" of Daniel, Chapter 7, Verse 8 — attempted to hasten the establishment of Satan's kingdom on the earth. He magnified himself and pretended to be the end-time Beast. Accordingly, he eventually invades the Holy Land, successfully occupies Jerusalem, destroys and wickedly desecrates the holy sanctuary by sacrificing a swine on it, and abolishes the Jewish daily sacrifices.

10. With respect to the Four Gentile World Powers — The Babylonian, the Medo-Persian, the Grecian, and the Roman Empires — the fulfillment of Daniel's prophecy regarding their successive rise and fall has already taken place. In accordance with the interpretation of King Nebuchadnezzar's image, the disintegration and demise of the Fourth Empire, the Roman Empire, has also been fulfilled. Daniel had foreseen how the Fourth Empire would first divide into two branches, two legs — the Roman and the Byzantine — and then degenerate into ten toes (Dan. 2:43) and then almost into nothingness. Through a gradual disintegration and demise of the Fourth Empire, its leader, the fourth beast, is likewise symbolically wounded to death and awaiting resurrection.

11. As the Fourth Empire will be revived, at the end time, through a ten-nation coalition and on the territories of the Old Roman Empire, the fourth beast will be likewise resurrected and healed. This death and subsequent healing of the Beast become symbolically his identification throughout the Bible, particularly when speaking of him (Rev. 13:3; 17:8, 11). It is God's plan to make sure that this Beast is well known to mankind of his day.

12. Yet, disregarding the many clues and predictions provided by Daniel the prophet to King Nebuchadnezzar of Babylon quoted in this work, many well-meaning, well-seasoned Bible scholars have not paid special attention to such instructions and, perhaps in their zeal for some interpretation, have succumbed to their misunderstandings. Concerning the "ten horns" (Dan. 7:7), the "little horn," and the three horns "plucked up by roots" (Dan. 7:8), the following are but a few such suggestions Matthew Henry's Commentary presents.

13. Some consider the *little horn*, according to Matthew Henry's Commentary, "to be the Turkish empire, which rose in the room of Asia [Minor], Greece, and Egypt. Others make this fourth beast to be the kingdom of Syria, the family of the [Grecian] Seleucidae." And as for the *"ten* horns, [they] are then supposed to be ten kings that reigned successively in Syria; and then the *little horn* is Antiochus Epiphanes, the last of the ten, who by one means or another undermined three of the kings, and got the government." The ten horns are said to have been the ten kingdoms of which the Roman empire was "comprehended: Italy, France, Spain, Germany, Britain, Sarmatia, Pannonia, Asia, Greece, and Egypt."[5]

14. Concerning the *ten horns*, which ultimately represent ten kingdoms that are, in some way, connected to the Roman Empire, both in its past form and in its future revived form, Walvoord points out, apparently with dissatisfaction, the views of two writers of prophecy, Young and Leupold, saying:

> Both of them [Young and Leupold] find literal fulfillment impossible because there are no ten kings reigning simultaneously in the Roman period. Young, however, considers fulfillment of the Roman Empire in the past, and no further fulfillment is necessary. Leupold finds ultimate fulfillment at the second coming of Christ, rather than in past history. Adherents of Premillennial persuasion offer a third view, providing literal fulfillment: ten actual kingdoms will exist simultaneously in the future consummation.[6]

15. Speaking about verse 9 of Revelation, Chapter 17, Feinberg comments as follows: "The seven mountains (or hills) are proof that mystical Babylon cannot be ancient literal Babylon, which was situated in a plain and not on mountains. However, it is known that Rome is built on

seven hills... classical writers familiarly spoke of 'the city of seven hills.'"[7]
It is interesting to notice how a prominent verse that opens up its words
with an invitation to figure out what the words mean: "And here is the mind
which has wisdom" (Rev. 17:9), Feinberg dismisses it with an ancient
account about Babylon, completely ignoring the challenge. For this verse's
interpretation, see Appendix B.

16. Dealing with verse 10 of the same chapter, Feinberg, likewise,
(quoting Charles), resorts to old tired explanations, giving us ancient leaders of ancient Rome, such as: "Augustus, Tiberius, Caligula, Claudius, and
Nero, then Vespasian, and finally Titus."[8] Again, completely disregarding
the fact that these prophecies belong to the future, to "the things which
shall be hereafter" (Rev. 1:19), and not in the past. For the interpretation
of this verse, see Appendix B.

III. The Symbolic Horns

17. In Daniel, Chapter 7, Verses 7 and 8, the word "horn" or "horns"
somewhat dominates the scene. It is extremely important to establish the
identity of these horns individually and collectively, to provide a reasonable description for them, to seek out and to clarify any signification that
could be attached to them both prophetically and historically, and, finally,
to thoroughly study and present a Scripturally sound interpretation of their
role in the program of God for the end time. Chronologically, they are: (1)
The ten horns; (2) The little horn; and (3) The three horns plucked up by
roots.

a. The ten horns

18. In our study of the "methods and clues of interpretation" provided in Appendix B, it is clearly demonstrated that a *horn* stands for a
king, or a leader, or a kingdom, or a system of government, or, symbolically, for a mountain, when that mountain stands for a ruler, etc. In other
words, a *horn*, simultaneously and interchangeably, may at once stand for
a *king*, his *kingdom,* and the specific *system* of government he rules
over. Symbolically speaking, a *horn* corresponds and represents a *toe*

and, by the same token, the *ten horns* of Daniel, Chapter 7, Verse 7, represent the ten toes of the image King Nebuchadnezzar had seen in his vision (Dan. 2:41, 42).

19. In his interpretation of King Nebuchadnezzar's dream, Daniel lastly mentions the ten toes of the image. These toes symbolically represent the last stage of the Gentile World Power, namely, the fourth kingdom, as exemplified by the Old Roman Empire. But this Old Roman Empire, which in a way was the culmination and embodiment of its three preceding Gentile World Powers — the Babylonian, the Medo-Persian, the Grecian Empires — was to be broken into pieces by "the stone . . . cut out of the mountain without hands" (Dan. 2:40-45). It would likewise be healed and revived in the form of ten horns, or ten toes, or ten kingdoms. Accordingly, the present-day European Union, although composed of a rapidly growing coalition of more than ten states, may very well be a precursor that will represent the end-time, Revived Roman Empire.

20. It is very important to know the time when this ten-nation coalition of ten kingdoms will take place. While the exact time of its formation and its unification may not be easy to pinpoint for all such developments come about gradually, it was clearly made known to Daniel that it would come about during the events surrounding the Beast of the end time. Daniel was clearly instructed about the time of the fulfillment of his vision by none other than "the man Gabriel," saying: "Understand, O son of man: for at the time of the end shall be the vision" (Dan. 8:17[b]). The book of Revelation also indirectly corroborates the time when these ten kings, which correspond to the ten toes and the ten horns of Daniel, will run their course. For we read:

> *And I . . . saw a beast rise up out of the sea, having seven heads and ten horns, and upon his horns [were] ten crowns [or diadems]. . . (Rev. 13:1).*

> *And the ten horns which thou sawest are ten kings, which have received no kingdom as yet; but receive power as kings one hour with the beast (Rev. 17:12).*

21. Before leaving this segment, it is essential to mention here a few additional facts about the ten horns. It should be clearly understood that, in terms of power and government, these ten horns are always closely associated with the end-time Beast. These additional facts are cited in the book of Revelation and presented here chronologically: (1) These ten horns first appeared on the head of the Beast as he rises up out of the sea. (Rev. 13:1). (2) They are also cited as kings who receive power possibly symbolically for "one hour," or one year or more with the Beast. (Rev. 17:12). (3) They unanimously "give their power and their strength unto the beast." (Rev. 17:13). (4) They will fulfill God's will by destroying the "whore" and make her desolate. (Rev. 17:16, 17). And (5) they will make war with the Lamb who will overcome and destroy them. (Rev. 17:14).

22. The word "horn," as employed in prophecy, especially in the book of Daniel and the book of Revelation, symbolizes power, strength, and support for the entity carrying it. Just like a ram, or a bull, that has horns with which to defend itself and which are located on its head, such is the case with the end-time Beast, who will symbolically carry ten horns on his head from whom he receives his support for the domination, if possible, of the entire world. Accordingly, a horn symbolizes a rule, a ruler/king, or a kingdom. The ruler, or the king, may also be identified as a leader, or a mountain (Rev. 17:9).

23. Daniel declares that, at the end time, ten horns, corresponding to the ten toes of King Nebuchadnezzar's image, will rise out of the fourth kingdom, the Old Roman Empire. Subsequently, "another [little horn/king] shall rise after them [after the ten horns]; and he shall be diverse from the first [ten], and he shall subdue three kings" (Dan. 7:24). To properly understand what is taking place here with respect to the three subdued horns/kings, it is absolutely important to notice the striking difference of meaning, in terms of tense and voice employed for the verb used.

24. In Biblical Aramaic, the language Daniel used, the Aramaic verb **eth'aqaru**, translated in the King James Version of the Bible as, *were plucked up by the roots*, of Verse 8, or *destroyed*, Verse 24, as some

Bible scholars of prophecy have erroneously translated; the verb is in the indicative passive of the past tense. It should be made amply clear here that, at best, the translation of its King James Version is an "over-kill." A better etymological and contextual rendering would have been, *removed*, or *taken out*, or *excluded*. In Verse 24 of the same chapter, basically the same idea is again expressed by the Aramaic verb, **yehashphil** *he shall subdue*, which is the simple future of the active voice. Again, an additional yet better rendering would have been similar to the verb Syriac used for its translation in the *Peshitta* Aramaic Version of the Bible, which is **nammikh** *to demote, to humiliate*.

25. Based on the proper translation of tenses, voices and roots of the two verbs mentioned above, especially in light of their meaning in Biblical Aramaic and their rendering in the Peshitta Aramaic, one may conclude that: (1) Since the "little horn," is not the subject, but the surrogate subject of the verb, **eth'aqaru** *were uprooted*, it is not then the Beast who *destroys* or *uproots* the three horns, as most scholars of Bible prophecy believe. (2) When the Beast joins the ten horns, the three horns were already *demoted*, *subdued*, or *removed* (Dan. 7:24) but not *destroyed*. And this demotion, or exclusion, was made before the "little horn," the Beast, joined this European Alliance, and was, most likely carried out unilaterally by the ten horns, possibly as a precondition set forth by the Beast for his joining the new coalition. (3) It appears, the Beast, the "little horn," attaches himself to this pusillanimous federation partly by invitation and partly through diplomacy and persuasion. (4) From Revelation, Chapter 13, Verses 2 and 5, we learn that the Beast does not use force to join this Revived Roman Empire, especially since he is depicted in prophecy as having only a bow without the arrows during the first half of the Tribulation Period (Rev. 6:2).

b. The Little Horn

26. The expression, "the little horn," is mentioned twice in the book of Daniel (Dan. 7:8 and 8:9). In addition to its first mention, references to it as a horn, or as a king, or as the Beast, are also provided by Daniel. These references provide for us the Scriptural interpretation of who really this "little horn" is. In the interpretation of the vision, Daniel was told that a horn is a king:

> *And the ten horns out of this kingdom are ten kings that shall arise: and another [little horn, or king] shall rise after them [the ten horns/kings]; and he shall be diverse from the first [beast, representing the Old Roman Empire], and he shall subdue [remove] three kings [horns] (Dan. 7:24).*

27. That this little horn symbolizes a human being, is apparent from the eyes and the mouth that are attributed to him, and from the role he plays in the fulfillment of prophecy, which corresponds to the end-time Beast. Through the interpretation of Daniel's vision which he received from "one like the Son of man" who came to the "Ancient of days," we further learn from Daniel, Chapter 7, Verse 24, the verse just quoted above, that the little horn corresponds to a king. Daniel's vision concerning this end-time judgment equates this horn/king with the end-time Beast at the time when he is finally judged. Notice the following verse:

> *Then I saw that, because of the voice of many great words this horn was speaking, the beast [this horn] was slain, his body was destroyed and was given to the burning fire[9] (Dan. 7:11).*

28. It is very important to understand that this little horn is none other than the Beast himself, the Antichrist, who will rule over the world during the Tribulation Period. After the rapture of the Church and the departure of the Holy Spirit with it from the earth, he will be heralded to be the world's new Leader and Saviour. In the absence of the Holy Spirit and the Church, the Dragon finds it very conducive to declare the Beast the redeemer of mankind. In order to understand the very essence of this little horn, we must understand some of the terms and statements very cleverly associated with the Beast. The following three significant attributes, or statements, which need ample explanation and understanding, are prescribed to or associated with the Beast: "another," "little," and "plucked up by the roots."

1. "Another," Called Horn

29. Let it be said that the Holy Bible does not contain any superficial language. Every word, every expression, every phrase, every sentence in it is there for a reason. The use of the adjective *another* in Daniel, Chapter 7, Verse 8, has a useful purpose. It implies that, contrary to what many interpreters of prophecy have said, this little horn is not one of the ten horns mentioned in the preceding verse, nor is he taken from among the ten nation-coalition that represent the ten nations. This horn is number eleven, coming out from elsewhere, from beyond the territories within the boundaries of the Old Roman Empire. Unlike the ten horns, which constitute the coalition of the ten states — geographically covering the Old Roman Empire — this little horn comes from another place, from outside of the Roman territories, from beyond the sea. It is very possible that this personage comes from beyond the sea, or "out of the sea" (Rev. 13:1), possibly representing "another" country across the ocean, as it shall be seen in due course.

2. Another, Called "Little Horn"

30. Etymologically and connotatively, the adjective "little," in Aramaic z`era, the language Daniel employed in his book, has two meanings; even in Hebrew it corresponds to the two ideas: size and a shorter duration of time. Described in the Bible as "dreadful and terrible, and strong exceedingly," it would be an oxymoron to identify the Beast with the attribute *little*. He must then represent a much more youthful, yet powerful country headed by a powerful personage qualified to assume the future leadership of a much larger empire that includes a two-tier government. At the same time, the Beast will assume the leadership of yet another coalition of a much larger alliance in strength and in geography, a coalition of seven kings with himself as king number eight to rule possibly over the Atlantic Alliance, or some other alliance like it.

31. As was mentioned earlier, in the book of Revelation, Chapter 13 and elsewhere, by the way of interpretation, a horn is a king, is a head, is a mountain, is a kingdom, is the system of government, especially as headed by any one of the four beasts. Accordingly, in Revelation, Chapter 13, Verse 1, we find the Beast rising "up out of the sea, having seven heads and ten horns" (Rev. 13:1). Since the words "horn" and "head" are synonymous, one and the same, in terms of their interpretation, both signify kings or kingdoms, or states. The expression "having seven heads and ten horns" could only be interpreted as follows.

32. It clearly appears, when the Beast comes to take power over the world, he will have two sets or alliances of fundamentally the same nations which, to a great extent, overlap in a two-tier government: one set, or group, is composed of only seven heads, or leaders, representing their seven governments which represent the ten nations; the other set is composed of ten kings, or leaders, representing their ten-nation coalition that constitutes the Revived Roman Empire. And these two sets, or two groups of governmental institutions, primarily respectively rule over the Revived Roman Empire of Europe and over the Atlantic Alliance in North America and Europe which would be dominated, as the author sees it, by the United States.

33. This two-tier arrangement of the two overlapping alliances, which support the Beast, is also substantiated by both Daniel and John. Notice carefully in Daniel, Chapter 7, Verse 8, where we find "another little horn," the Beast, to be joining this European coalition only after the three horns/kings, out of the original ten horns, are *removed*, thereby creating a new, eight-king coalition, composed of the original seven horns plus the "little horn" himself as the king number eight. In the Book of Revelation, Chapter 17, Verses 10 and 11, the same idea is expressed, saying: "And there are seven kings . . . [a]nd the beast [the little horn] . . . is the eighth [king], and is of the seven. . .", namely, he is allied with the seven kings who are chosen from the ten.

c. Three "Plucked Up By the Roots"

34. The King James Version's translation of the Aramaic verb, **ith'aqru** *were plucked up by the roots* used by Daniel, is an extremely exaggerated rendering. The fact that the ten horns, which are mentioned here in

Daniel, also appear in the book of Revelation intact, suggests that they were never destroyed. A better connotative translation for this verb would have been *to remove, to take out*, which is the meaning given by the Syriac verb used in its *Peshitta* Version of the Bible. Such an interpretation may be corroborated by the substitute verb used in Verse 24 of Daniel, Chapter 7, to express the same idea, except that here the horns are explained to be kings:

> *And the ten horns out of this kingdom are ten kings that shall arise: and another shall rise after them; and he shall be diverse from the first, and he shall subdue [take out, not plucke up or destroye] three kings. (Dan. 7:24).*

35. For the Aramaic verb **yehashphil** *to subdue*, which primarily means *to debase*, the *Peshitta* Aramaic version of the Bible uses the verb **nammikh** *to debase, to demote, to take out*. It should also be noted that while the little horn is not the subject of the second verb of Verse 24, it is neither the subject of the first verb, *plucked up by the roots*. Furthermore, reference for this action is also made in Verse 20 of the same Chapter, where the surrogate subject of the intransitive verb *fell* is "the three horns":

> *And of the ten horns that were in his head, and of the other [horn] which came up, and before whom three fell; even of that horn that had eyes, and a mouth that spake very great things, whose look was more stout than his fellows. I beheld, and the same horn made war with the saints, and prevailed against them (Dan. 7:20, 21).*

36. In conclusion, it should be reiterated that the three horns were never subjected to destruction as most Bible scholars have thus far suggested. They were only removed from a new Super Alliance which the Beast joined to be made up of only seven major representatives from among the ten-nation European Coalition which could very well correspond to the present Atlantic Alliance. The Beast's appearance — having seven heads and ten horns at the same time — only signifies that when he joins the European coalition, he forms a Super Government that would not only include the original ten-nation coalition of the European Council as one Lower House, but also of an Upper House which is numerically smaller yet stronger and superior coalition made up of the seven stronger members also drawn from the ten-nation coalition.

37. To this Super Government, the end-time Ruler joins himself as the eighth king. That this beast is not "little" but "young," or "youthful," implies that his country is, likewise, much younger than the countries of Europe which are a direct legacy of the Old Roman Empire. Because of its relatively huge size and strength, such a country could only be the United States of America, which itself, too, is undeniably, primarily a legacy of the Revived Roman Empire as Gromacki also suggests.

CHAPTER 3

PRESENT DEVELOPMENTS

For the time will come when they will not endure sound doctrine; but after their own lusts shall they heap to themselves teachers, having itching ears; And they shall turn away their ears from the truth, and shall be turned unto fables (2 Tim. 4:3, 4).

I. New Trends

1. IN LIGHT OF TODAY'S EVENTS, it is easy to observe certain highly unusual political and religious trends developing right before our eyes. To those who are versed in the Scriptures, these developments are not unusual. As a matter of fact, these events are taking place in the fulfillment of the prophetic Word of God. While the specifics and the exact timing of these happenings, whether they be political, moral, or religious, may not always be perceptible, the fact that they do occur is usually anticipated by the child of God.

2. Just in the realm of politics, intensive diplomatic exchanges will and are even now taking place between and among many regional and distant countries, in the main, seeking security alliances and trade arrangements. It is very possible that many of today's international organizations and alliances will eventually join forces with the Beast. With respect to religion, a One World Church has been for decades the goal of many Protestant and Orthodox churches. Presently, efforts are in the making to bring under one umbrella all Christendom, and most likely, this includes the Roman Catholic Church which has lately, under John Pal II, become more amenable to the idea.

II. Political Trends

3. As it was mentioned earlier, it is obvious that the establishment of

A EUROPE UNITED

The forerunner of the 15-nation European Union was the 6-nation Common Market. Now the EU is considering expanding to more than two dozen countries. Turkey repeatedly has been rejected for membership

Phase 1 Common Market   **Phase 2** European Union   **Phase 3** Immediate consideration   **Phase 4** Future consideration

The Washington Times

this One World Government — the nucleus of which could very well be the European Union, namely, the ten-nation Revived Roman Empire — will take place mostly through peaceful and diplomatic means and gentle persuasion. The policy of "carrot and stick" could very well be masterfully employed. This European Union, joined by an eleventh member, an outsider, most likely from across the Atlantic Ocean, would constitute a mighty power that — through its sheer magnitude, its territorial size, its economic dynamism, and its military strength — could become a desirable shelter for many smaller countries.

4. It is highly likely that many of today's existing international organizations will join forces with the Beast's Revived Roman Empire. Just within the last several months, a number of political pronouncements have appeared in *The Washington Times* pointing to a greater desire on the part of North America, primarily the United States and Canada, and Western Europe to establish stronger economic and security ties between the two sides.

5. On June 21, 1995, it was reported by three European defense ministers — Malcolm Rifkind of the United Kingdom, Joerjin Kosmo of Norway, and Antonio S. Lopes of Portugal — on "the Washington Conference on Transatlantic Security," saying:

> 'America still has a fundamental security and economic interest in Europe: We are the major export market for the United States. . . . Europe and North America share many common objectives around the world. . . . The Atlantic Community must embrace many walks of life, not just security and defense, if it is to succeed, but politicians on both sides of the Atlantic must give a lead.'

6. On July 15, 1995, Martin Sieff comments:

> 1. At a time when angst over America's future has been raised to an art form, it is both bracing and disconcerting to come across a rousing geopolitical call to arms by a visionary elder who sees

this country's commitment to democracy and its federal system as the keys to achieving the dream of *world government* in the next century (Italics added).

2. In an era when millions of Americans regard the growth of their own federal government with suspicion and fear, and are implacably opposed to submerging US. national interests in any increased international commitment, Mr. Strausz-Hupe boldly writes: 'The issue before the United States is *the unification of the globe under its leadership within this generation.*' (Italics added).

3. Americans respond to great altruistic challenges and to the championing of the principles of democracy, he argues, and the success and relative efficiency of the American federal system of government — balancing strong local government against the ambitions of national government — make it both a model for the rest of the world and the seed of an expanded federal system that should eventually embrace other democracies.

III. Religious Trends

7. Imitating King Nebuchadnezzar of Babylon, who some 26 centuries earlier erected his image of gold, in the plain of Dura, to be worshipped, the Beast, too, demands the universal worship of his own image. As sinful and unfaithful as the Apostate Church has been, it will desist the worship of the image of the Beast. The Church united under the "titular leadership" possibly of the Pope, will unanimously refuse to worship the image. The Apostate Church refuses, because such an action would make its Supreme Church Leader subordinate to the Beast.

8. In his fury, the Beast will soon direct the "ten horns" of the General Council of the ten-nation coalition to "hate the whore, and [they] shall make her desolate and naked, and shall eat her flesh, and burn her with fire" (Rev. 17:16). The Apostate Christendom is unwilling to bow down to the Beast, or to surrender its power and its authority to the Beast; it will not yield its supremacy to the Beast. Especially since the Apostate

Christendom thinks — albeit falsely — that it derives its authority from the Almighty God. And so, the Beast, having consolidated his power over the people of the world, will now decide to destroy this unyielding apostasy. John writes:

> *And the ten horns which thou sawest upon the beast, these shall hate the whore, and shall make her desolate and naked, and shall eat her flesh, and burn her with fire. For God hath put in their [the ten horns] hearts to fulfill his will, and to agree, and give their kingdom unto the beast until the word of God shall be fulfilled (Rev. 17:16, 17).*

9. With respect to this One-World Church, Pope John Paul II recently made two new pronouncements which were separately printed. One dealt with the subject of the church unity; the other dealt with the women's right and role in the church. These two declarations are not only significant, but also timely.

1. On May 31, 1995, Larry Witham reported in The Washington Times on *Papal Overture Seeking Christian Unity*.

Without renouncing his authority in the seat of St. Peter, Pope John Paul II yesterday *issued an encyclical that proposed reforming the Roman Catholic papacy* to seek unity with Protestant and Orthodox churches. . . . At the end of the 115-page document, John Paul stated a desire to 'heed the call' of most Christian traditions 'to find a way of exercising the *primacy* which, while in no way renouncing what is essential to its mission, is nonetheless open to a new situation.' He did not propose a new model for *papal primacy* but spoke of the papacy's role as '*moderator*' in the early church and said the reform was an 'immense task' that could take years of talks. (italics added)

2. On July 11, 1995, Larry Witham again reported in The Washington Times on the subject of *Wrongs Against Women*, saying:

Pope John Paul II yesterday apologized for the Roman Catholic Church not standing by women strongly enough in their fight against historical bias but called for an alliance that would join their social equality with traditional roles. 'In every time and place this conditioning has been an obstacle to the progress of women,' he said in a 16-page message addressed 'to every woman.' The Pope also said: 'Women will increasingly play a part in the solutions of the future. . . .'

10. Obviously, the trend the papacy follows, both with respect to a One-World Church unity and with the women's role in it, is not lost on those who are keen on the Word of God. Godly women have always played a godly role in the Church. The Pope's call here is not for the strengthening of the traditional role women have always exercised in the Church. Under pressures from today's feminists, especially those within his own church, the Pope is responding, though obliquely at the present, to their demands. Neither is the adoration of women in the Roman Catholic Church a new phenomenon to the Catholic adherents.

III. Adoration of Mary

11. The Catholic Church teachings with respect to Mary have always been a means by which to glorify femininity thereby distracting the attention of the "faithful" from Christ the Saviour to the Virgin Mary. The Roman Catholic Church's tradition portrays Christ on the crucifix as an ever crucified, ever helpless, hopeless, dying Son of God. The exuberant and ever youthful Mary, the Mother and the Supreme Guardian of the little "baby jesus," has become the Supreme Mother, the Intermediary, the Regent, the Mother Coredemptrix, through whom prayers and supplications are made daily. As the Supreme Mother, she has gradually become, at least to the innocent faithful, the main object of worship. Today, it appears that more prayers and worship are made in the Catholic Church to Mary than to any other single Person of the Trinity.

12. How conveniently Satan has succeeded in transforming the blessed mother of our Saviour, into a modern-day Ashtoreth of Mesopotamia,

Diana of the Greeks, and Ishtar of the West, the ancient goddess of love and fertility. By giving undue prominence and devotion to Mary, both God the Father and God the Son are downgraded and their deity sacrificed. Sound biblical doctrines have been subtly misinterpreted in order to give Mary her present lofty status in the Catholic Church. Since Mary is the mother of Christ who is God, she has also become the mother of God Himself. Since God the Son dies on the Cross, God the Father ultimately dies with Him on the

"La Pieta"

cross. If God the Father and God the Son are dead, the *Immaculate* Mother must now reign supreme and become the object of all worship and prayers. In a Catholic Girl's Manual and Sunday Missal, the following "blessing" was written — a blessing, which I believe, most Catholics would not approve of. Here is the quotation in its format:

> May Jesus
> *Through Mary,*
> The Mother of God
> And Your Merciful Mother
> Come and Live in You,
> To Purify,
> Vivify
> And Sanctify You
> For the Greater Honor and Glory
> of the Most Blessed Trinity
> (*Italics added*).[1]

13. Also in another report quoted from a book on the persecution of Christians, the name of an order founded by a Roman Catholic priest in North Vietnam was, "The Congregation of the Mother Coredemptrix."[2] Observe carefully the slogan, "the Mother Coredemptrix," co-saviour;

namely, Mary here is portrayed as co-equal with the Savior in her ability to save sinners. Where are the Scriptures that promulgate a basis for such an usurpation of salvation that has been bought through the precious blood of our Savior, the Redeemer? The blessed mother of Jesus would stand in judgment against such a teaching that no true Catholic believer would want to defend.

14. Numerous miracles have of late been attributed to Virgin Mary everywhere, or to one of her patrons. Christ is all but forgotten. Or, if remembered, He is eternally seen hanging haggardly and miserably on the cross of the crucifix. To millions of worshippers, He is never risen! As the end-time approaches, Satan must now hasten to transform Mary into a "female goddess." On the pretext of granting women their dignity and an equal status with men, the One-World Catholic Church, which has been preparing for the end time, could very well allow and even encourage women to become priestesses, bishops, cardinals, and eventually even a Pope. Of course, this apostasy is not limited to the Catholic Church alone; it likewise takes place, with different parameters yet very serious, among the great majority of the Protestant Churches.

15. In Revelation, Chapter 17, Verse 3, John declares: "I saw a woman sit upon a scarlet colored beast, full of names of blasphemy. . . ." While the term, "woman," here speaks of the end-time Apostate Church in its entirety — Protestant, Orthodox and Catholic — the ecumenical Apostate Church could very well also be led by a woman. Prophetically, it is possible that the term "woman" could have a double application and a double interpretation — a One-World, Apostate Church led by a woman. And why not!? If the sinless Eve became the better target for Satan's deception in the Garden of Eden, why shouldn't Satan install a "woman-Pope," to become the head of the end-time, One-World Church. Eventually, a woman could become an easy prey to the Beast's plans and plots against the Almighty God, just before the returning of our blessed Savior to the earth.

16. The doctrine of a "co-redeemer" is not only in contradiction to the teachings of the Scripture, but it also finds no basis in the entire Word of God for its justification. On the contrary, the Bible is very clear and distinct in its message about such a doctrine. The Word of God tells the believing Christians that there is only one mediator between God and men, the Lord Jesus Christ. It is this mediator that will impart salvation for all those who accept Jesus Christ as their Saviour. God's provision for salvation is eternal and has no equal. "For he [God] is not a man, as I am," says Job, "that I should answer him, and we should come together in judgment" (Job 9:32). Job recognizes the one God in heaven, who is far above every man on the earth, and He does according to His pleasure. "Neither is there any daysman betwix us, that might lay his hand upon us both" (Job 9:33). Thusly, Paul says to Timothy:

> For there is one God, and one mediator between God and men, the man Jesus Christ; who gave himself a ransom for all, to be testified in due time (I Tim. 2:5)

> For I am not ashamed of the gospel of Christ: for it is the power of God unto salvation to every one that believeth; to the Jews first, and also to the Greeks. For theirin is the righteousness of God revealed from faith to faith: as it is written, the just shall live by faith (Rom. 1:16, 17).

> Even the righteousness of God which is by faith of Jesus Christ unto all and upon all them that believe: for there is no difference: For all have sinned, and come short of the glory of God (Rom. 3:22, 23).

IV. Cultural Trends

17. Just within the past few decades, I saw America slip from its pristine goodness to its callous ungodliness. While I was recently gassing my car, another well-dressed motorist came up on the other side of the pump stand. As he looked towards me, apparently gauging the situation possibly out of apprehension, I greeted him, "Hello." Reluctantly he responded and turned his head away. I told him that I was on a campaign. "Campaigning for what?" He retorted without looking towards me. "Every time I see a person, I like to say to him 'Hello.' Do you remember the time when, many years ago," I continued my monologue, "people were very friendly?" "Yah!" he responded reluctantly and left. The spiritual calamity that has befallen us in America lately is vividly and prophetically described by Paul to Timothy:

> *This know also, that in the last days perilous times shall come. For men shall be lovers of their own selves, covetous, boasters, proud, blasphemers, disobedient to parents, unthankful, unholy, [w]ithout natural affection, trucebreakers, false accusers, incontinent, fierce, despisers of those that are good, [t]raitors, heady, highminded, lovers of pleasure more than lovers of God; [h]aving a form of godliness, but denying the power thereof. . . . Ever learning, and never able to come to the knowledge of the truth (II Tim. 3:1-5, 7).*

18. This falling away affects not only America, but also the entire world. The same spirit of selfishness, greed, lies, despising God, making a mockery about everything that is decent, prevails today all over the United States and even all over the world. We now have a shallow culture; a culture based upon how one feels about everything. It is a "me" generation; a generation that does not have anything in common with its past, or with its parents. If it makes me feel good, I will do it. It is my business to do whatever pleases me, and benefits me. I do as I want! I am the king of my life! In the book of Judges we read:

> *In those days there was no king in the land of Israel, every man did that which was right in his own eyest (Judges 21:25).*

19. In America, and I suppose in many other countries, the name of God is likewise taken very lightly nowadays. Religion has no place in the lives of most Americans today. Profanity and taking God's Name in vain is very common among all the levels of our population. Even among the government employees of all ages and of both genders, foul-mouth speaking is rampaging throughout the governmental institutions across America. Most people lie and swear to achieve a convincing argument. Lying to God appears in many forms and in many shapes. The following article is taken from Danis Shea who wrote on "Lying as a coping strategy," posted July 28, 1998, on the MSNBC Web site.

1. This article which is entitled, "Lying to God," was reported in The Washington Times, on August 6, 1998.

In an earlier time, lying while invoking God's name was considered a very big deal. The presumption was that few, if any, would risk the punishment that God would mete out in the afterlife to those who falsely swore. That's why there once were no laws against perjury. To expose oneself to the wrath of God of the Creator was considered an incredibly dopey thing to do. Today, of course, very few people on the witness stand perform eschatological cost-benefit calculations before testifying. And the act of swearing an oath no longer, in any meaningful way, serves to enhance the swearer's credibility. . . .

2. The following article was written by Rabbi Yahuda Levin and quoted from a lecture he had given on "Religion and Homosexuality" in a conference sponsored by the Family Research Council.

For the past three decades, our biblically-based morals and beliefs have been under attack by those who seek to lower the bar of decency and an acceptable code of conduct to subterranean level. Our enemy has established dominant position in all our cultural institutions from grammar school to university, from town hall to the White House. Our families and children are bombarded by deviancy and degeneracy masquerading as art and civil rights. . . . As they shove 'Ellen' onto our TV screens and legislate same-sex marriage — desecrate churches, screaming 'We are here, queer and in your face' — religious people must get off their McDuffs and draw a line in the sand.

3. Written by Kenneth A. Myers, on "Popular Culture and the Family," in the July-August issue of Family Policy; September 25, 1998.

> Prior to the invention of modern technologies of communication and travel, all culture was local culture. . . . Since culture was 'produced and consumed' locally, the values communicated through cultural forms were values of the local community. Moral notions that did not fit 'community standards' were not publicly tolerated. In contrast, most of our cultural life is now defined by distant strangers; today's popular culture is *mass-mediated culture*. As such, the moral dynamic of cultural activity has changed radically. We have moved from being creators and participants in culture to being simply consumers of culture. . . . Partly because of aggressive efforts in the name of free speech and partly because of the carelessness of a generation raised on television, the centrality of local life in the shaping of culture has given way to mass-produced culture from Hollywood, New York, and Nashville.

20. The Rev. Jim Wright was asked to open, on 6-4-1999, the new session of the Kansas Senate. Everyone was expecting the usual politically-correct generalities. But what they heard instead was a stirring prayer, passionately calling our country to repentance and righteousness. Here is that prayer as Commentator Paul Harvey aired it successfully on his radio program.

> THE PRAYER:

> Heavenly Father, we come before you today to ask Your forgiveness and to seek Your direction and guidance. We know Your Word says, 'Woe on those who call evil good,' but that's exactly what we have done. We have lost our spiritual equilibrium and reversed our values.

> We confess that:
> We have ridiculed the absolute truth of Your Word and called it pluralism.

We have worshipped other gods and called it multi-culturalism.

We have endorsed perversion and called it an alternative lifestyle.

We have exploited the poor and called it the lottery.

We have neglected the needy and called it self-preservation.

We have rewarded laziness and called it welfare.

We have killed our unborn children and called it a choice.

We have shot abortionists and called it justifiable.

We have neglected to discipline our children and called it building self-esteem.

We have abused power and called it political savvy.

We have coveted our neighbor's possessions and called it ambition.

We have polluted the air with profanity and pornography and called it freedom of expression.

We have ridiculed the time-honored values of our forefathers and called it enlightenment.

Search us, O God, and know our hearts today; cleanse us from every sin and set us free. Guide and bless these men and women who have been sent to direct us to the center of Your will. I ask it in the name of Your Son, the living Savior, Jesus Christ. Amen.

CHAPTER 4

THE TRANSFER OF GOD'S THRONE

And I heard a great voice out of heaven saying, Behold, the tabernacle of God is with men, and he will dwell with them, and they shall be his people, and God himself shall be with them, and be their God (Rev. 21:3).

I. The Heavenly Places

1. IN ORDER FOR OUR LORD to carry out His purpose and design on the earth, according to God's blueprints for the end times, the very throne of God will be "relocated" from the uppermost heaven to the lowest, to the "heavenly places" (Eph. 3:10). God has always desired to be close to man whom He had created for His fellowship. The Almighty God has made man the very center of His loving concern since the foundations of the world. Of this relocation, both the Old and the New Testaments are, explicitly or implicitly, permeated with such references. The tabernacle of Moses in the wilderness is just one such example of how God occasionally dwelt amongst His people, despite their sins and shortcomings. In preparation for the judgment of the enemy, the Devil, for having wrecked havoc against mankind, David, the Psalmist, said:

O thou enemy, destructions are come to a perpetual end: and thou hast destroyed cities; their memorial is perished with them. But the Lord shall endure for ever: he hath prepared his throne for judgment. And he shall judge the world in righteousness, he shall minister judgment to the people in uprightness (Ps. 9:6-8).

2. Immediately after seeing the "little horn" and in conjunction with that horn, Daniel likewise saw God, the "Ancient of days," seated on a throne. And Daniel says: "I beheld till the thrones were cast [placed] down, and the Ancient of days did sit, whose garment was white as snow, and the hair of his head like the pure wool: his throne was like the fiery flame, and his wheels as burning fire" (Dan. 7:9). Likewise, in conjunction with the Beast, the Apostle John saw an identical vision of the tabernacle, or the throne of God, and of them that dwell in heaven, or heavenly places (Rev. 13:6 and 15:5). This transferring of the throne of God, possibly from the upper heaven to be established in the air, in high places (Eph. 3:10; 6:12), is clearly described for us by Daniel in his vision:

> *I saw in the night vision, and, behold, one like the Son of man came [down] with the clouds of heaven, and came to the Ancient of days, they brought him near before him. And there was given [to] him dominion, and glory, and a kingdom, that all people, nations, and languages, should serve him. . . . (Dan. 7:13-14).*

3. Chapter 4 of the book of Revelation is almost entirely devoted to the description of this transferring to and the relocation of God's throne to the air region. Remember, John is shown in his vision the things which would come about "hereafter." The first thing John saw was *the setting of a throne in heaven* (Rev. 4:2). Since God's throne is eternally established in upper heaven, not "heavenly places necessarily", what John saw at this moment was undoubtedly a transfer of God's throne from the upper heaven to the air, to our atmosphere. It is to these heavenly places, which are closer to the saints of God who are to rule over the earth with Christ, that the throne is now brought down.

4. The relocation of the throne of God comes about in preparation for the great things the Almighty God and His Son will undertake there immediately after Christ's return to the cloudy air. First, there will be the Judgment Seat of Christ to judge the believers; secondly, there will be the Marriage of the Lamb; thirdly, the Marriage Supper of the Lamb; and, fourth, just before Christ descends to the earth to begin His rule over the Millennial Kingdom, there will be the resurrection of the martyrs who had been slain on the earth during the Tribulation Period. Of this transfer of the throne from heaven to heavens or the heavenly places, David says:

The Lord hath prepared his throne in the heavens[1] [not heaven, but the heavenly places]; and his kingdom ruleth over all [the earth] (Ps. 103:19).

5. The throne of God is set in the heavenly places for another reason; to judge the wicked of the earth for their wickedness and their arrogance against the God of heaven. This throne "will not, for example, be like the 'Great White Throne' of Revelation 20:11-15 — the last judgment scene. There, of course, Deity is unveiled in absolute finality of judicial holiness and brightness. There, the heaven and earth have *fled away.* ... But here in chapter 4 and 5, the question is, Who shall execute the 'judgments written' regarding *this earth*, and vindicate God's ways in its *government?*"[2]. When God deals with the affairs of man, both the believer and the sinner, He carries out His dealings in the presence of man, the righteous man. We must never forget that God's love for man has always been supreme; man always remains the center of the Almighty's preoccupation. (*Italics added*)

6. Moreover, with respect to this relocation of the throne of God in heaven, John says, "[R]ound about the throne were four and twenty seats: and upon the seats I saw four and twenty elders sitting, clothed in white raiment; and they had on their heads crowns of gold" (Rev. 4:4). Most assuredly, because these twenty-four elders were clothed "in white raiment," and the fact that they had crowns on their heads, indicate that they are "believers of a prominent statute," whose position in the coming kingdom of our Saviour has just been determined at the Judgment Seat of Christ in accordance with the durability of their works and the faithfulness in which these works were carried out. That twelve of these elders must be presumed to be the disciples of Christ, can be inferred from the fact that, while on the earth, they were specifically instructed by our Lord that they would be judging the twelve tribes of Israel during the Millennial Kingdom. Of this event, in the book of Matthew, Christ makes the following remark:

And Jesus said unto them, Verily I say unto you, That ye which have followed me, in the regeneration[3] when the Son of man shall sit in the throne of his glory, ye also shall sit upon twelve thrones, judging the twelve tribes of Israel (Matt. 19:28).

7. According to the beloved disciple, John, the throne of God is established on a sea of glass, possibly on a platform which the Son of God will occupy to deal with the affairs of mankind during His future reign over the world. "Come and hear, all ye that fear God, and I will declare what he hath done for my soul" (Ps. 66:16). It is God's ultimate plan that He may henceforth dwell among His children. Of this, John says:

And I heard a great voice out of heaven saying, Behold, the tabernacle of God is with men, and he will dwell with them, and they shall be his people, and God himself shall be with them, and be their God (Rev. 21:3).

II. The Throne of God

8. It must be clearly stated here that, in order for God to live among His people, it has been His ultimate purpose to bring together, both Jews and Gentiles, into one fold. Even during the dispensation of grace, the Church itself is one body made up of both Jews and Gentiles who are saved through the precious blood of Christ. There is no longer a distinction between the two bodies of holiness: the saved Jews and the saved Gentiles. The mystery that both, Jews and Gentiles, were to become one fold, Paul received from God and declares it to the Ephesians:

How that by revelation he made known unto me the mystery. . . [w]hich in other ages was not made known unto the sons of men, as it is now revealed unto his holy apostles and prophets by the Spirit; [t]hat the Gentiles should be fellowheirs, and of the same body, and partakers of his promise in Christ by the gospel (Eph. 3:3ᵃ, 5, 6. See also Eph. 1:9, 10, 18-22).

9. God had promised that he would establish the throne of David for ever and ever. God had made also a promise to His people that a kingdom would be offered to them; a kingdom that had no end. Furthermore,

God promised that this kingdom would be eternal and David would once again rule over it. Nathan, the prophet, spoke about David saying: "But I will settle him in mine house and my kingdom for ever: and his throne shall be established for evermore" (I Chro. 17:14). Knowing full well that David like his descendants would die, God made a promise to Judah through the mouth of Jacob, the third Patriarch, that He would bless the tribe of Judah eternally:

> *The sceptre shall not depart from Judah, nor a lawgiver from between his feet, until Shiloh come; and unto him shall the gathering of the people be (Gen. 49:10).*

10. Of course, we now know that not only King David has died, but also his children and the scepter has discontinued in the flesh. The whole kingdom has disappeared for many, many centuries. So what happened to the kingdom which was promised to David and to his descendants? Because of sin, the kingdom has deceased for a long time, and in its place there is now the Church of our Saviour to which Church the Lord has been adding "daily such as should be saved" (Acts 2:47[b]).

11. God has never negated his promises to man. "For all the promises of God in him are yea, and in him Amen" (II Cor. 1:20[a]). And so the Lord, sooner or later, fulfills His promises to his people. Particularly, this eternal promise of the kingdom was first made to Judah through Jacob on his death bed. It is this better promise made in Hebrews, Chapter 8, Verse 6[b], that God mediates between Himself and His people; namely, that the scepter would be reinstated and David the King would be resurrected and re-established as the King of Israel during the Millennial Age. In Ezekiel and Jeremiah, we read:

> *And David my servant shall be king over them; and they all shall have one shepherd: they shall also walk in my judgments, and observe my statutes, and do them (Ez. 37:24).*

> *And I will set up one shepherd over them, and he shall feed them, even my servant David; he shall feed them, and he shall be their shepherd. And I the Lord will be their God, and*

*my servant David a prince among them; I the Lord have spo-
ken it (Ez. 34:23, 24).*

*But they shall serve the Lord their God, and David their
king, whom I will raise up unto them (Jer. 30:9).*

12. The throne of David is the throne of Jesus Christ who is the King
of kings and the Lord of lords. While the throne of David is limited to the
Jewish people, the throne of God and His Christ extends also to the entire
humanity, to the saved heathen nations. "God reigneth over the heathen:
God sitteth upon the throne of his holiness" (Ps. 47:8). It is this throne that
the Lord has prepared in the heavens, "in the heavenlies" (Eph. 1:20^b), in
order to extend his rule over the saved Gentiles as well. "The Lord hath
prepared his throne in the heavens [in the heavenly places]; and his kingdom ruleth over all" (Ps. 103:19).

III. The Throne Confirmed to David

13. Yet, it is this throne, whether it be in conjunction with the rule over
the people of God or the rule over the saved Gentiles, that the Lord swore
to David that someone of his seed would sit upon this throne. "The Lord
hath sworn in truth unto David; he will not turn from it; of the fruit of thy
body will I set upon thy throne" (Ps. 132:11). God's throne is established
for ever to be a tabernacle for David's rule among his people. Isaiah
declares, saying:

*And in mercy shall the throne be established: and he shall
sit upon it in truth in the tabernacle of David, judging, and
seeking judgment, and hasting righteousness (Isa. 16:5).*

14. It is interesting to notice how God intertwines his throne with the
throne of His Son, the Lord Jesus Christ, and then with the eternal throne
of David. God's dealing with his people, both the Jews and the Gentiles,
is so close to His heart, that he makes Jerusalem the very center for worship and judgment. The Lord will make Jerusalem the capitol of the entire
world from whence He will rule all the heathen nations in addition to Irael.

*At that time they shall call Jerusalem the throne of the
Lord; and all the nations shall be gathered unto it, to the
name of the Lord, to Jerusalem: neither shall they walk any-
more after the imagination of their evil heart (Jer. 3:17).*

15. Particularly as regards the end of the judgment of nations, Daniel
describes not one throne but many thrones as being just located in the
heavenly places for the sole purpose of being a seat for the Lord God
Almighty. After describing this "Ancient of days," Daniel tells us that the
throne of the Almighty God is now ready to be sat on and be used for
judging not only the sinful nations, but also the Dragon, the Beast, and the
False Prophet. In the books of Revelation and Daniel, we read:

*And he opened his mouth in blasphemy against God, to
blaspheme his name, and his tabernacle, and them that dwell
in heaven (Rev. 13:6).*

*I beheld then because of the voice of the great words which
the horn spake: I beheld even till the beast was slain, and his
body destroyed, and given to this burning flame (Dan. 7:11).*

16. Confirming Christ's superiority, as the Son of God over the angelic beings, the writer of the book of Hebrews points out that this Lamb
of God has a throne that is by far more excellent and more everlasting,
and its "sceptre of righteousness is the sceptre of the kingdom" (Heb.
1:8^b). The same writer demonstrates to us how, "[w]e have such an high
priest, who is set on the right hand of the throne of the Majesty in the
heavens" (Heb. 8:1^b). It is this "throne of the Majesty" that God has
decided to take down to the lower heavens, to the heavenly places, to the
realm of the air, where He will closely commune with His people as He
governs them, and be with them, in righteousness and justice.

17. John describes this throne of God in this fashion: First, the throne
was placed upon "a sea of glass like unto crystal" (Rev. 4:6). Secondly, in
the midst and around the throne there were "four beasts full of eyes before
and behind" (Rev. 4:6). Thirdly, the noble personage that sat on the throne
looked "like a jasper and a sardius stone" (Rev. 4:3). Fourth, round

about the throne were four and twenty seats occupied by "four and twenty elders sitting, clothed in white raiment, and they had on their heads crowns of gold" (Rev. 4:4). The scene is majestic; the thrones are ready; God and His Son are seated in the midst of the throne; it is time to now open the book of books.

IV. The Lord Opens the Book

18. It is interesting to observe that, in Revelation, Chapter 5, the Lamb of God stood in the midst of the four beasts and of the four and twenty elders. The Lamb is seen standing; He is about to do something. While all else had failed to open the book, "the Lion of the tribe of Judah, the Root of David, hath prevailed" (Rev. 5:5), and He is the One to open the book. The Lamb of God comes forward and takes "the book out of the right hand of him [God] that sat upon the throne" (Rev. 5:6). As the Lamb takes the book, "the four beasts, or creatures, and the four and twenty elders fell down before the Lamb" (Rev. 5:8). At this moment, it appears that the entire heaven broke into singing:

> *And they sung a new song, saying, Thou art worthy to take the book, and to open the seals thereof: for thou wast slain, and hast redeemed us to God by thy blood out of every kindred, and tongue, and people, and nation; [a]nd hast made us unto our God kings and priests: and we shall reign on the earth (Rev. 5:9, 10).*

19. As the Lamb opens the book, which no one else could open, the angels of heaven began singing praises to Him that unfolded the book. The angelic choir is joined by the four beasts and by the four and twenty elders in singing. The number of the angelic choir is limitless and innumerable. It is an incomprehensible number (Rev. 5:11)! They all began singing in unison to the Lamb of God with a loud voice that almost shook the heaven and the earth from their foundations, saying: "Worthy is the Lamb that was slain" (Rev. 5:12). He is proclaimed the Mighty God, the Saviour of mankind. Perhaps, they also could join Isaiah the prophet in his exaltation of the redeemer, saying, "And righteousness shall be the girdle of his loins, and faithfulness the girdle of his reign" (Isa. 11:5). But the angels continue to sing praises to the Lamb:

> *And I beheld, [says John] and I heard the voice of many angels round about the throne and the beasts and the elders: and the number of them was ten thousand times ten thousand, and thousands of thousands; Saying with a loud voice, Worthy is the Lamb that was slain to receive power, and riches, and wisdom, and strength, and honour, and glory, and blessing (Rev. 5:11, 12).*

20. A large congregation of singers which includes every creature — whether from heaven or from the earth — soon began to sing the praises of the Lamb, saying, "Blessing, and honour, and glory, and power, be unto him that sitteth upon the throne, and unto the Lamb for ever and ever" (Rev. 5:13b). Oh what a choir! And what a chorus! Finally, heaven and earth are joined together to sing God's praises and adoration to the Lamb of God which was slain for the sake of our redemption. They rendered glory to His name for ever and ever. And now the universal ensemble, made up of the heavenly and earthly creatures, are joined together in unison singing praises to God and adoration to the Lamb.

> *And every creature which is in heaven, and on the earth, and under the earth, and such as are in the sea, and all that are in them, heard I saying, [b]lessing, and honour, and glory, and power, be unto him that sitteth upon the throne, and unto the Lamb for ever and ever. And the four beasts said, Amen. And the four and twenty elders fell down and worshipped him that liveth for ever and ever (Rev. 5:13, 14).*

21. And now the throne of God and of His Christ Jesus is brought down from above, from upper heaven, and is placed in the heavenly places, in the realm of the clouds, from where God, the Lord Jesus, and the saints of every dispensation and every hue and tinge, will commune and judge the entire living world not only during the Millennial Kingdom but also for eternity thereafter. We could declare with the angels, saying, "Behold, the tabernacle of God is with men" (Rev. 21:3).

22. How wonderful is Thy Name, O Lord! How great are Thy works! Sons of men will ever praise Thee, for the beautiful things Thou hast done for them. They did not deserve They did not deserve Thy goodness; but Thou art always good. They did not merit Thy mercies; but Thou art always merciful. They are not worthy of Thy redemption; but Thou has delivered them from the power of Satan. Thou hast granted to them eternal life, despite their own weakness. Thou hast made them heirs of thy good things and coheirs with Christ, Thy Son. Thou hast given unto them to live and to rule with thee eternally. And now, thou hast blessed them with thy presence among them. Praised be thy Name! Amen.

CHAPTER 5

THE LORD'S RETURNING

For as the lightening cometh out of the east, and shineth even unto the west; so shall also the coming of the Son of man be. And he shall send his angels with a great sound of a trumpet, and they shall gather together his elect from the four winds, from one end of heaven to the other (Matt. 24:27, 31).

I. The Coming Prince

1. IF WE BELIEVE IN CHRIST and in the Scriptures that have proclaimed His first coming, then most assuredly, we must likewise believe in His second coming. In general, the Messianic prophecies, especially with respect to the second coming of our Lord, are so intertwined in the Bible that there is no excuse for us to dismiss or underestimate them. If all the passages that bespeak the second coming of our Lord Jesus Christ and the hope of eternal life through the Saviour were compiled together, we would definitely have in our hands a sizable book. As a matter of fact, such a book, or something very similar to it, does already exist in print which is entitled: *All the Messianic Prophecies of the Bible.*[1]

2. Perhaps no future event given in the prophetic message is more cherished and more anticipated by the Bible-believing Christians than the second advent of our Lord Jesus Christ. The blessed second appearance of our Saviour is in itself a test, or a scrutiny, of the hearts and souls of both the saved and the unsaved. To the saved, it is a time of joy and justification for their faithful obedience to the high calling of our God; to the unsaved, it is a time of judgment, bewilderment, and condemnation for having spurned the simple message of salvation. Of the blessed hope which the Christian has in the re-appearing of our Lord, the Apostle Paul says: "Wherefore comfort one another" (I Thes. 4:18).

3. It should not come to us, the children of God, as a surprise that the Lord's coming is near, on the horizon. The Lord Jesus Himself, on several occasions, made this matter known to His disciples. John records what the Lord said to His distraught followers with respect to His return:

> *Let not your heart be troubled: ye believe in God, believe also in me. In my Father's house are many mansions: if it were not so, I would have told you, I go to prepare a place for you. And if I go and prepare a place for you, I will come again, and receive you unto myself; that where I am, there ye may be also (John 14:1-3).*

> *I will not leave you comfortless [orphans]: I will come to you (John 14:18).*

> *And ye now therefore have sorrow: but I will see you again, and your heart shall rejoice, and your joy [over my return for you and to be with you] no man taketh from you (John 16:22).*

4. In a private meeting with their Master, on Mount Olives, the disciples — wanting to know more about His departure to the Father, about future events during His absence, and about His return for them — asked: "[W]hat shall be the sign of thy coming, and of the end of the world?" (Matt. 24:3b). As to the specific time of His return, the Savior's answer was general. With respect to the many events that would come about just before His return to the earth, the answer He gave was specific enough. Speaking to the disciples, as the Jews of the Old Testament dispensation, Jesus, likewise, provided them with an answer commensurate to the people of the seventieth week of Daniel, which covers the Tribulation Period and which would not be fulfilled until immediately before His return to the earth. Jesus said to them:

> *Immediately after the tribulation of those days. . . [there] shall appear the sign of the Son of man in heaven: and then shall all the tribes of the earth mourn, and they shall see the Son of man coming in the clouds of heaven with power and great glory (Matt. 24:29, 30).*

5. Many are those who, now and then, come up with all sorts of explanations and interpretations that supposedly pinpoint the exact timing of the Savior's second coming. Dr. Joseph Brown,[2] Manna Bible Baptist Church, said: "Those who attempt to pinpoint the exact timing of Christ's second coming are, first, making Christ a liar, and, secondly, they make His Word a lie." For, Christ said to His disciples that no man knows either the *day* or the *hour* in which the Son of Man comes. For we read in Matthew:

> *But of that day and hour knoweth no man, no, not the angels of heaven, but my Father only (Matt. 24:36).*

> *Watch therefore, for ye know neither the day nor the hour wherein the Son of man cometh (Matt. 25:13).*

6. The general longing of God's people has always been to focus attention on the return of our Lord to the earth; yet, they must not worry about the specific moment. It is useless to assume that we *can* know the precise timing of this future event, especially when our Saviour has already warned us against such an attempt. It is not only absurd, but it also leads many innocent believers into confusion, bewilderment, and discouragement. Moreover, such predictions, no matter how well-meaning, give an occasion to the non-believers to deride our faith and scoff at this cherished doctrine. Of such scoffers, Apostle Peter warns:

> *Knowing this first, that there shall come in the last days scoffers, walking after their own lusts, [a]nd saying, Where is the promise of his coming? For since the fathers fell asleep, all things continue as they were from the beginning of the creation. . . . The Lord is not slack concerning his promise, as some men count slackness; but is long-suffering to us-ward, not willing that any should perish, but that all should come to repentance (II Pet. 3:3, 4, 9).*

II. The Manner of His Return

7. The Scriptures do not tell us about the exact time of our Lord's second coming; to the contrary, both the Saviour and the Apostles, have amply warned us against any such speculations. The Lord knew very well that the disciples and their followers could very easily be subjected to deceit and treachery. He was also cognizant that the Devil would make every attempt to mislead the Apostles and their followers with respect to the exact timing of the Lord's return. In response to the disciple's direct question about the sign (and the time) of His return, both in the Olivet discourse and at the time of His ascension, Jesus said to them:

> But of that day and that hour knoweth no man, no, not
> the angels which are in heaven, neither the Son, but the Fa-
> ther. Take ye heed, watch and pray: for ye know not when
> the time is (Mark 13:32, 33).

8. While the exact time of His appearing is not known, there are, however, many hints that are clearly associated with the Second Advent of Christ. Throughout His ministry, whenever the Lord spoke of His return, Jesus mentioned only the end-time events that would be associated with it. Following after the footsteps of the Master, Apostle Paul admonishes the Thessalonians for the same, saying:

> Let no man deceive you by any means: for that day shall
> not come, except there come a falling away [apostasy] first,
> and that man of sin [the Antichrist] be revealed, the son of
> perdition [which is the Beast]; who opposeth and exalteth
> himself above all that is called God, or that is worshipped. . .
> (II Thes. 2:3, 4ª).

9. Perhaps no part of the Scriptures has captured the vision and the manner in which the Lord of glory would be revealed from heaven to the believer, as the passage the Apostle Paul wrote by inspiration to the converts at Thessalonica. Paul later recognized their bewilderment over the time of Christ's second coming. Five events will take place, Paul says, when the Lord shall descend from heaven: (1) He will descend with a shout that no man can ignore; (2) He will come down with the loud voice of the archangel; (3) He will arrive with the trumpet of God; (4) He will come down in a cloud; and (5) He will be accompanied with power and great glory.

10. Convinced possibly by false teachers of the early days of the Church, the followers of Christ were disturbed and had thought "that the persecutions from which they were suffering were those of the 'great and terrible day of the Lord,' from which they had been taught to expect deliverance by 'the day of Christ, and our gathering together unto him.'"[3] And so, Paul had already warned them, saying:

> *For the Lord himself shall descend from heaven with a shout, with the voice of the archangel, and with the trump of God: and the dead in Christ shall rise first: Then we which are alive and remain shall be caught up together with them in the clouds, to meet the Lord in the air: and so shall we ever be with the Lord. Wherefore comfort one another with these words (I Thes. 4:16-18).*

11. With respect to the manner in which the Lord will return from heaven, it is very interesting and even heartwarming for the child of God to observe how beautifully the cloud, or clouds, figure in the Scriptures with the second coming of our Saviour. Just as His ascension was in clouds, so too, the coming of the Lord will be in clouds.[4] Likewise, the raptured Church will be caught up together in the cloud (I Thes. 4:17). It is interesting to observe how God uses even such seemingly fleeting and unstable objects, such as the cloud, for His glory. Time would not allow us, even if as an unintended diversion, to refer to all such instances in the Bible where a cloud has indeed rendered profitable service in the hands of the Almighty God its creator. Christ tells us in the Gospel of Matthew the following:

> *And then shall appear the sign of the Son of man in heaven: and then shall all the tribes of the earth mourn, and they shall see the Son of man coming in the clouds of heaven with power and great glory (Matt. 24:30).*

12. In like manner, the second coming of the Lord, physically, was very clearly and emphatically announced to the eleven disciples by the two "men" which appeared to them in white apparel at the time of Christ's ascension. The two angels not only did testify of Christ's return, but also confirmed that His return would be "in like manner," which also means "physically," and yet glorified. And so we read in the book of Acts:

> *And while they looked steadfastly toward heaven as he [the Lord] went up, behold, two men stood by them in white apparel; [w]hich also said, Ye men of Galilee, why stand ye gazing up into heaven? This same Jesus, which is taken up from you into heaven, shall so come in like manner as ye have seen him go into heaven (Acts 1:10, 11).*

III. Preparations for His Return

13. The events leading to the second coming of Christ provide us with an unprecedented drama. In this drama, there are two major acts: the descent of Christ into the air where He will meet His bride; and His descent from there to the earth, seven years later, where His feet will touch the Mount of Olives. Often the second act is called *parusia*, or *unveiling*, or *openness to the public*; it is the time when Christ manifests Himself physically to the entire living world on the earth. This time, however, He comes not as the meek and lowly one, the lamb of God to be slain for the sins of the world, but as the Judge and the Ruler of the entire world. When Christ comes in the air, the first act in this drama, He will be met there by His Bride, the Church, which is composed of the believers of all ages and dispensations. Of this event Paul says:

> *[A]nd the dead in Christ shall rise first. Then we which are alive and remain shall be caught up together with them in the clouds, to meet the Lord in the air (I Thes. 4:16^b, 17^a).*

14. Before this blessed reunion takes place in the air, however, this vast extraterrestrial domain, which Apostle Paul calls in Ephesians, "the heavenly places," must be utterly liberated from Satan and his demonic forces and be cleansed from all vice. For it is here that God will subsequently establish His throne, the headquarters from which He will first judge the world through His Son, the Lord Jesus Christ, and rule over the saints of the Millennial Kingdom. Of the ugly defeat that the dragon, that old Serpent, suffered at the hands of Michael, the archangel, the Psalmist by inspiration declares: "Thou [God] hast made his glory to cease, and [hast] cast his throne down to the ground" (Ps. 89:44).

15. In his epistle to the Ephesians, Paul, describing the object of the warfare of the believers, refers to this region of heaven, which is directly situated above the earth, the atmosphere, as the "heavenly places" (Eph. 3:10). This place is located in the lower parts of the heavens, and it is synonymous with the term "air," and the term "cloud," in which Satan and his cohorts have dwelled since their rebellion against God and his being cast out of heaven at the time of creation. It should be pointed out that while God is omnipresent, He has allowed Satan, the old Serpent, Lucifer, to reside there until the end time. Through inspiration, Paul tells the Church at Ephesus where this region is:

> *For we wrestle not against flesh and blood, but against principalities, against powers, against the rulers of the darkness of this world, against spiritual wickedness in high places (Eph. 6:12).*

> *To the intent that now unto the principalities and powers in heavenly places might be known by the church the manifold wisdom of God, [a]ccording to the eternal purpose which he purposed in Christ Jesus our Lord (Eph. 3:10, 11).*

> *Wherein in time past ye walked according to the course of this world, according to the prince of the power of the air, the spirit that now worketh in the children of disobedience (Eph. 2:2).*

16. Of this lower heaven, or the heavenly places, where "the prince of the power of the air" dwells, God declares that, along with the earth,

He will shake the heavens mightily in order to reveal the temporal things from the eternal, the durable and long-lasting elements of God, from the impermanent endeavors of Satan. God will finally draw a distinction between the wicked forces of Satan and the righteous hosts of the Almighty. The writer of the book of Hebrews admonishes the Hebrew believers concerning this destruction. Isaiah appertains this destruction to the wrath of God towards the Wicked One. Haggai has already emphasized this shaking of the "heavenly places," along with the wicked earth. Observe their declarations:

> See that ye refuse not him that speaketh. . . from heaven: Whose voice then shook the earth: but now he hath promised, saying, Yet once more I will shake not the earth only, but also heaven. And this word, Yet once more, signifieth removing of those things that are shaken, as of things that are made, that those things which cannot be shaken may remain (Heb. 12:25-28).

> Therefore I will shake the heavens, and the earth shall move out of her place, in the wrath of the Lord of hosts, and in the day of his fierce anger (Isa. 13:13).

> For thus saith the Lord of hosts; Yet once, it is a little while, and I will shake the heavens, and the earth, and the sea, and the dry land; And I will shake all nations. . . . (Hag. 2:6-7a).

17. In the long run, this long awaited general shaking and cleansing of the heaven and the earth undertaken by God the Almighty, covers not only Satan and his forces, but also the vestiges of evil committed by his demonic forces both in the "heavenly places" and also amongst the "children of disobedience" on the earth. At a predetermined time, God's fierce wrath will be unleashed once again, "against principalities, against powers, against the rulers of the darkness of this world, against spiritual wickedness in high places," according to Paul (Eph. 6:12). It is very important to recognize that Isaiah, likewise, spoke about this heavenly sphere, the "heavenly places" in the air, where Lucifer was banished from before the throne of the Holy God:

> *How art thou fallen from heaven, O Lucifer, son of the morning! How art thou cut down to the ground, which didst weaken [through your guile] the nations! Yet thou shalt be brought down to hell, to the sides of the [deep] pit (Isa. 14:12, 15).*

18. This cleansing of wickedness begins with the heavenly places, from where "the prince of the power of the air," Satan himself, has directed his evil operations against humanity and strengthened and sustained the "children of disobedience" in their supportive actions to Satan against the children of God. From this territory, which is the uppermost part of the global earth, Satan and his cohorts have carried out their wicked operations against the entire human race. It is time now that it be taken over, be vacated of Satan and of sin, and be purged, purified and readied, according to the Master's master-plan. For it is here, in the heavenly places, that the throne of God will be re-established (Rev. 15:5; 21:3); to where the Lord Jesus Christ will descend to receive His Bride; and from which to rule the entire world during the Millennial Kingdom.

IV. "Jesus Is Coming Again"

19. There is absolutely no doubt of the fact that the Lord Jesus Christ is coming soon. No Christian believer doubts the imminence of the second coming of our Saviour. This is the glorious belief all true Christians have maintained since the time when "he was taken up; and a cloud received him out of their sight" (Acts 1:9b), and when "two men stood by them in white apparel" (Acts 1:10), saying: "Ye men of Galilee, why stand ye gazing up into heaven? [T]his same Jesus, which is taken up from you into heaven, shall so come in like manner as ye have seen him go into heaven" (Acts 1:11b). The same message still reverberates and resounds in the heart and mind of every believing Christian today. Jesus Christ is coming soon and in the same manner and the same physical likeness and form as he has gone away.

20. The throne of God is now ready; it has been transferred from upper heaven to the lower one, to the heavenly places (Eph. 3:10), the hevenlies (Eph. 6:12), where God the Father and God the Holy Spirit will congregate and witness God the Son receiving His Bride. The throne is now ready to receive the redeemed ones who are just arriving from the earth. Yes, God has appointed for us a day that we should see our Bridegroom and be with Him eternally.

> *For the grace of God that bringeth salvation hath appeared to all men, [t]eaching us that, denying ungodliness and worldly lusts, we should live soberly, righteously, and godly, in this present world; Looking for that blessed hope, and the glorious appearing of the great God and our Saviour Jesus Christ; Who gave himself for us, that he might redeem us from all iniquity, and purify unto himself a peculiar people, zealous of good works (Tit. 2:11-14).*

> *Faithful is he that calleth you, who also will do it (I Thes. 5:24). And being fully persuaded that, what he had promised, he was able also to perform (Rom. 4:21).*

21. The following hymn was written by Mabel Johnston Camp,[5] 1871-1937. The words in it will warm your soul and prepare your heart for the second coming of our Saviour.

HE IS COMING AGAIN

> Lift up your heads, pilgrims aweary!
>> See day's approach now crimson the sky;
> Night shadows flee, and your beloved,
>> Awaiteth with longing, at last draweth nigh.
>
> He is coming again, He is coming again,
> The very Lord Jesus rejected of men;
> Pow'r and great glory, He is coming again!

O blessed hope! O blissful promise!
      Filling our hearts with rapture divine;
O day of days! Hail Thy appearing!
      The transcendent glory forever shall shine!

Dark was the night — sin warred against us!
      Heavy the load of sorrow we bore;
But now we see signs of His coming —
      Our hearts glow within us, joy's cup runneth o'er!

Even so, come, precious Lord Jesus!
      Creation waits redemption to see;
Caught up in clouds, soon we shall meet Thee —
      O blessed assurance, forever with Thee.

CHAPTER 6

SATAN: HIS ORIGIN AND HIS FINALE

Ye are of your father the devil, and the lust of your father
ye will do. He was a murderer from the beginning, and abode
not in the truth, because there is no truth in him. When he
speaketh a lie, he speaketh of his own: for he is a liar, and the
father of it (John 8:44).

I. The Origin of Satan

1. IN THIS CHAPTER WE shall see that Satan, who in Isaiah, Chapter 14, Verse 12, is called Lucifer, was very likely the highest ranking angelic being among the archangels God had created. In both rank and responsibility, Lucifer — the bright one — outranked, in many ways, even the other two archangels: Gabriel and Michael. Observe the following remark: "Thou art the anointed Cherub that covers; and I have set thee so; thou wast upon the holy mountain of God. . . ." (Ez. 28:14). God further says, I have put you upon My holy mountain (Ez. 28:14^{b}). Gabriel is portrayed in the Scriptures primarily as the news bearer to the people of God; Michael is the warrior angel who fights on behalf of God and of His people. By God's people, it is meant here the believers of all ages and of all dispensations, be they the believing Jews or the believing Gentiles.

2. It appears that God had given Lucifer the responsibility of caring for, or covering, the mankind that was yet to be created. Lucifer was not only the closest to God in his position, but was also the greatest in his responsibilities. He was an anointed "Cherub that covereth" (Ez. 28:14); he was "set so" by God Himself. He was set upon the holy mountain of God. Now this holy mountain was "the mount of the congregation" (Is. 14:13), where the children of God, Adam and his posterity, would have been dwelling once they were created. It points to the fact that Lucifer would have had the responsibility of caring for and "covering" mankind once they were called into existence.

3. There are a number of Bible prophecy interpreters that see Lucifer as a chief musician; this is sheer speculation, especially since some of these cherubim (Hebrew plural) do sing glory to God for His holiness. That he was, indeed, a cherub, there appears to be no doubt. About his position, however, we have scanty suggestions in the Word of God. Some important prophetic descriptions about Lucifer give us a clue of who he was and why he fell from God's grace. The Bible says: "Thou has been in Eden the garden of God. . . in the day that thou was created" (Ez. 28:13). What was this Archangel doing in the garden of Eden upon his creation? Of course, the garden of Eden was the place God had created for Adam and his succeeding generations. Hence, God had placed Lucifer in the garden of Eden, where this Archangel would take care of the man, which He would subsequently create and place there. For we read in the book of Genesis the following:

> . . . *Thus saith the Lord God; Thou sealest up the sum, full of wisdom, and perfect in beauty. Thou hast been in Eden the Garden of God; every precious stone was thy covering, the sardius, topaz, and the diamond, the beryl, the onyx, and the jasper, the sapphire, emerald, and the carbuncle, and gold: the workmanship of thy tabrets and of thy pipes was prepared in thee in the day that thou wast created. (Ez. 28:12[b]-13).*

4. The second proposition about Lucifer is that he was specially created to make a *covering*, that is to take care of the soon-to-be-created mankind. "Thou art the anointed cherub that covereth; and I have set thee so" (Ez. 28:14[a]). God had created and ordained this great Archangel to provide a covering for the children of men; and God emphasizes that He had willed it as such. To this great Archangel, who was possibly the leader of the cherubim, God would have entrusted the responsibility of the man once created. God tells Lucifer that He was created to become a covering and a protection to the would-be created mankind. The man whom I will create will become the pupil of my own eyes; you will "cover" him for me. That the word "cover" means connotatively to "protect" or to "take care of," is evident from the syntactic usage of the term. In Isaiah we read how God employs the word to mean: "Let mine outcasts dwell with thee, Moab: be thou a *cover* to them from the face of the spoiler; for the extortioner [Satan] is at an end. . . ." (Is. 16:4ᵃ). (*Italics added*).

5. Another meaningful proposition the Lord God of heaven makes about this Archangel is: "[T]hou was upon the holy mountain of God" (Ez. 28:14ᵇ). The expression, "the holy mountain of God," usually implies "the holy congregation of God." Other than its usage with respect to the congregation of angels, the word also means the very center of God's holy people. Initially, God had created His people holy and righteous; they were to remain pure eternally. Lucifer would provide for the people, "the holy congregation of God," all their needs to live in the presence of the Almighty. Alas! Satan, early on, successfully beguiled man, thereby causing his plunge into sinfulness and, accordingly, into the lake of fire.

6. Lucifer's illustrious position under God was not acceptable to him; he decided to rebel against the Almighty. He struck out alone; subsequently, he also subverted mankind and brought it under his sway, holding its dead captives, or hostages, in sheol for himself (Ps. 68:18; Eph. 4:8; 2 Tim. 2:26). The Creator could either let go of Adam and his descendants eternally, or redeem him through the precious and commensurate price, the blood of the Lord Jesus Christ.

7. The Hebrew word for Lucifer is **Heylil**, which means "the bright one." In Hebrew, **ben shakhar** means "son of the morning," which implies, "early," or "the first born," thereby indicating that Lucifer was the first angel God ever created. **Heylil** is also the name of the planet Venus. According to Ezekiel, Chapter 28, Verses 12 to 17, Satan is called by this name, because, like the planet Venus, he was bright and brilliant, full of intelligence and had great propensity to accomplish things. Ezekiel describes Lucifer's creation as follows:

> *Thou art the anointed Cherub that covereth; and I have set thee so: thou wast upon the holy mountain of God; thou hast walked up and down in the midst of the stones of fire. Thou wast perfect in thy ways from the day that thou wast created, till iniquity was found in thee. (Ez. 28:14-15).*

8. Despite his lofty position among the creatures of the Almighty God, Lucifer found it necessary to rebel against the Lord of heaven in an attempt to place his throne above that of Jehovah. The Lord reveals to this misguided Devil his treachery and casts him down to the earth. But before doing so, God describes him as he is, the Wicked One, and declares him guilty before the entire creation. In Isaiah, God says:

> *How art thou fallen from heaven, O Lucifer, son of the morning! How art thou cut down to the ground, which didst weaken the nations! (Isa. 14:12).*

9. God knows every thought we have and every idea we harbor; He singles out our opinions and even provides for us their results. He knows how we think and what we say even before we think or say anything. His holiness has so permeated His being that He cannot stand any falsehood. He must eradicate evil before it starts to become a major stumbling block. Men's hearts are wide open before our God, and He knows their contents very well (Rev. 2:23; 1 Chro. 28:9). God opens wide the heart of Lucifer, the old Serpent, Satan himself, and tells him his exact thoughts. And so, God tells Lucifer:

> *For thou hast said in thine heart:*
> *I will ascend into heaven,*
> *I will exalt my throne above the stars of God:*
> *I will sit also upon the mount of the congregation,*
> *[I will sit] in the sides [neighborhood] of the north:*
> *I will ascend above the heights of the clouds;*
> *I will be like the most High [God] (Isaiah 14:13-14).*

10. Seeing the roots of Tyre's wickedness, Ezekiel prophetically speaks of Lucifer's downfall. The Prophet realizes that this evil that has so captured the world is rooted in the Devil himself. He, too, reveals it and forthwith condemns it. The Prophet knows very well that when sin is discovered, it must immediately be made known and condemned. Man, though sinful and wicked himself, deserves from God the ultimate of truthfulness. And God tells it as it is; He, through the mouth of His prophet, exposes the Wicked One as he is.

*Thou wast perfect in thy ways from the day that thou
wast created, till iniquity was found in thee. . . . thou hast
sinned: I will cast thee as profane out of the mountain of
God: and I will destroy thee, O covering cherub. . . . Thine
heart was lifted up because of thy beauty, thou hast corrupted
thy wisdom by reason of thy brightness: I will cast thee to the
ground. . . (Ez. 28:12-17).*

II. Satan's Confrontation with God

11. Satan, having lost his original position over the affairs of mankind
which God had created for him, now engineers a new and most subtle
plan of rebellion for humanity to follow. Unfortunately, man did, indeed,
follow the plan of the Old Serpent. Adam and Eve ate of "the tree which
is in the midst of the garden" (Gen. 3:3). They disobeyed God, transgressed against God's will, and fell from his fellowship and association
with Him. The two transgressed against God. God told them that since
they, too, had become sinners through their disobedience of His command, He would drive them out of Paradise.

*Therefore the Lord God sent him forth from the garden of
Eden, to till the ground from whence he was taken. So he
drove out the man; and he placed at the east of the garden of
Eden Cherubims, and a flaming sword which turned every
way, to keep the way of the tree of life (Gen. 3:23, 24).*

12. Having finally gained dominion over the affairs of mankind since
Adam's fall, Satan now realizes that, sooner or later, he will lose that
power. He knows that the Lord Jesus Christ, whose throne he attempts
to usurp, is coming down to the earth to restore the Royal Seat and to
reestablish the Millennial Kingdom on the earth. The Dragon does not
want to give up his claim upon the earth and over the people of the earth.
He wants to secure his control over its inhabitants.

13. Behind the scenes, Satan works out his ultimate plan for confrontation with Christ, making full use of "the children of disobedience," to
resist Christ's descent to the earth. In order to frustrate Christ's planned

invasion of the earth, the Old Serpent reinforces his power in the air, in the high places. Satan also knows full well that he must fight to hold on to his territory in the air, in the heavenlies, where his throne is, to prevent Christ's descent to the clouds where He will establish His throne and meet His Bride, the Church. (I Thes. 4:16, 17).

14. Before Christ Jesus comes down to the clouds, God commands Michael, the warrior archangel, to recapture this region from Satan and his cohorts in preparation for the setting of His throne there. In a desperate move, Satan, the Old Serpent, the Devil, puts forth a show of force in heaven, or the heavenlies, and, at the same time, he bolsters his position on the earth. In the "woman with child," Satan thinks he has a suitable hostage. The one-third, remnant of Israel as a nation, which has now accepted Christ as its Messiah, is now at his mercy. He threatens to destroy her. For we read:

> *And there appeared another wonder in heaven; and behold a great red dragon, having seven heads and ten horns, and seven crowns upon his head. . . . And the dragon stood before the woman which was ready to be delivered, for to devour her child as soon as it was born (Rev. 12:3, 4[b]).*

15. It is apparent that the Devil knows quite well that he has established his claim over a sinful humanity through the person of his own "son," the Beast. Accordingly, he displays his symbolic power to the world: the "seven heads and the ten horns" (Rev. 13:1). But God in His mercy, has His own plans for the woman, the remnant of Israel, to escape into the wilderness of Moab. It is very likely that the woman will resort to Petra, in today's Jordan, where provisions, ahead of time, will be prepared for her by God according to the Scriptures. Isaiah tells us how God commanded Moab to protect the woman. For we read in Isaiah:

> *Let mine outcasts dwell with thee, Moab; be thou a covert to them from the face of the spoiler; for the extortioner is at an end, the spoiler ceaseth, the oppressors are consumed out of the land (Is. 16:4).*

III. War in Heaven

16. We are talking now about the warfare that has been taking place in the universe perhaps since the fall of Lucifer. In its enlarged scope, this struggle is a conflict between the Almighty God and His angels and saints, on the one hand; on the other, Satan and his demonic angels, along with the children of disobedience who follow him, are putting up a battle with the Lord God Almighty. In a way, this confrontation is between Good and Evil. At certain intervals and as dictated by the Almighty God, the battle becomes very serious and unrestrained.

17. God, the Creator, has allowed Satan and his cohorts to exist since the foundation of the world, since the fall of Lucifer; for whatever reason, the Almighty has, throughout the course of human history, permitted the Devil and his cohorts to excruciate mankind. Albeit, this angel of light has since become a thorn in the side of God's saints. However, Satan's catastrophic end is sure. He will not escape God's swift punishment. Jesus said to His seventy disciples after they returned from their highly successful mission of evangelization: "I beheld Satan as lightening fall from heaven" (Luke 10:18).

18. The Lord Jesus Christ called Satan "a liar and father of it" (John 8:44b). Notice the expression "father of it"; which means that he is the father and the contriver of all lies. It is interesting to observe how the Antichrist, Lucifer, invented the lies; he is the father of all falsehood. He is not only a liar; he is, likewise, a murderer from the very beginning. Christ told the apostate Jews of His days, "If God were your Father, ye would love me" (John 8:42). "Ye are of your father the devil, and the lust of your father ye will do" (John 8:44a).

19. Before Christ begins His descent to the air to set up His throne, Satan, whose headquarters are still in the air, in the high places (Eph. 6:12), must first be dislodged, along with his cohorts, and that territory be vacated and cleansed from all evil. Michael and his angels attack and mercilessly defeat and rout Satan and his evil forces from this region. The great archangel, Michael, casts the Dragon and his cohorts out of the air, out of the high places, into the ground. For we read in the book of Revelation the following:

> And there was war in heaven: Michael and his angels fought against the dragon; and the dragon fought and his angels, [a]nd prevailed not; nor could they keep their place in heaven anymore. And the dragon was cast out, that old serpent, called the Devil, and Satan, which deceiveth the whole world: he was cast out into the earth, and his angels with him (Rev. 12:7-9).

20. On the earth, at the beginning of the second half of the Tribulation Period, Satan now intensifies his wrath against the saints of God, both Jews and Gentiles, the new believers on the earth. As a result of his defeat in the air and his pending doom on the earth, he now prepares to harm the living believers of the earth. Any one confessing Jesus Christ as his or her Saviour is immediately destroyed or beheaded. Of this John records:

> Woe to the inhabiters of the earth [Jews] and of the seas [Gentiles]! For the devil has come down unto you, having great wrath, because he knoweth that he hath but a short time (Rev. 12:12b).

> And to the woman were given two wings of a great eagle, that she might fly into the wilderness, into her place, where she is nourished for a time, and [two] times, and half a time[1], from the face of the serpent (Rev. 12:14).

> And the dragon was wroth with the woman, and went to make war with the remnant of her seed, which kept the commandment of God, and have the testimony of Jesus Christ (Rev. 12:17).

IV. Michael's Victory

21. God's cleansing of the entire universe from sin and wickedness covers the first stage of its implementation; at the time of his initial rebellion, the altercation takes place in the air, in the heavenly places, the atmospheric region directly above the earth. It is here where almost the entire forces of the Evil One are located. It is from here, from this wicked region, Satan and his demonic forces have ceaselessly conspired against God and His saints. It is to this "celestial" territory that Lucifer and his cohorts were banished from the presence of the Almighty God as a result of Lucifer's initial rebellion. It is this evil-infested region that must now be thoroughly cleansed before the blessed Lord meets His resurrected, glorified, and raptured Bride, which is composed of the believers of all ages and of all dispensations. It is precisely to this area that Michael, the great archangel of war, is sent to begin his sweeping campaign of conquest and cleansing.

22. To prove his prowess and his serious intentions, while yet in the presence of God in the heavenly places, Satan, like his son, the *scarlet-colored* Beast (Rev. 17:3), appears now as a *red* Dragon, full of confidence and ready for battle. His threats of destruction against the woman, Israel, and his attempt to devour her man-child, the Lord Jesus Christ, continue unabated. In order to demonstrate his capabilities, he literally goes berserk; with one sweep of his tail, he casts the stars of heaven to the earth, where the woman resides under his sway (Rev. 12:3-4). But before he is able to destroy Israel, the woman flees into the wilderness.

23. In order to arrive at a proper understanding of Satan's attempt to devour the "man-child," it is essential to realize that some aspects of this threat have already been fulfilled at the time of our Saviour's birth and immediately thereafter. Through the instrumentality of Herod, the king of the Jews, (and at the behest of Satan,) the children of Bethlehem, two years and below, were put to death in a hopeful attempt to destroy the baby Jesus. Out of their fear for the child and through God's command, Joseph and Mary took Jesus into Egypt for His safety until the death of this butcher king. Subsequently and on numerous occasions, the Wicked One made every attempt to discredit, destroy, and distract the Saviour from fulfilling His mission on the earth. Satan's temptation of Christ on a high mountain and in the Garden of Gethsemane were such attempts; albeit, they were unfruitful undertakings.

24. Great importance should be attached to this battle between Michael and the Dragon. In the program of God for the end times, Satan and his forces must, step-by-calculated-step, be defeated and destroyed, and his territories reclaimed and cleansed, until finally the old enemy is crushed and put to eternal "unrest" in the fires of hell. This victorious battle by Michael is the first in a series of final battles God and His angels and saints will launch against the Dragon and his cohorts. In the eternal program of God, Satan is already defeated; at the same time, He has allowed this sinful creature, for a short season, to exercise his wickedness over the earth almost without restrictions. Because of this, the Apostle Paul identifies Satan as "the prince of the power of the air, the spirit that now worketh in the children of disobedience" (Eph. 2:2).

25. This great victory of Michael, the archangel and his angelic forces, over the dragon and his wicked forces, gives cause to the multitudes of heaven, in heavenly places, to express with loud voices: (1) their great joy over the defeat of the "accuser of our brethren"; (2) to warn, with woes the inhabitants of the earth and the sea [Jews and gentiles], against the wrathful descent of the dragon to the earth. Of this episode, John writes:

> *Woe to the inhabiters of the earth [Jews], and of the sea [Gentiles]! for the devil is come down unto you, having great wrath, because he knoweth that he hath but a short time (Rev. 12:12[b]).*

V. A Brief Summary:

26. Christ prepares to come down to the earth. On His way, He will first stop in the air, the heavenly places. There, He will commune with His Bride for seven years, while on the earth there will be the tribulation period. But the upper air, the heavenly places, is the abode of Satan and his demonic cohorts since the fall of Lucifer (Is. 14:12-17). This region, then, must be purified from wickedness. To do so, Satan, the old Dragon, must first be banished and driven out of it, and be cast out to the earth. Michael and his angels are tasked to do the job. The mighty archangel fights the dragon and his demonic angels; he overcomes him and his forces, and casts them down to the earth.

27. Now that the air region, the heavenly places, is cleared and cleansed from sin and from iniquity, God moves His tabernacle and His throne into this purified domain from which to give Satan a final blow, to reclaim what is His, and to rule the world during the Millennial Kingdom. In this realm, seated by the right hand of Majesty, the Lord Jesus Christ will meet His Bride, the Church.

28. While tribulation rages on the earth, three glorious events will transpire in this sphere, in the heavenly places. The Lord will establish His judgment seat, the *bema* of Christ, to judge the believers for their works and prepare His Church for the Marriage of the Lamb. The Marriage of the Lamb is finally consummated. Likewise, the Marriage Supper takes place in heaven. The last resurrection of believers martyred during the Tribulation Period takes place just immediately before the Lord Jesus comes down to the earth. Preparations to finally invade the earth itself take place. Having defeated His enemies on the earth, Christ judges the living nations of the earth who had escaped the tribulation's trials. Christ restores the "usurped" throne of Israel, sets the resurrected David upon that throne (Ez. 37:24, 25), and proclaims Himself as THE KING OF KINGS, AND LORD OF LORDS. All the kings and lords of the redeemed nations are now brought under Christ's immediate rule (Rev. 19:16)

29. As for Lucifer, that Old Dragon, God says to him, "You are finished"! You have run your course and committed the most heinous crimes against the children of God. The bottomless pit awaits you for a thousand years. You will be shut in it until I bring you up again and for a special purpose. Although Satan is still under the eternal condemnation of God, and eventually he will be thrown into the fire and brimstone for eternity, the Almighty God has some more work for this Wicked One to do at the very end of the Millennial Age. When the Millennial Age has ended, the Almighty God will, once again, call out the Devil from the bottomless pit. The Lord will loose the Devil free from the bottomless pit to accomplish one more major objective on the earth, as we shall see later.

30. In heaven there is a great tumult concerning the mighty victory Michael, the archangel, has over the dragon and his emissaries. The end of the Dragon and his associates is very close. The victory of this archangel is celebrated in heaven by all of its inhabitants. This victory is sure, and it is eternal; it has brought shame and disdain not only upon the Dragon and his cohorts, but also upon the Beast, the False Prophet, and their followers. Joyful praises are sung about Michael's victory. For we read in the book of Revelation the following:

> *And I heard a loud voice saying in heaven, Now is come salvation, and strength, and the kingdom of our God, and the power of his Christ: for the accuser of our brethren is cast down, which accused them before our God day and night. Therefore rejoice, ye heavens, and ye that dwell in them. . . (Rev. 12:10, 11).*

CHAPTER 7

THE RAPTURE OF THE CHURCH

For the Lord himself shall descend from heaven with a shout, with the voice of the archangel, and with the trump of God: and the dead in Christ shall rise first: Then we which are alive and remain shall be caught up together with them in the clouds, to meet the Lord in the air: and so shall we ever be with the Lord (1 Thes. 4:16, 17).

I. The Glorified, Exalted Church

1. THAT THE RAPTURE of the church takes place at the end time is a well known fact for the believing Christian; when the exact timing of this glorification and exaltation of the Church occurs, however, is now a subject for speculation only. In the preceding chapter, especially in the summary, a number of events associated with the second coming of Christ were cited. It is very clear, however, that God the Father with His Son must first descend from heaven and establish His throne in the air, in the "heavenly places," which Michael has just recaptured from Satan and cleansed it (Rev. 12:9; Ps. 89:44). Simultaneously, with Christ's descent to the air, the believing Church, the Bride of Christ, both dead and alive, shall also be caught up together in the clouds to meet her Bridegroom in the heavenly places.

2. Perhaps no other more significant event of prophecy exists that is so very closely associated with the second coming of Christ as the rapture of the believing Church. The fact that the word "rapture" is not used in the Scriptures, does not matter; it is clearly implied. Paul firmly warns the believers at Thessalonica that they should not be deceived by any means with respect to the exact time when "the day of Christ [will be] at hand" (II Thes. 2:1, 2). The Apostle Paul chronologically relates the following two major events that should come about before Christ's return. While no exact time-table is specified for the rapture of the Church, two end-time events must take place, at this juncture in time when the rapture occurs. These two events are: First, there must be a spiritual falling away, an apostasy in the Church. Secondly, the Man of Sin, the Son of Perdition, that is, the Beast, must also be revealed (II Thes. 2:3). The problem with these two events is that neither of them provides any specific point in time for their occurance.

3. It has already been explained how in the end time there will come about a general falling away from the truth — an apostasy in religion. Such an apostasy will certainly manifest itself in the every-day moral conditions of mankind, and more so in political affairs. Accordingly, the Beast cannot be revealed and formally declared as the new Saviour of mankind, while the Holy Spirit and the Church are yet on the earth. Remember, the Tribulation Period is a time of wrath; it is a time when God pours out His judgments and His indignation upon the inhabitants of the earth and upon the new Master of the world. Indwelt by the Holy Spirit as it is, the Church could not remain on the earth at a time when Satan has been given by God a full sway over the affairs of mankind. And when the Beast is declared openly, Satan has almost full control of the earth. Of this, Paul declares:

> Let no man deceive you by any means: for that day [the day of Christ] shall not come, except there come first a falling away [apostasy], and secondly that man of sin [the Antichrist] be revealed, the son of perdition. . . . For the mystery of iniquity doth already work: only he who now letteth [hindereth] will [continue to] let [hinder], until he [the Holy Spirit] be taken out of the way. And then shall that wicked [one] be revealed. . . (II Thes. 2:3, 7-8).

II. A Premillennial Position

4. Various Christian denominations differ in their viewpoint regarding the exact timing of the rapture with respect to the periods of the Tribulation and the Millennial Age. This author strongly believes and tenaciously advocates the Pretribulationist-Premillennialist position. This position is based on a compelling reason to adhere to a literal interpretation of the Bible prophecy. This position is adhered to by practically all fundamental, conservative, Bible believers. Accordingly, the Church's glorification and her exaltation take place immediately before the Tribulation Period begins, and before the Beast — the Antichrist, the ruler of the end-time Gentile World Empire — is presented to the world at large.

5. For those who believe in a literal second coming of Christ, the Church's rapture takes place immediately before or simulataneously when the Tribulation Period begins. This position, regarding the time of the rapture vis-a-vis the Tribulation Period, allows for a literal and physical return of Christ and for a literal interpretation of the prophetic passages of the Scripture. Despite its richness in symbolism, the prophetic portions of the Bible, including the books of Daniel and Revelation, become more readily subject to a literal interpretation from a Pretribulational-Premillennial position than from any other position. Unless the Bible clearly states against a verbatim interpretation of a prophetic passage, most pretribulational, premillennial Bible scholars have strongly advocated such an interpretation.

6. The second coming of Christ, as it was mentioned in the Fifth Chapter, must be viewed as a drama having two main acts: Christ's descent to the air, where He is to be met by the just raptured Church, and Christ's advent to the earth, to the Mount of Olives, accompanied by the armies of His saints. Between the two descents — first to the air, then to the earth — there will be a lapse of about seven years. With respect to the Church in the air, several important events will take place during the seven years, in preparation for the re-establishment of the Davidic Kingdom: (1) God Almighty will descend from heaven with His Son to establish His throne in the air. (2) There will be the setting up of the *Bema* of Christ (John 19:13; II Cor. 5:10), also known as the Judgment Seat of Christ, from which the Lord Jesus will judge the works of the believers only. (3) There will be the Marriage of the Lamb, which is immediately followed by (4) the Marriage Supper of the Lamb. And (5) there will be the resurrection of the millions of saints martyred during the Tribulation Period just before His descent to the earth.

7. The pivotal point with regard to the second coming of our Saviour is not whether or not Jesus is coming, but rather that He could come today, at this very hour. If this is the premise which the Word preaches and the Apostles taught, then Christ should indeed appear at any moment. Fundamental Christians believe that Christ could come at any time; however, they confess that they know nothing about the exact timing of His appearing. This is the position advocated by the *premillennialist* believers all over. The *amillennialists*, on the other hand, do not believe that there would be a literal second coming of our Lord. References referring to the second coming of Christ are dismissed by the adherents of the Catholic faith and by the liberal clan as allegorical.

8. The *postmillennialists* advocates believe that the second coming of the Saviour will be preceded (1) by the Christianization of the entire world, (2) by the generally diminishing of the tribulation experience in the Church, and (3) by a comprehensive improvement of conditions by the end in the world. All these "glorious" experiences would eventually produce conducive circumstances for the realization of the Kingdom Age. Once these ordeals have taken place, they advocate, the Lord would come down from heaven to establish His throne and to rule over the earth.

III. Jesus' Testimony of Rapture

9. The Bible presents certain signs for the Church about the second coming of the Lord. On Mount Olives, during the Olivet discourse, the disciples asked the Master the following question: "Tell us, when shall these things be? [A]nd what shall be the sign of thy coming, and of the end of the world"? With respect to the first question, Jesus did not provide an answer to His disciples; but He told them of the events that would happen at the end time. First, Jesus warned them about many false Christs coming in His name to deceive them. He also told them: They would hear of "wars and rumours of wars" (Matt. 24:6), that "nation shall rise against nation, and kingdom against kingdom and [that there would] be famines, and pestilences, and earthquakes, in divers places" (Matt. 24:7). These would be the signs for His second coming.

10. In the second portion of His response to His disciples, Jesus mentions several things that would take place during the second half of the Tribulation Period: First, they shall "deliver you up to be afflicted, and shall kill you: and ye shall be hated of all nations for my name's sake" (Matt. 24:9). Secondly, many "shall betray one another, and shall hate one another" (Matt. 24:10). Thirdly, "many false prophets shall rise, and shall deceive many" (Matt. 24:11). And fourth, "because iniquity shall abound, the love of many shall wax cold" (Mat. 24:12). Having enumerated these events that will take place, especially during the second half of the Tribulation Period, Christ then emphatically declares:

> *But he that shall endure unto the end, the same shall be saved. And this gospel of the kingdom shall be preached in all the world for a witness unto all nations; and then shall the end come" (Matt. 24:13-14).*

11. Despite this gloomy picture Christ puts forth for His disciples, He also told them the following: "For I say unto you, Ye shall not see me henceforth, till ye shall say, Blessed is he that cometh in the name of the Lord" (Matt. 23:39). Representing the last generation of the Jews of the Old Testament, Christ declared primarily to the unbelieving Jews of His day, "Ye shall not see me henceforth, till ye shall say, Blessed is he that cometh in the name of the Lord." The Lord Jesus knows well that while the Jews, by and large, would not acknowledge Him as their Messiah in His earthly ministry, the time would come when they would recognize Him as their Saviour. Only when the re-gathered Israel repents and turns to the Lord, only then Jesus would once again make Himself known to His people. Right now a large majority of the Jewish people does not want to accept Christ as its Messiah. We read in Hosea the following:

> *For the children of Israel shall abide many days without a king, and without a prince, and without a sacrifice, and without an image, and without Teraphim: Afterward shall the children of Israel return, and seek the Lord their God, and David their king; and shall fear the Lord and his goodness in the latter days (Hos. 3:4, 5).*

12. Jesus went on to warn His disciples and the entire Jewish nation of His sudden appearance to mankind, when He returns, and asked them to be prepared, saying: "For as the lightning cometh out of the east, and shineth even unto the west; so shall also the coming of the Son of man be" (Matt. 24:27). Here, Jesus is speaking of His return to the earth at the end of the Tribulation Period (See Mar. 13:24-26). He then warns the disciples saying: "Therefore be ye also ready: for in such an hour as ye think not the Son of man cometh" (Matt. 24:44). Again He warns His innocent followers saying: "Watch therefore, for ye know neither the day nor the hour wherein the Son of man cometh" (Matt. 25:13).

13. Many Christian believers confuse the rapture of the Church with the second advent of Christ. It was stated earlier that the second coming of Christ is a drama having two acts: First, Christ comes to the air to receive the just raptured Church; secondly, the second advent entails Christ's reappearance to the earth with His Bride. This reappearance is often known as *parusia*, when the whole world will see the Son of Man coming down in glory. And so, after He has judged the living nations that have come out of the Tribulation Period — the sheep and the goats — He will then re-establish the Davidic Kingdom and set over it none other but David, His servant, whom He has resurrected, glorified and raptured to rule over Israel for a thousand years. However, Christ Himself will exercise His eternal role, He will become the King of kings and Lord of lords over the whole world.

14. Dr. Bob Jones, Sr., the Founder of Bob Jones University, used to say: First, any church that does not preach the prophetic message of the Bible, is either spiritually dead, or it is on its way to spiritual demise. Secondly, he would also say that the Second Coming of our Lord takes place in a two-fold manner: First, He comes into the air to meet His bride; secondly, seven years later, He will come down to the earth, to reestablish His throne.[1]

IV. God's Program for Israel

15. It should be made clear here that God's program for Israel is distinct during the Tribulation Period. As we shall see later, this period is primarily a time of Jacob's trouble. During the Millennial Kingdom, on the other hand, both Jews and Gentiles will be required to serve the Lord on almost an equal basis. While the temple at Jerusalem will be rebuilt, according to the book of Ezekiel, and services of obedience will be re-instituted. The Children of Israel, the **kohanim** *the priests*, will conse-crate service in that temple to the Lord. The Gentiles from all nations will likewise come up to Zion to worship and to render service of obedience to the Son of God.

16. During the Tribulation Period, as God's concern for the unbeliev-ing Jews grows greater, His efforts to "salvage" as many as possible from among them likewise grows stronger. In Revelation, Chapter 7, Verses 2 and 3, we are told that an "angel having the seal of the living God", told the four angels that were about "to hurt the earth and the sea," not to do so, "till we have sealed the servants of our God in their foreheads" (See Rev. 7:2, 3). Later, John tells us: "And I looked, and lo, a Lamb stood on the mount Sion, and with him an hundred forty and four thousand, having his Father's name written in their foreheads" (Rev, 14:1).

17. Speaking about the same 144,000 sealed servants of our God, Pentecost comments on them, saying: "The fact that God is again dealing with Israel on this national relationship [level], setting them [the sealed servants of our God] apart to national identities, and sending them as special representatives to the nations in place of the witness of the Church, indicates that the Church must no longer be on earth."[2] While the Church is not on the earth during this time of trouble, many Gentile nations are, like the Jews, in need of salvation. The Bible makes it amply clear that there are millions of martyrs of both Jews and Gentiles at and about the throne of God in heavenly places as a living testimony of what the 144,000 sealed servants of our God have done clandestinely through their preach-ing and teaching of the Word of God.

V. The Song of Deliverance

18. As the rapture of the Church takes place, the world below finds itself in agony and anguish. Sinful humanity is now confused and frus-trated by the sudden, clandestine disappearance of the so called "Christian believers." The entire world is wrathful at these cowardly "believers" who caused the innumerable catastrophes and calamities upon the earth as a result of their sudden disappearance from the face of the earth. The people of the earth are callously pointing their fingers and gnashing their teeth at all those Christians who have abandoned the cars they drove and the trains and the planes they piloted, causing the unexpected and unprecedented death of possibly millions. They point at how multitudes of these "nervous nellies" have just departed leaving no trace behind them. They have simply slipped away and vanished!

19. This rapture embodies the very first grand resurrection of the believers in Christ. It contains all the saints of the past and the present, both the Jews and the Gentiles. "Because I live, ye shall live also," said the Lord Jesus (John 14:19[b]). Adam's posterity finally has received its redemption and its complete glorification. Perhaps, this is the most happy group of people that ever lived. "Blessed and holy is he that hath part in the first resurrection: on such the second death hath no power" (Rev. 20:6[a]). Believers from every corner of the earth are now on their way to be received by the clouds of the air; ready and anxious to meet the Lord their Saviour and their God. As they rise in unison towards the heaven, both the "dead" and the living in Christ, who are now resurrected, regenerated and glorified, feel the joy of singing the song of redemption.[3]

TO MEET THE LORD IN THE AIR
(I Thes. 4:17)

Hark! the sound of the Trumpet.
        The angel's call shall declare:
Come ye bidden of the Lord,
        Come meet your Lord in the air.

The dead shall rise so swiftly;
        New bodies pure they shall share
With the living on their way,
        To meet the Lord in the air.

In the twinkling of an eye,
     All the chosen and the fair;
New garments white shall put on,
     To meet the Lord in the air.

Bye, Bye, farewell, thou cursed world,
     Enough of your sins and snare;
Freedom at last has prevailed,
     We'll meet the Lord in the air.

Threats and curses from below,
     Rise so ugly in despair;
Go ye 'shameful', Leave us here!
     We shall manage our affair.

Yet so many — mother, son,
     Husband, daughter — Spirit share;
Look to Christ and then confess,
     To meet the Lord they prepare.

No more for self do they care;
     True to their faith, the world dare:
"Kill the body! The soul spare!"
     We'll meet the Lord in the air! (ZSS©)

CHAPTER 8

THE INDIVISIBLE CHURCH

For as the body is one, and hath many members, and all the members of that one body, being many, are one body: so also is Christ. For by one Spirit are we all baptized into one body, whether we be Jews or Gentiles, whether we be bond or free; and have been all made to drink into one Spirit. For the body is not one member, but many. (I Cor. 12:12-14).

I. The Church Is a Mystery

1. ABOUT THE CHURCH AND in connection with his preaching of the Gospel of Christ to the Gentiles, it was made known to Paul, through a mystery, how this body of Christ would be made universal. To the Apostle Paul this Church unity was to be worldwide in its scope and eternal in its duration. Based upon the sure foundation of the Lord Jesus Christ, the Church would be invincible, indivisible and would remain victorious throughout the ages. The Lord told Simon Peter: "and I say unto thee, [t]hat thou art Peter, and upon this rock[1] I will build my church; and the gates of hell shall not prevail against it" (Matt. 16:18). Observe what Paul writes to the believers at Ephesus:

> *How that by revelation he made known unto me the mystery . . . [w]hich in other ages was not made known unto the sons of men, as it is now revealed unto his holy apostles by the Spirit; that the Gentiles should be fellowheirs, and of the same body, and partakers of his promise in Christ by the Gospel . . . that I should preach among the Gentiles the unsearchable riches of Christ; [a]nd to make all men see what is the fellowship of the mystery, which from the beginning of the world hath been hid in God, who created all things by Jesus Christ (Eph. 3:3, 5-6, 8-9).*

2. The unity of the Church of our Saviour is well documented in the Scriptures. This unity transcends the dispensation of grace. The Holy Word says that, "it pleased the Father that in him [in Christ] should all fullness dwell" (Col. 1:19). This inclusion covers everything that takes place in heaven and on the earth. God puts everything under the feet of His Son, the Lord Jesus Christ. The Almighty Saviour wants to present us, the believers, unto God the Father, "holy and unblameable and unreproveable in his sight" (Col. 1:22^b). For we read in Colossians the following:

> *And he is before all things, and by him all things consist. And he is the head of the body, the church: who is the beginning, the firstborn from the dead; that in all things he might have the preeminence. For it pleases the Father that in him should all fullness dwell; [a]nd, having made peace through the blood of his cross, by him to reconcile all things unto himself; by him, I say, whether they be things in earth, or things in heaven. And you, that were sometime alienated and enemies in your mind by wicked works, yet now hath he reconciled [i]n the body of his flesh through death, to present you holy and unblameable and unreproveable in his sight (Col. 1:17-22).*

3. In light of this, notice how Newell describes the resurrection and glorification of the nation of Israel: "Howbeit, it must be remembered that our Lord has a glorified body, while the saved remnant of Israel, and also, *as I see it*, the faithful Israelites raised when our Lord returns, will all have flesh and blood [unglorified] bodies — as earthly people."[2] How this is possible, is not explained. Apparently, the author lost sight of what the blessed Christ told the Sadducees when they had asked him about the woman who had married seven brothers. They had asked, "Therefore in the resurrection whose wife shall she be of the seven, for they all had her" (Matt. 22:28). "Jesus answered and said unto them, Ye do err, not knowing the scriptures, nor the power of God. For in the resurrection they neither marry, nor are given in marriage, but are as the angels of God in heaven" (Matt. 22:29, 30). The resurrected Jews and Gentiles will be like the angels of God in heaven. (*Italics added*).

4. In the book of Romans, Chapter 3, Verses 9-20, the Apostle Paul discusses, both theologically and argumentatively, the concordance of man in his sinfulness. Likewise, the Great Apostle emphasizes in Romans, Chapter 3, Verses 21-28, that salvation is "by faith of Jesus Christ unto all and upon all them that believe: for there is no difference: For all have sinned, and come short of the glory of God" (Rom. 3:22^b-23). Paul concludes his remarks by saying: "Therefore we conclude that a man [any man] is justified by faith without the deeds of the law" (Rom. 3:28). And then Paul goes on to summarize his argument through the following two passages of Scripture:

> *Is he the God of the Jews only? [I]s he not also of the Gentiles? Yes, of the Gentiles also. Seeing it is one God, which shall justify the circumcision by faith, and uncircumcision through faith. Do we then make void the law through faith? God forbid: Yea, we establish the law (Rom. 3:29-31).*

> *[God has given the Church gifts] For the perfecting of the saints, for the work of the ministry, for the edifying of the body of Christ: Till we all come in the unity of the faith, and of the knowledge of the Son of God, unto a perfect man, unto the measure of the stature of the fulness of Christ (Eph. 4:12, 13).*

5.   The entire body of believers of all ages and of all dispensations has just one song to sing; the song declares that Jesus Christ, who died for each and every one of us sinners, is the Lord of all and Master of the universe. There is absolutely no way for any of us to think that the Jews and the Gentiles would remain distinctly separated in their resurrection, in their justification, in their glorification, and in their other spiritual functions during the Millennial Kingdom. Every saved sinner of every dispensation will gladly join the late Dr. Bob Jones, Jr.[3] and sing the penitent's hymn of contrition:

THE SHAME HE SUFFERED

The shame He suffered left its brand
      In gaping wound in either hand;
Sin's penalty He deigned to meet
      Has torn and scarred His blessed feet.

The condemnation by Him borne
      Marred His brow with print of thorn;
Trespass and guilt for which He died
      Have left Him with a riven side.

Mine was the guilt, the penalty
      The sin was mine, it was for me.
He let the nails, the thorn, the spear;
      For love of me the scars appear.

In hands and feet and side and brow
      Beholding them I can but bow;
Myself a living sacrifice
      To Him who paid so dear a price.

II. Who Are the Members of the Bride?

6. Some Bible scholars believe that the Bride of Christ is composed of only the believers of the New Testament, excluding entirely the saints of the Old Testament, including the Jews. Accordingly, they consider the Old Testament saints' presence at the marriage supper of the Lamb (on the earth) to be only that of the guests, or of the invited friends of the Bridegroom. This they conclude primarily on the basis of the parable of the 'great supper' which Jesus gave to His disciples (Luke 14:16-24; Matt. 22:1-14). However, we must not lose sight of the fact that a parable — any parable — has only one point of illustration to make, including this parable. It is very clear that, indeed, this figurative story of the great supper provides us with only one illustration; namely, it points to the fact that the invited guests, which supposedly symbolize Israel, made light of the king and rejected his invitation, nullifying any interpretative possibility of considering Israel to be the honored guest (friend) of the Bridegroom.

7. Those who follow such a double interpretation, such as Ryrie,[4] and Newell — though the latter somewhat grudgingly — in order to prove the point that Israel is that special guest at the Marriage Supper, are impelled to make every effort, even to the extent of twisting or ignoring the meaning of other relevant Scriptures to present the nation of Israel as the friend of the Bridegroom. Such a slanted approach to the interpretation of the prophetic message will never produce a proper conclusion. This parable, if it is to fulfill Israel's role as a friend, condemns that nation in reality, rather than praises her for making trivial excuses.

8. To begin with, the parable gives us outright prevaricated lies. One of those invited said, he had bought "a piece of ground"; the other said, he had bought "five yoke of oxen"; and another, "I have married a wife" (Luke 14:18-20). None of these guests accepted the invitation of the "king which made a marriage [supper] for his son" (Matt. 22:2[b]). The parable's conclusion was: "For I say unto you, That none of these men which were bidden shall test of my supper" (Luke 14:24). The invited guests all lied; the very trivial excuses they gave provided witness against them. How can one buy a piece of ground, or purchase five yoke of oxen, etc., without first seeing them, inspecting them, and trying them?

9. There are also some interpreters of prophecy who consider John the Baptist to be a symbol of the Old Testament saints for having declared himself to be "the friend of the bridegroom." Those who insist on such an interpretation, also insist that the Marriage Supper must take place on the earth, after Christ's descent to it, thereby complicating the matter even further. John's friendship to the Lord Jesus Christ, the Bridegroom, was not symbolic; it was a real friendship. The two were cousins. Such an interpretation is oblivious to the following Scripture from the book of Hebrews, where it is stated that all believers of the two Testaments receive the promises of God at the same time at the very end:

And these all [the Old Testament saints] having obtained a
good report through faith, received not the promise: God having
provided some better things for us [the saints of the New Testa-
ment], that they without us should not be made perfect [and be
rewarded ahead of time] (Heb. 11:39-40).

10. There are a number of reasons why the Scriptures, including the
above reference, cast a great deal of doubt upon such an interpretation,
usually fully nullifying such an assumption. If we are to have a "friend" of
the Bridegroom at the Marriage Supper, that "friend" could most likely be
represented by "a great multitude, which no man could number" (Rev.
7:9), who were martyred during the tribulation period. Although not as
yet resurrected, not raptured with the Church or Glorified, and not judged
for their works, they, nevertheless, are a group of millions of believers,
both Jews and Gentiles, saved and martyred during the Tribulation Period, and whose souls are now present at the throne of God. The following four groups of countless souls robed in white — but not "in fine linen"
which would emphasize their being glorified — and spoken about in the
Book of Revelation, should be a sufficient example.

1. Under the altar —

And when he had opened the fifth seal, I saw under the
altar the souls of them that were slain for the word of God,
and for the testimony which they had: And they cried with a
loud voice, saying, How long, O Lord, holy and true, dost
thou not judge and avenge our blood on them that dwell on
the earth? And white robes were given unto every one of
them. . . (Rev. 6:9-11[a]).

2. Before the throne —

After this I beheld, and, lo, a great multitude, which no
man could number, of all nations, and kindreds, and people,
and tongues, stood before the throne, and before the Lamb,
clothed with white robes, and palms in their hands; [a]nd
cried with a loud voice, saying, Salvation [belongeth] to our

God which sitteth upon the throne, and unto the Lamb. . .
(Rev. 7:9, 10).

And one of the elders answered, saying unto me, What
are these which are arrayed in white robes? and whence came
they? And I said unto him, Sir, thou knowest. And he said to
me, These are they which came out of great tribulation, and
have washed their robes, and made them white in the blood
of the Lamb (Rev. 7: 13, 14).

3. On the sea of glass —

And I saw as it were a sea of glass mingled with fire: and
them that had gotten the victory over the beast, and over his
image, and over his mark, and over the number of his name,
stand on the sea of glass, having the harps of God. And they
sang the song of Moses the servant of God, and the song of
the Lamb, saying, Great and marvelous are thy works, Lord
God Almighty; just and true are thy ways, thou King of saints
(Rev. 15:2, 3).

4. In the throne —

And a voice came out of the throne, saying, Praise our
God, all ye servants, and ye that fear him, both small and
great. And I heard as it were the voice of a great multitude,
and as the voice of many waters, and as the voice of mighty
thunderings, saying, Alleluia: for the Lord God omnipotent
reigneth (Rev. 19:5, 6).

11. When one studies closely the above four passages, it becomes at
once clear that: (1) the four groups are all composed of the martyrs of the
tribulation period; (2) they are believers from "all nations, and kindreds,
and people, and tongues," and, doubtless, of both, Jews and Gentiles; (3)
each group is given the "white robes" of righteousness; but they are not
"arrayed in fine linen, clean and white," which is limited to the resurrected
and glorified saints, the Bride of Christ; (4) mention is made of the twenty

and four elders and also of the four beasts; (5) in each case, the Lamb is mentioned and exalted; and (6) God is, all the while, seated on the throne to Whom songs of praises are made.

III. The One Eternal Church

12. Perhaps no other passage of the Scripture gives us as crystal clear an answer for the question of the unity of the Church as does Revelation, Chapter 21. While in heaven, John was shown "the bride, the Lamb's wife" (verse 9). He was also shown "the great city, the holy Jerusalem, descending out of heaven from God" (verse 10), "[h]aving the glory of God" (verse 11). But the city also had twelve gates each bearing the name of a tribe of Israel (verse 12). The walls of the city had twelve foundations each bearing the name of one of the twelve apostles of the Lamb. At almost the very end of the Millennial Kingdom, John is told that the Bride is the wife of the Lamb, and that the city in which the wife dwells has twelve gates named after the twelve names of the twelve tribes of Israel, and that it also has twelve foundations the name of each being "the name of one of the twelve apostles of the Lamb" (Rev. 21:12^b). The very unity of the heavenly Jerusalem and the very concept of its depicted oneness bespeaks the oneness of the Eternal Church. Of this point, Paul tells the Gentile Galatians the following:

> *For there is neither Jew nor Greek [Gentile], there is neither bond nor free, there is neither male nor female: for ye are all one in Christ Jesus. And if ye be Christ's, then are ye Abraham's seed, and heirs according to the promise (Gal. 3:28-29).*

> *But Jerusalem which is above is free, which is the mother of us all. Now we, brethren, as Isaac was, are the children of promise. . . . So then, brethren, we are not children of the bondwoman, but of the free (Gal. 4:26, 28, 31).*

13. In the book of Romans, Paul presents an argument concerning Abraham's conversion from the unbelieving Gentiles to God and his obedience to the Almighty through simple faith. The Apostle makes it clear that Abraham's faith in God was primarily through his conviction and trust and not by works. "For if Abraham were justified by works," Paul contended, "he had whereof to glory; but not before God" (Rom. 4:2). The fact that Abraham's conversion was through simple faith, was sufficient for the Gentiles now to trust the same God of Abraham and His Son, the Lord Jesus Christ, for their salvation. Paul gives this verse from the book of Romans to justify his argument:

> And he received the sign of circumcision, a seal of the righteousness of the faith which he had yet being uncircumcised: that he might be the father of all them that believe, though they [the Gentiles] be not circumcised; that righteousness might be imputed unto them also" (Rom. 4:11).

14. Second to the question of defending the legitimacy of his own apostleship, Paul was also quite concerned with another equally important inquiry. The Gentile believers almost everywhere felt inferior to the Jewish believers in the early days of the church. As the membership of the Gentiles grew larger and larger, they began questioning their perceived inferiority. To address the problem properly, Paul reminded the believers, time and again, of their position in Christ and that there was no difference between the Jews and the Gentiles. To the converts of the church at Ephesus, Paul wrote:

> Now therefore ye are no more strangers and foreigners [non-Jews], but fellowcitizens with the saints [believing Jews], and of the household [Jews and Gentiles] of God, and are built upon the [one] foundation of the apostles and prophets, Jesus Christ himself being the chief corner stone (Eph. 2:19, 20).

15. In order to provide comfort to the Gentile believers, Paul emphasizes to them that their position in Christ Jesus was as solid as that of the believing Jews. Whether Jews or Gentiles, their election through faith in Christ was eternal, and that this election took place "before the foundation of the world" (Eph. 1:4). Christ had "made known unto us the mystery of his will, according to his good pleasure which he hath purposed in himself" (Eph. 1:9). Paul continues to write:

> That in the dispensation of the fullness of time he might gather [bring] together in one [fold] all things in Christ, both which are in heaven, and which are on earth; even in him (Eph. 1:10).

16. Finally, Paul emphasizes the oneness of the Church — in its past, in its present, and in its future — to be rooted in the unity of the Trinity. Unlike his "speech" which, according to his antagonists, "was contemptible" (Gal. 10:10), he had a complete mastery of the written language. The written language for him was a very flexible and a multifaceted tool that he could use effectively to get his message across. With his rich educational background, especially the depth and the breadth of his training in the Law of Moses under Gamaliel, the greatest of scholars in his day, Paul was able to analyze, understand, and express whatever subject he dealt with. A careful analysis of Paul's writings will clearly demonstrate the richness of his intelligence. Writing to Ephesians, especially in Chapter 2, Paul employs such powerful terms, expressions, and phrases with respect to this *common* salvation, common to the Jews and the Gentiles, as follows:

> Gather together; in one all things; in whom ye also trusted; he quickened us together with Christ; he raised us up together; made us sit together in heavenly places [in the air]; you [both] are made nigh by the blood of Christ; who hath made both one; who hath broken down the middle wall of partition between us [two]; he might reconcile both [Jews and Gentiles] unto God in one body [the church, the one fold]; he preached peace [to the] far off and to [the] nigh.

17. The song of every redeemed sinner is the same throughout the ages. He knows who died for him. The wounds in His hands, His feet, and His side are for the atonement of the entire humanity. He suffered, and bled, and was crucified, and died, and was buried, and finally He arose from the dead triumphantly. Through His condemnation, the entire human race could be made perfect; through His death and resurrection, the entire mankind could be redeemed, glorified, and preserved for eternity. After all, how many "Christs" do we have? How many types of salvation does God cultivate? How many Paradises has God made for His many peoples? If we deny the oneness of our humanity with regard to sin and salvation, we are denying the oneness of our God and His Trinity. For the Ephesians, Paul makes it very clear saying:

> *There is one body, and one Spirit, even as ye are called in one hope of your calling; One Lord, one faith, one baptism, One God and Father of all, and through all, and in you all (Eph. 4:4-6).*

18. Samuel T. Stone,[5] the hymn writer, describes the Church's unity very well in the following hymn, declaring that the Church of Jesus Christ has just one foundation who is none other than the Lord Jesus Himself. Reading the above quotations carefully, one will find out how marvelous God's ways are as He has subjected all things to the Son. For it is this Son who has given His life a ransom for the Church, the Bride of Christ. The hymn writer declares:

THE CHURCH'S ONE FOUNDATION

The Church's one foundation
    Is Jesus Christ her Lord;
She is His new creation
    By water and the word:
From heav'n He came and sought her
    To be His holy bride;
With His own blood He bought her
    And for her life He died.

Elect from ev'ry nation,
        Yet one o'er all the earth,
Her charter of salvation
        One Lord, one faith, one birth;
One holy name she blesses,
        Partakes one holy food,
And to one hope she presses,
        With ev'ry grace endued.

Mid toil and tribulation
        And tumult of her war,
She waits the consummation
        Of peace for ever more;
Till with the vision glorious
        Her longing eyes are blest,
And the great Church victorious
        Shall be the Church at rest.

Yet she on earth hath union
        With God the Three in One,
And mystic sweet communion
        With those whose rest is won:
O happy ones and holy!
        Lord, give us grace that we,
Like them, the meek and lowly,
        On high may dwell with Thee.

IV. Could the Marriage Supper Be on Earth?

19. Moreover, those who advocate that Israel and the Old Testament saints, are the guests at the Marriage Supper; they, likewise, usually insist upon a Marriage Supper that is conducted on the earth. The notion that this Supper takes place on the earth, is in total contradiction, especially to the chronological order of the heavenly events that are described in Revelation, Chapter 19, Verses 1 through 14. There, the sequential order of the "heavenly" events is clearly presented: (1) the gathering of the twenty-four elders and four living creatures (beasts) around the throne of God to sing His praises and to declare His power, Verses 5 and 6; (2) the Marriage of the Lamb, Verses 7 and 8; (3) the Marriage Supper of the Lamb, Verse 9; (4) The resurrection of the martyrs of the Tribulation Period; (5) Christ's descent from heaven on "a white horse," Verse 11; and (6) He was followed with the armies of His saints — all the glorified saints, including now the martyrs of the Tribulation Period — which were "clothed in fine linen, white and clean," Verses 11 and 14.

20. Obviously, it is more logical to think that the millions of martyrs of the Tribulation Period, who most likely will not be resurrected until the very end of that period and just before Christ descends to the earth, are the only saints that could possibly witness this Marriage Supper as His friends. Being already in heaven, present at the Marriage Supper, in the presence of the Almighty God, and wearing white robes of righteousness, only these as yet non-glorified saints — both Jews and Gentiles — could possibly be considered the friends of the Bridegroom. Once the "heavenly events" are consummated, including the Marriage Supper of the Lamb, the Lord of Glory resurrects now the martyrs of the Tribulation Period. With all the saints of the Old and New Testaments with Him, Christ descends to the earth victoriously, having defeated the Devil and his emissaries — the Beast, the False Prophet and the unbelieving sinners, the children of disobedience.

CHAPTER 9

GLORIOUS EVENTS IN HEAVEN

Husbands, love your wives, even as Christ also loved the church, and gave himself for it; [t]hat he might sanctify and cleanse it with the washing of water by the word, [t]hat he might present it to himself a glorious church, not having spot, or wrinkle, or any such thing; but that it should be holy and without blemish (Eph. 5:25-27).

I. The Judgment Seat of Christ

1. THE BELIEVING CHRISTIANS have now arrived in the presence of God and His dear Son in the heavenly places. The Judgment Seat of Christ is already set up in the air. "But the Lord shall endure for ever: he hath prepared his throne for judgment. And he shall judge the world in righteousness, and shall minister judgment to the people in uprightness" (Ps. 9:7-8). It is apparent that the very first important thing that takes place in heaven, during the seven years of tribulation on the earth, is the judgment of the believers' works. Why the judgment, and why so early? The Marriage of the Lamb is about to take place; it is soon followed by the Marriage Supper of the Lamb. Preparations for these two occasions are essential. Many of the believing Christians are about to serve the Master in the two celebrations. Their selection is based upon their faithfulness to the Lord Jesus Christ and to the Word of God during their lives on the earth. The judgment is open — fair and square — and is conducted before all the believers, whereby, in choosing the faithful servants, the Lord justifies Himself among His followers.

2. Of this judgment seat of Christ, Paul makes it absolutely clear that all believers shall appear before the Lord to be judged for their works. This judgment has nothing to do with the question of sin and salvation; namely, whether a person is saved or unsaved. Since only the saved believers will be raptured to meet the Lord in the air, only they will appear before this Judgment Seat of our Saviour. That this judgment pertains only to works, Paul clearly instructs the Roman and the Corinthian Christians as follows: to these believers, Paul says,

> *"[F]or we shall all stand before the judgment seat of Christ" (Rom. 14:10).*

> *For we must all appear before the judgment seat of Christ; that every one may receive the things done in his body, according to that he hath done, whether it be good or bad (II Cor. 5:10).*

3. In preparation for the Marriage of the Lamb, for the Marriage Supper of the Lamb and for their rule in the Kingdom, the saints of God must first undergo a final assessment of their works, an appraisal based primarily upon the faithfulness of the individual in performing his works. It is apparent that, at this *Bema*[1] of Christ, each believer's works will be appraised for special awards. These trophies, most likely, are in the form of crowns that signify positions of leadership to rule with Christ during the Millennial Kingdom. They are not bestowed on the believer on the basis of a great work, or of many works, accomplished on the earth, but on the basis of absolute faithfulness to the Lord and obedience to the Word of God demonstrated while performing these acts. Of this judgment, Paul explains to the Corinthians in this manner:

> *For other foundation can no man lay than that is laid, which is Jesus Christ. Now if any man build upon this foundation gold, silver, precious stones, wood, hay, stubble; every man's work shall be made manifest: for the day shall declare it, because it shall be revealed by fire; and the fire shall try every man's work of what sort it is. If any man's work abide which he hath built thereupon, he shall receive a reward. If any man's work shall be burned, he shall suffer loss: but he himself shall be saved; yet so as by fire (I Cor. 3:11-15).*

4. Fire has the power to consume the perishable and to purify the imperishable (I Pet. 1:7). With regard to sin and to unrighteousness, our

God is a consuming fire, we are told in Hebrews, Chapter 12, Verse 29. At the Judgment Seat of Christ, the holiness of our God will be so bright and so consuming that nothing rubbish — wood, hay or stubble — will withstand it. For the believer, the sin question has already been taken care of at the foot of the Cross. The test at the Bema of Christ examines only the believer's quality of works and, accordingly, establishes just rewards. Interestingly, the quantity of a Christian's works does not come into account at all. It is not how much or how great a work we have done that matters; but how faithful we have been with the "talents" the Saviour has entrusted to us.

5. Our service in the Church of our Lord must always be commensurate with our individual capabilities and talents. God's children must exercise all those gifts the blessed Saviour has so graciously and benevolently bestowed upon each one of us (I Cor. 12:4-11). A godly smile, a strong and hearty handshake, a helpful hand, an encouraging word, a kind compliment, teaching a Sunday School class, praying for the sick and the needy, visiting the bedridden, teaching the Word, etc., are just some of the things for the child of God to do for the Lord. Such good services and good deeds the believer is exhorted to render to the glory of the Almighty. The love of Christ must constitute the constraints and the impetus to serve the Master daily and faithfully (II Cor. 5:14). It is our faithfulness to Him who serves faithfully in God's house on our behalf, and who is "Called of God an high priest after the order of Melchisedec" (Heb. 5:10).

6. The Christian who receives one or more awards for his faithfulness in good and abiding works — works of gold, silver, and precious stones — shall be indeed blessed with eternal compensations and with unspeakable joy which our limited mind can hardly comprehend presently. Those whose works are puny— works of wood, hay, and stubble — shall suffer loss of rewards with the fire of God's testing. It must be clearly stated here that this loss is not of life but of rewards. No raptured believer who participates in the first blessed resurrection and who has come before the Bema of Christ will ever lose his life, or spend some time in purgatory, as some churches have taught. No born again Christian, regardless of his poor works, will ever lose his eternal life, no matter whether he receives awards or not. Figuratively speaking, such a person has become tanta-mount to a "second class citizen" of heaven: he will have nothing to show forth; nothing to cast at the feet of the Saviour; ever unable to rule with Christ in the Kingdom. Nevertheless, he is a child of God who enjoys eternal life with Him. Every believer will be judged according to his cir-cumstances.

7. The most tangible reward a born again Christian receives, at this Judgment Seat of Christ, is in terms of different crowns. He may get one, or two, or more such crowns. And it is these crowns that the believer casts at the feet of the Master (Rev. 4:10^b). And the Saviour deserves them all! What a joy! What a satisfaction! Briefly quoted here, non-verbatim, is Pinch's description of each crown.[2]

(1) The Crown of Life (Rev. 2:10) — This crown is given to honor those believers who spared not their life in the service of the Lord whom they loved. It is the martyr's crown.

(2) The Crown of Righteousness (II Tim. 4:8) — This is given to those who have the hope of, are properly prepared for, and love His dear appearing.

(3) The Incorruptible Crown (I Cor. 9:24-27) — This is specifically given to those who exercise self-discipline over their own bodies and self-control in order to provide a better service to the Lord.

(4) The Crown of Rejoicing (I Thes. 2:19) — This is also known as the evangelist's crown and is given to the soul-winner. It is a crown of rejoicing over the salvation of souls won to Christ.

(5) The Crown of Glory (I Pet. 5:2-4) — This unique crown is rewarded to pastors who faithfully care and properly feed the flocks of God. They preach the sound doctrine, and stand, as good examples, for the Word of God and for the testimony of Christ the Saviour.

II. The Marriage of the Lamb

8. For the Church, the marriage of the Lamb is another blessed event that awaits her in the air, in the "heavenly places." It occurs immediately after the Judgment Seat of Christ. Once the rigorous test is over, the Church is now ready for adornment and marriage. The Marriage of the Lamb transpires immediately after the individual Christian is tested for his works. It is very possible that, through this judgment, the believer is also identified by rank, designated for a specific position and function to be performed during the Marriage of the Lamb, the Marriage Supper of the Lamb and during the Kingdom. Immediately after the *Bema* of Christ, the Bride "has made herself ready" (Rev. 19:7b) for the marriage. Of this joyful occasion, John writes:

> *And to her was granted that she should be arrayed in fine linen, clean and white: for the fine linen is the righteousness of saints (Rev. 19:8).*

9. Not by coincidence, the Marriage of the Lamb takes place almost immediately after the Judgment Seat of Christ in heaven and, mind you, after the destruction of the Apostate Church on the earth (Rev. 17:16). It appears that the saints of God, who had suffered greatly at the hands of this bloodthirsty, pernicious "whore" — in whom "was found the blood of prophets, and of saints, and of all that were slain upon the earth" (Rev. 18:24) — could not celebrate or attain full joy at this glorious and blessed occasion until God had avenged them on her, on this harlot. Hence, John writes:

> *Rejoice over her, thou heaven, and ye holy apostles and prophets; for God hath avenged you on her (Rev. 18:20).*

10. Now that the destruction of the Apostate Christendom has taken place on the earth, the entire realm of the "heavenly places" is engaged in a glorious celebration around the throne of God. Congregated around the throne are the twenty-four elders and the four living creatures (beasts), along with "much people in heaven," together worshipping the Almighty God and praising His Holy Name:

Alleluia, salvation, and glory, and honour, and power, unto the Lord our God: For true and righteous are his judgments: for he hath judged the great whore, which did corrupt the earth with her fornication, and hath avenged the blood of his servants at her hand. And I heard as it were the voice of a great multitude, and as the voice of many waters, and as the voice of mighty thunderings, saying, Alleluia: for the Lord God omnipotent reigneth (Rev. 19:1^b,2,6).

11. It should be borne in mind that, throughout the entire Bible, only twice the term "wife" is used with respect to the Bride of the Lamb. The term is used only after the Marriage of the Lamb has taken place in the air. It is very true that the term "wife," in the Old Testament, was used exclusively of Israel, as the nation of God. But it should be made very clear here, however, that when the term was so used, it almost always dealt with a backslidden Israel and its unscrupulous spiritual condition on the earth. Nevertheless, it is at this juncture in the air, when the marriage of the Lamb is about to be consummated and, possibly, during the time of feasting at the great Marriage Supper that the betrothed Church is now referred to as the *wife* of the Lamb. John beautifully reports:

Let us be glad and rejoice, and give honour to him [God]: for the marriage of the Lamb is come, and his wife hath made herself ready (Rev. 19:7).

III. The Marriage Supper of the Lamb

12. That the Marriage Supper of the Lamb is conducted in heaven, there is absolutely no doubt about it. We must not ignore the fact that the believers of all ages and dispensations are saved only by one means: through faith in the precious blood of Christ. The Lord made also clear that He will have only one sheepfold, and that He would also bring His other sheep, the believers of the Old Testament Dispensation, not just the Jews, to be joined with the new believers of the Church into one fold. John quotes Jesus, saying:

I am the good shepherd, and know my sheep, and am known of mine. . . . I lay down my life for the sheep. And other sheep I have, which are not of this fold: them also I must bring, and they shall hear my voice; and there shall be one fold, and one shepherd. (John 10:14-16).

13. Since the Marriage Supper is conducted in heaven, we must assume then that the Bride of Christ is made up of the saints of both Testaments. When considering the many Scriptural passages that, explicitly or implicitly, speak of the corporal unity of the one body of Christ, made up of the believers of all ages, it is only logical then to conclude that the Marriage Supper takes place in heaven rather than on the earth. Moreover, since in the mind of God, the believer's names are all written in the Lamb's book of life since "the foundation of the world" (Matt. 25:34[b]), it is only possible that the saints of the two Testaments were now united through the contemporaneous resurrection at the time of the rapture.

14. It would be contrary to the teachings of the Bible that Christ would have preached the Gospel "to them that are dead" (I Pet. 4:6), seeing that after death there is only judgment (Heb. 9:27). Likewise, the Saviour could not have preached the Gospel of salvation to "the spirits in the prison," supposedly hell (I Pet. 3:19), which is also supported by Peter's declaration. The only plausible interpretation here would be that this prison is the Hades (Is. 61:1) where the spirits of the Old Testament saints — the dead in the hoped-for, the coming Messiah, who were held hostages by Satan until God would provide for them the redemptive price, the ultimate ransom — had been residing since Adam's days.

15. And so, having accomplished the work of redemption on the Cross, having openly and loudly declared, "It is finished!" (John 19:30[b]), Christ did indeed, after His burial, go down into the lower parts of the earth, into Hades. It was there, "in prison," where the Old Testament saints were held captive (hostages) by Satan, that Christ went down and preached (announced) to them that He had now paid the price in full. Christ calls these Old Testament saints "other sheep." It should be clearly understood that these Old Testament saints were not all Israelites or Jews; in human history, the Jewish people did not start until the times of Abraham, Isaac and Jacob.

16. It should, likewise, be clearly understood that Christ, in His ordeal of death, would never go to "hell," as some have stated. Hell is created for the Devil and his cohorts. There is absolutely no reason for the Lord Jesus, who triumphantly declares from the Cross, "It is finished" (John 19:30), to enter into "hell." Those who insist that Christ went down to hell for our sins, and there, supposedly, after enduring the taste of death under Satan, He took from Satan the key to Paradise, are in a way blaspheming against the Saviour and against God the Almighty. Jesus Christ, the Son of God, will never submit to the Devil, at any time, nor will He become subject to Satan who has the full sway over the hell. Christ went down to shaol, to the Old Testament saints, and preached to them the good news of salvation accomplished. As it was just mentioned above, salvation is wrought on the cross and not through going down to shaol. Satan has no key to Paradise. Christ's death, burial and resurrection are only assurances for our salvation fulfilled according to the Scriptures.

17. Of this work of Christ, namely, making out of the two "sheep" one fold, the Psalmist says: "Thou hast ascended on high, thou hast led captivity [those who were captive to Satan] captive [to yourself]" (Ps. 68:18[a]). Over and again, the Lord Jesus makes mention, directly or indirectly, of the one fold. Paul makes it clear that God had through a mystery declared it to him that the Jews and the Gentiles were one body in Christ. Concerning the same, Paul writes to the church at Ephesus:

> *Wherefore he saith, [w]hen he ascended up on high [into heaven], he led captivity [of Satan, the Old Testament saints] captive [to Himself and carried them into Paradise], and gave gifts to men. Now that he ascended, what is it but that he also descended first to the lower parts of the earth. He that descended is the same also that ascended up far above all heavens [into Paradise]: 'Today thou shall be with me in Paradise' (Luke 23:43[b]), 'that he might fill [fulfill, or make perfect] all things' (Eph. 4:8-10).*

18. On this "that he might fill [fulfill or make perfect] all things," the promises which were made to the faithful saints of the Old Testament and of which they were worthy, were postponed to be received with the saints of the New Testament, most likely at the judgment seat of Christ. Certainly, it has been in God's planning that all mankind be reconciled to Himself through the person of His only begotten Son, the Lord Jesus Christ. Since salvation is possible only through Jesus Christ, the saved of all ages and dispensations become one sheepfold, under one shepherd. He is the one who makes perfect the elect, fulfilling all their expectations according to the promises of their God. Christ does indeed make the two groups of saints — the Jews and the Gentiles — perfect together at the end time. For we read in Ephesians the following:

> *For he is our peace, who hath made both one, and hath broken down the middle wall of partition between us; [h]aving abolished in his flesh the enmity, even the law of commandments contained in ordinances; for to make in himself of twain one new man, so making peace. And that he might reconcile both unto God in one body by the cross, having slain the enmity thereby: [a]nd came and preached peace to you which were afar off, and to them that were nigh. For through him we both have access by one Spirit unto the Father. Now therefore ye are no more strangers and foreigners, but fellowcitizens with the saints, and of the household of God: [a]nd are built upon the foundation of the apostles and prophets, Jesus Christ himself being the chief corner stone (Eph. 2:14-20).*

19. To place such a *time* and *space* dissimilitude between the Marriage of the Lamb and the Marriage Supper — the former in heaven; the latter on the earth — would be a gross misinterpretation of the Scriptures. The whole concept of a MarriageSupper on the earth, as adhered to by some Bible prophecy interpreters, primarily stems from a desire to consider the phrase "Friend of the Bridegroom" to be Israel. With respect to spiritual matters, filial relationships do not guarantee friendships. The Lord defined a friend as the one who keeps His commandments. "Ye are my friends," Christ said, "if ye do whatsoever I command you" (John 15:14).

Accordingly, interpreting the word "friends" to signify Israel would drastically lead to the misinterpretation of the passage in view, not to mention the misinterpretation of many other related passages.

IV. The Resurrection of the Martyrs

20. All the saints who had been martyred for "the testimony of Jesus and for the Word of God," during the Tribulation Period, and whose souls were found to be resting near the throne of God, are now ready for their blessed resurrection. From the passage found in the book of Revelation, Chapter 20, Verses 4 through 6, we also learn that all the souls who were martyred for the testimony of Christ, were resurrected from the dead. It is apparent that this resurrection took place while the Lord was still in heaven[3] with His Bride. It is also apparent that this resurrection materialized as the very last act accomplished in heaven, during the seven years period, before Christ was ready to come down to the earth. This is the very last group of believers to be resurrected as part of the first resurrection. This resurrection comes last in heaven, just before Christ returns to the earth, because its members were daily increased by the continued persecution and martyrdom occurring on the earth. We read in the book of Revelation the following:

> *[A]nd I saw the souls of them that were beheaded for the witness of Jesus, and for the word of God, and which had not worshipped the beast, neither his image, neither had received his mark upon their forehead, or in their hands; and they lived and reigned with Christ a thousand years. But the rest of the dead lived not again until the thousand years were finished. This is the first resurrection (Rev. 20:4[b], 5).*

21. Christ now is ready to descend to the earth; the angel accompanying the brightly moving procession of Christ blows the trumpet. The souls of the martyrs of the Tribulation Period are now quickened, their bodies are forthwith resurrected from the dead, and they are glorified into eternal life. This is the very last segment of the resurrection of the believers in Christ who had as yet not been raised. They are counted among

those who had a part in the first resurrection. Most assuredly, they likewise did receive the rewards they deserved from the Master. To them
God says:

> *Blessed and holy is he that hath part in the first resurrec-*
> *tion: on such the second death hath no power, but they shall*
> *be priests of God and of Christ, and shall reign with him a*
> *thousand years (Rev. 20:6).*

CHAPTER 10

THE RISE OF THE BEAST

And I stood upon the sand of the sea, and saw a beast rise up out of the sea, having seven heads and ten horns, and upon his horns ten crowns, and upon his heads the name of blasphemy (Rev. 13:1).

I. Search from Within

1. AS IT WAS STATED EARLIER, the Revived Roman Empire will most likely be ruled by a "General Council" composed of representations of the ten (or more) states, corresponding to the ten horns of Daniel's vision (Dan. 7:7) and the ten toes of King Nebuchadnezzar's image (Dan. 2:43). The need for a qualified leader to take over this extensive new realm will be indisputable; but attempts to find this Supreme Sovereign from amongst its own ranks will be frustrated by national jealousies, downright suspicions, and historical mistrust. The ten-horn Union will abandon its attempt to produce a commonly agreed-upon Supreme Ruler, and the General Council will, of necessity, go elsewhere to find such a leader.

2. From the following three words of Daniel, "another little horn" and from the general prophetic message's context, one may also conclude the following: First, such a leader, before accepting the invitation, must already be the head of another state, an eleventh country (representing the eleventh horn, the "little horn" of Daniel). Secondly, the state this Commander-in-Chief rules, must likewise be much younger and exuberant; yet it must have the most powerful organizations politically, economically, and militarily. It must conform with Daniel's description of him as "the king of fierce countenance" (Dan. 8:23), or "whose look was more stout than his fellows," the ten kings. (Dan. 7:24). Thirdly, the leader of this most powerful eleventh country must be a personage who is greatly qualified to assume, in addition to the leadership of his own country, the leadership of a much larger alliance composed of a number of alliances, specifically of both the Revived Roman Empire and possibly of a newly instituted Super Alliance that constitutes seven kings taken out of the ten-nation Revived Roman Empire and himself as the eighth king.

3. The "mother" of all questions should then be: "What country in the entire world of today could qualify to play such a magnificent role and provide a powerful Commander-in-Chief to lead this newly forged Super Union of the United Europe?" It is absolutely imperative that this leader's main characteristics and idiosyncrasies be commensurate with those Daniel ascribes to the little horn, namely, "the king of fierce countenance" (Dan. 8:23). It is likewise necessary that this new Superman be both imperious and exalted at the same time. As a human being, from the very outset, this "little horn" as the Beast, will in all reality, represent the best mankind has ever to offer. For this Antichrist must, as a counterfeit of the Lord Jesus Christ, be Satan's "unblemished lamb." Humanly speaking, he will be the most intelligent intellectual who ever existed, a most charming politician, an imposing personality, a majestic configuration, whom the entire world will gladly venerate and worship.

II. Search from Without

4. If such a leader is not found among the ten-nation coalition, where else could he come from? Could he come out of the Russian Federation? From Ezekiel, Chapters 38 and 39, as we shall see later, Russia "in the later years," as distinct from "the end time," (Ez. 38:8, 16), and possibly immediately after, or simultaneously with the beginning of the Tribulation Period, will inevitably invade the Holy Land. With its historical pride of its own grandeur, with its mighty nuclear arsenal, and with its huge armed forces, though weak as Russia is today, the wounded Bear of the North will never accept an artificial merger, or a second-rate partnership with the European Union, the precursor of the Revived Roman Empire. Right now, Russia is strenuously objecting to an alliance with NATO, and is strongly resisting that Organization's perceived encroachments upon its western borders.

5. Even at this very moment and in order to reinforce its opposition to the western alliances, Russia is strengthening her former coalition and is establishing new ones, in particular with China and the other countries of southeast Asia. Undoubtedly, covertly and overtly, the wounded Red Bear is already preparing possibly for its impending military incursion into the Middle East, directly into Israel. At this very moment, Russia is establishing stronger ties with Iran (the old Persia) and is providing the Middle East's third-rate countries with armament of all kinds. Once such weapons are made available to these countries, it is only a matter of time until its military and civilian technicians follow.

6. If the ten-nation Union fails to find a leader from among the member states, or from Russia, what other country then is sufficiently qualified to produce such an extraordinary Statesman? It is only logical to assume that a Super Leader could only come from an already existing Super State. Certainly, not from among the countries of Central or South America; much less from Japan, China or Australia. While the terms "sea, seas, waters," etc., in prophecy, usually signify the gentile world; it is also very likely that these terms (Rev. 13:1) have here a double interpretation and a double application. Since the Beast rises "up out of the sea," it is very likely that he comes out of a gentile country lying beyond the sea, and with respect to Europe, beyond the Atlantic Ocean.

7. As a matter of fact, Bible scholars have often suggested for some terms and passages of prophecy, a *double interpretation* and a *double application*. For the term "sea," has already been suggested by some to imply both the "Gentile nations" and erroneously the "Mediterranean Sea," even before America was discovered or was in the picture. Accordingly, for the sentence, "[I] saw a beast rise up out of the sea. . ." (Rev. 13:1), scholars of prophecy have interpreted that the Beast comes out of the Gentile nations, and that he also comes from beyond the Mediterranean Sea. Unfortunately, while their application was sound, their interpretation was in error. Because the Beast comes out of the Gentile nations but not from the Middle East, as some have advocated. The sea in question can only be the Atlantic Ocean. Since the "sea," discussed here is with respect to the Revived Roman Empire's territories, which itself is beyond

the Mediterranean Sea, this Little Horn comes out from beyond the Great
Sea, which could only imply here the Atlantic Ocean.

8. There is a great deal of credibility in the interpretation of the word
"sea," here, to signify the Atlantic Ocean. Apart from its geography, when
considering world events, especially given the time in which the earlier
scholars lived and the moderate level of interpretation the subject of prophecy had then attained, such a double interpretation and a double application became the most logical and the most appropriate. The Little Horn
then could only represent a great and young leader from beyond the sea,
from beyond the Ocean, from a Gentile nation. In light of the present
world circumstances, such a nation could only be the United States of
America. For only America, which is situated beyond the sea , shares
with the countries of the Revived Roman Empire the same heritage and,
for the most part, the same lineage and basically the same culture.

9. The President of Bob Jones University, Dr. Bob Jones III, raised
the all important question from the pulpit of that University during a recent
Bible Conference, saying: "Does America play a role in the end-time events
described in the Scriptures?" This writer's humble answer is yes. America
will, indeed, play a decisive role, the role of the very Beast himself. When
considering the indispensable position of the United States of America as
the leading power in the world, particularly with respect to its involvement
and often its dominance in the United Nations Organization, the North
Atlantic Treaty Organization, the Atlantic Alliance, the new European Union,
and the Arab-Israeli conflict, etc., etc., it becomes crystal clear that America
is indeed destined to play the leading role in the fulfillment of the end-time
prophecy. The forces and the plans that aim at bringing together the United
States and Canada (and possibly Mexico and some other Hispanic countries of this hemisphere) in a Super-Alliance with the European Union are,
most probably, in action right now.

10. Presently, there exist a number of alliances, associations, coali-
tions, and unions, on both sides of the Atlantic Ocean, that almost with the
stroke of a pen could be turned into a Gentile Alliance between North
America and Western Europe. The existing alliances, such as these, are

already far-reaching and the most powerful in the world. It is interesting to observe that the description provided for the symbolic Babylon in the book of Revelation, Chapter 18, can in its totality be applied only to America today. America is so great and powerful today which makes it the only state that deserves such a description as a Super Power.

11. Of this American greatness — and, in my opinion, its readiness to assume the leadership of the world — here is what *Washington Post* reporter, Paul Taylor, saw while looking from 8,000 miles away as he put it: "An America that had colonized the planet with democracy, language, currency, computers, movies, music and fast food. An America whose inflation and unemployment were low and whose stock market was booming. An America that had slain communism just as it had earlier slain fascism. An America at peace."[1] This America could very well become the "little horn," of Daniel and play the greatest role in the establishment of any future European power for the dominance of the world.

12. It is never pleasant to think of one's own country becoming a tool in the hands of Satan to carry out his wicked program on the earth, or its president becoming the embodiment of Satan. That the Word of God must be fulfilled, there is no escaping; but that America — the land of the Bible and of the unprecedented world-wide missionary effort for almost two centuries or more — becoming a tool in the hands of the Wicked One, there is indeed a great deal to be sad about. Of this anomaly, Paul says to the Church at Rome the following: "Where sin aboundeth, grace did much more abound" (Rom. 5:20). But wickedness and lawlessness are rampaging our country, sad to say, even this very day and are multiplying daily.

III. Russia and the Tribulation Period

13. Of this Russia's attitude toward the Atlantic Alliance, Charles Aldinger reported what Russian Defense Minister Pavel Grachev said to his US and Ukraine counterparts: "We will be obligated to reexamine our views on the role and place of tactical nuclear weapons, review our treaty obligations in the military sphere."[2] In order to rival the nations of the

Atlantic Alliance, as it was concluded earlier, Russia presently is most likely feverishly reorganizing its government, strengthening and equipping its armed forces, consolidating its worldwide position, and streamlining its diplomatic relations among all nations. It is highly unlikely for Russia to join, at this critical time — critical to Russia, that is — any European or American-led alliance; at least not prior to its invasion of the Holy Land and the destruction of Israel's military power "in the glorious holy mountain" (Dan. 11:45). Until that time, the Russian Federation with its allies will remain a painful thorn in the side of every Western alliance.

14. Once Russia completes its reorganization and modernization, it will seek to enhance and maintain its perceived pre-eminent position in the world. To secure its access to the abundant energy sources of the Middle East and, at the same time, to deprive the United States and its allies of this precious commodity, Russia will find itself constrained (Ez. 38:4) to carry out an unexpected foolhardy *tour de force* that will take it into Israel, "the client-state of the West," where eventually it will suffer its catastrophic deconstruction and demise as a superpower. Russian failure to achieve its pre-planned goals in the Middle East, particularly in the Holy Land, will be thwarted by the Lord Jesus Christ Himself, as we shall see in due course.

15. In harmony with the end-time scheme of events, it is highly likely that the Russian Invasion of the Holy Land will occur, as it was stated earlier, immediately *after* or *concurrently* with the rapture of the Church. Only after the following two major events — the rapture of the Church led by the Holy Spirit and Russia's invasion of the Holy Land — take place, only then will the Beast be formally and ceremonially presented to the world as their new "Messiah," and the "true Saviour" of mankind.

IV. The Beast As the Antichrist

16. Since the day Lucifer rebelled against the Almighty God (Isa. 14:12-15), the Devil has fervently and feverishly sought to dethrone the King of Heaven. His plans and his wiles against God and against the redeemed mankind are numerous and subtle. His most effective blueprint thus far has been that of deception and intimidation. He can never deceive the Almighty; he is, however, capable of misleading mankind to disobey God. In order to distract sinful humanity from seeking the Lord for salvation, or from "[l]ooking unto Jesus the author and finisher [perfector] of our faith" (Heb. 12:2), the Dragon is busy misleading mankind. The ubiquitous Satan knows full well that the eternal and godly Trinity has gloriously succeeded in providing for man a free plan of salvation by which it will be reconciled freely with God. Accordingly, this Old Dragon, too, must now create his own Satanic Trinity, of which the Beast is one of the three persons.

17. Except in purpose, a wicked, earthly Trinity must, in all aspects and in every detail, correspond to the heavenly Trinity. In addition to Satan himself, who is the counterfeit of God the Father, he must also have a counterfeit son, the Antichrist, or the Beast (Rev. 13:1), who simulates God the Son. For the third person of this evil Trinity, Satan has the False Prophet (Rev. 13:11), who endeavors to imitate the Holy Spirit. Together, God the Father, God the Son, and God the Holy Spirit, have their wicked counterparts, in this world of sin, emulated in a Trinity made up of Satan, the Beast, who is the Antichrist, and the False Prophet.

18. Throughout the ages, this Satan-led Trinity has endeavored to outsmart and outwit the Holy Trinity among the sinful men. Knowing its demise is sure and imminent, it makes every effort to disrupt God's plan of salvation among men. While remaining the chief antagonist of the Almighty God and of His Kingdom; nevertheless, Satan's main objective has, throughout the ages, been focused on distracting the would-be sons and daughters of God from entering the eternal Kingdom. Through deception, Satan steers away as many souls as he can from all that is good, pure, and godly.

19. Contrary to the agnostic's false claims, Good and Evil are not the two infinite antagonists. Good is eternal, and this eternity is one of God's immutable attributes. Evil is created through transgression and rebellion against God; it has a beginning and is relatively temporal; it emanates from a lie. Quoting Jesus, the Apostle John says of this Wicked One: "He was a murderer from the beginning, and abode not in the truth, because there is no truth in him. When he speaketh a lie, he speaketh of his own: for he is a liar, and the father of it" (John 8:44^b). Since Evil has a beginning, it will most assuredly have an end too. Its end will be sudden and lethal. This expiration will come about at the very end of the Millennial Age. For we read in the book of Revelation:

> *And the devil [Satan] that deceived them was cast into the lake of fire and brimstone, where the beast and the false prophet are, and shall be tormented day and night for ever and ever (Rev. 20:10).*

20. The rise of the Beast is a process by which sin gradually and at an ever escalating pace rampages humanity to a much greater degree of wickedness as time goes by. Knowing that his doom is at hand (Rev. 12:12), Satan hastens to establish his own kingdom on earth, a pretentious kingdom, in an attempt to imitate the Kingdom of God. Satan does not send his son into the world; he affectionately chooses him from the best of mankind. He embraces someone who is congenial, sociable and gregarious; someone the unpolished sinful world will more readily embrace (John 5:43). In both the Old and the New Testaments, the teachings of the Scripture are many concerning the Beast, as he is aided and abetted to take over the world, and concerning his never ceasing attempts to assume leadership of the world.

21. It should not be lost to the believer that the Beast, in reality, is the Antichrist himself. Obviously, he is called the Antichrist, because he diametrically opposes Christ and, likewise, the entire Trinity — God the Father, God the Son, and God the Holy Spirit. Some Bible scholars have suggested that the Beast will be resurrected from the dead, brought back from the abyss. As an antagonist of our Saviour, whom, at the fullness of time, God sent to the world; likewise, Satan's Superman, is chosen from amongst the living and not the dead; in due time, he will declare the Beast's appearance to the world. Of this appearance, the apostle John says:

> *Little children, it is the last [end] time: and as ye have heard that antichrist shall come, even now are there many*

antichrists; whereby ye know that it is the last [end] time (I John 2:18).

V. The Beast's Debut

22. In the midst of this anarchy created primarily by the absence of the Church on the earth and also by the Russian invasion of Israel, the sinful world is greeted by none other than the Dragon himself. This outcast Evil, who was just chased down from the "heavenlies," is now present on the earth shamelessly advocating new schemes against God and His saints. He assures the confused world of his program for a new world government that is superior to the previous "Bible-tarnished, Judaeo-Christian" system. He "anoints" his chosen one, his Antichrist, to be the new "Messiah," the new hope of humanity. He gives him strength, authority and a throne from which to rule mankind (Rev. 13:2). In the book of Revelation, we read:

And they worshipped the dragon which gave power unto the beast: and they worshipped the beast, saying, Who is like unto the beast? [W]ho is able to make war with him? (Rev. 13:4, 5).

23. At least in his beginnings, the Beast is strongly supported and directed by the "woman," the One-World Apostate Church of the end time (Rev. 17:3). Normally, this end-time church proclaims itself to be godly, especially as it confesses a traditional faith. But the Bible has a different view of this apostasy; it calls it "the great whore" (Rev. 17:1). To fully understand the exact meaning and implication of the symbolically used word "whore," we should read in Hosea. Not only is the word greatly clarified there; but the end-result is also well understood. The calamity that befalls such a whore is also clearly stated.

Plead with your mother, plead: for she is not my wife, neither am I her husband: let her therefore put away her whoredoms out of her sight, and her adulteries from between her breasts; [l]est I strip her naked, and set her as in the day that she was born, and make her as a wilderness, and set her like a dry land, and slay her with thirst (Hos. 2:2, 3).

24. From such passages of the Scriptures as Revelation, Chapter 13, Verse 1, and Chapter 17, Verses 10 and 13, we learn that, not too long after his formal presentation by the Dragon, the Beast receives the unanimous support of all ten horns/kings, "having seven heads and ten horns" (Rev. 13:1). It is at this juncture in the prophetic history of the end-time events that John, the beloved disciple, while standing before the throne of God, declares:

> *And I stood upon the sand of the sea, and saw a beast rise up out of the sea, having seven heads and ten horns, and upon his horns ten crowns, and upon his head the name of blasphemy (Rev. 13:1^a).*

> *[A]nd the dragon gave him his [own] power, and his [own] seat, and great authority (Rev. 13:2^b).*

> *And there was given unto him a mouth speaking great things and blasphemies; and power was given unto him to continue [a relatively peaceful and prosperous reign for] forty and two months (Rev. 13:5).*

25. Up to the moment of his proclamation, the Beast is just another great politician, another significant ruler, who has a total sway, possibly, over the newly forged "Atlantic Alliance," a far-flung Empire, embracing the two shores of the Atlantic Ocean. Now that he has finally received his power and his throne directly from the Dragon (Rev. 13:2), and is "sanctioned," that is, anointed, and supported by the False Prophet (13:11-17), the Beast is ready to be presented to the world as its new Saviour. Of the "exalted" appearance of the Beast, John says: "[A]nd behold a white horse: and he that sat on him had a bow; and a crown was given unto him: and he went forth conquering, and to conquer" (Rev. 6:2). And of course, the Beast, as the Antichrist riding "a white horse," attempts to imitate the Lord Jesus who is about to descend from heaven to the earth on a white horse. (Rev. 19:11-14)

26 Most Bible scholars are generally agreed that the Beast, who "rises up out of the sea," is most likely a Gentile. That he appears, "having seven heads and ten horns," signifies that the Beast has the full support of a two-tier government which he had earlier assisted in its establishment. The eighth-member Presidium -- which is headed by the seven kings elected from the ten-nation coalition of states and the Beast himself as the king number eighth -- has the dominion over the Atlantic Alliance. The General Council, on the other hand, is the ruling body of the ten horns that administers the internal affairs of the Revived Roman Empire only.

27. The second beast, who is "coming up out of the earth" (Rev. 13:11), is undoubtedly a Jew. This may be amply attested by the fact that the word **ha-Arets** *the earth, the land*, particularly in Israeli Spoken Hebrew, usually signifies *Israel*. The sentence, **Af pa'am lo biqqartiy ba-Arets** can only mean, *I have never visited Israel*. The fact that the False Prophet appears having "two horns like a lamb" (Rev. 13:11), it undoubtedly bespeaks of him as the counterfeit of the Holy Spirit, who is supported by the two end-time Apostate Religious Systems: Christendom and Judaism. For the term "horn," which in biblical Hebrew is **qérn**, is used most commonly to connote *power*. And it is this power, which the two religious bodies provide, that the False Prophet makes use of — at least for a limited time.

VI. The New System of Worship

28. Now that the False Prophet is openly committed to the support of the world, he demands of the world, particularly from his coriligiously Jews, the following: First, that a highly "computerized" image be made for the Beast to which he gives the ability to speak and to work miracles that deceive the world. Secondly, that all the people worship the image of the Beast, and those who refuse to do so be put to death. Thirdly, "[a]nd he causeth all, both small and great, rich and poor, free and bond, to receive a mark in their right hand, or in their foreheads" (Rev. 13:16). After more than 25 centuries since the days of King Nebuchadnezzar, whose "image of gold" was likewise erected in the plain of Dura to be worshipped, history repeats itself once again. Now, another more powerful miracle-working image is once again constructed for this end-time Beast to be worshipped throughout the new Gentile World Empire.

29. Now that the Beast is formally presented to the world as the new "Messiah" to rule over it, a new system of worship is declared — a secular religion of self-gratification, most likely, based primarily upon the teachings of the present-day humanism and centered around the image of the Beast. As the mightiest ruler of the Atlantic Alliance, representing the richest and the most powerful state in the world, the United States of America, the Beast is worshipped and adored by millions of peoples and nationalities all over the world. Those who openly refuse to bow down to the image are forthwith martyred.

30. On the earth, the believing Christians who have been living undercover, find it hard to obtain subsistence or to find jobs. Possibly many are helped, out of kindness and kinship, by their unbelieving family members, acquaintances, or neighbors. Those that are caught, whether they are believers or their supporters, are destroyed forthwith. Those who reject their faith and accept the Beast's number for survival, forfeit their relationship to Christ. There is only one way about the matter: You either are Christ's, and you become subject to persecution and even martyrdom; or you become one of the followers of the Beast, and perish spiritually.

31. Contrary to what some have ignorantly taught; God's grace, during the Tribulation Period, is no longer on the earth. Those who teach that God somehow will take care of anyone who has become a believer after the rapture are altogether misguided. While salvation is still through faith in Jesus Christ, any compromise with the cohorts of the Beast is tantamount to a spiritual betrayal and double-crossing of the Saviour. There is not one single verse in the entire prophetic message that speaks of God's grace functioning on the earth during the Tribulation Period. Being the seventieth week of Daniel, the personal relationship of the believer with Christ during this period is identical to that which the Old Testament saints had with Him. In His sermon on the mount, speaking about this period, Christ clearly stated: "But he that shall *endure unto the end*, the same shall be saved" (Matt. 24:13). The believers of the Tribulation Period must *endure to the end to be saved*. (*Italics added*).

VII. The Beast's Image

32. Immediately after his "rising to the throne" and his being presented to the world, the Beast is given unchallenged power "over all kindred, and tongues, and nations" for forty-two months (Rev. 13:5, 7). Through his crafty diplomacy, eloquent speech, charismatic persuasion, clearly without ever using military force, the Beast will *speedily* gain much power and great territorial expansion (Dan. 11:21). Initially, supported by the two apostate religious systems, Christendom and Judaism, especially by the former, "the woman" (Rev. 17:3-6), the Beast, during the first 42 months of the Tribulation Period, fully consolidates his dominion over the Revived Roman Empire, over the greater Atlantic Alliance, and over much of the rest of the world. The relative absence of peace, widespread famine, frequent deaths and many other such erratic disturbances are all explained away by this Demagogue and his followers.

33. With one stroke of genius, the Beast, through his treaty with Israel — apparently, his first major diplomatic accomplishment — achieves several significant objectives: First, he satisfies the immediate security needs of Israel — not from its Arab neighbors who militarily have never been an equal, but primarily from another major power similar to Russia which had just invaded the Holy Land and miserably withdrawn from it. It should be emphasized here that Russia, which had already carried out its invasion of Israel, became a symbol. Secondly, he secures the unanimous, worldwide support of the Jewish people, many of whom will be misguided and will undoubtedly, at least initially, consider him to be their promised Messiah. His miraculous entry into the world and his presentation by the Dragon in fanfare and in "brouhaha" will make him acceptable to all mankind. Thirdly, he ensures the tranquillity of the entire strategic, oil-rich region of the Middle East for himself and for his allies. Fourth, having significantly consolidated his throne, he is now free from any immediate or foreseeable challenges and is hence ready to compel the universal worship of his image. It is this worship of the Beast by mankind that the

Dragon longs for; for any worship of the Beast becomes tantamount to the worship of the Dragon, of Lucifer himself. This has been Lucifer's ultimate goal from the very beginning.

CHAPTER 11

THE NORTHERN INVASION

And the word of the Lord came unto me, saying, Son of man, set thy face against Gog, the land of Magog, the chief prince of Meshech and Tubal, and prophesy against him, [a]nd say, Thus saith the Lord God; Behold, I am against thee, O Gog, the chief prince of Meshech and Tubal: I will turn thee back, and put hooks into thy jaws. . . . I will bring thee against my land, that the heathen may know me, when I shall be sanctified in thee, O Gog, before their eyes (Ez. 38:1-4ᵃ, 16ᵇ).

I. God's Hook in Gog's Jaws

1. EZEKIEL OPENS CHAPTER 38 of his book with an indictment upon the forces of the Northern Confederation and its allies. This Northern Confederation is unmistakably spelled out almost in detail and parts of which are even repeated twice. Not only does the prophet narrate for us who the chief of this federation is, but also his name is given, the name of his land, the names of his two cities, and the names of the five countries that are allied with him. God tells the prophet to prophesy against Gog, and against the land of Magog, the chief prince of Meshech (Moscow) and Tubal (Tubolsk), apparently the two main cities of Magog (Russia), at that time.

Son of man, set thy face against Gog, the land of Magog, saying, . . .I will bring thee forth, and all thine army, horses and horsemen, all of them clothed with all sorts of armour, even a great company with bucklers and shields, all of them handling swords: Persia, Ethiopia, and Libya with them; all of them with shields and helmet: Gomer, and all his bands: the house of Togarmah of the north quarters, and all his bands: and many people with thee (Ez. 38:2, 4-6).

2. In the Scriptural passage we have just quoted above, Gog is identified with his land, the Magog, and he is called "the chief prince of Meshech and Tubal." God promises that He will put a hook in Gog's jaws and bring him forth into the land of Israel. In addition, God will order an army, a great company, from Persia, Ethiopia, Libya, Gomar and Tugarmah, to be joined with those of Gog's land. "In the latter years," God will bring forth a great company of soldiers "into the land that is brought back from the sword, and is gathered out of many people, against the mountains of Israel" (Ez. 38:8). Notice how the phrase states it: "in the latter years," and in Ezekiel, Chapter 38, Verse 16, the same phrase is repeated as "in the latter days" and not at the end time.

3. It is interesting to observe that the Scriptures do not say here "in the end time," as some have suggested. This small distinction in terms of time is sufficient to clarify for us that the occasion of this Northern Invasion differs from the time of the Battle of Armageddon. These two battles — the Northern Invasion and the Battle of Armageddon — should not be confused with each other. Furthermore, this invasion speaks of Gog and the "many nations," which are numbered, that are united with him to go up to the mountains of Israel and to capture it. With respect to the Battle of Armageddon, there will be practically "all nations" united to wage war not only on Israel, as the Beast had initially thought, but also on the God Almighty Himself and on His Son, the Lord Jesus Christ and His armies of saints.

4. It should be clearly understood that the bringing forth of Gog and his great company into the land of Israel will not take place in the middle of the seven years of the Tribulation Period as some Bible scholars have recommended. Earlier it was stated that this Russian Invasion will take place simultaneously with the Rapture of the Church or, most appropriately, immediately after the Rapture, and possibly after the Beast is identified and presented to the world as their new Leader. Such an excursion would have to preclude any possibility of interrupting the unique reign of the Beast on earth, an unequivocal rule given to him by the Dragon himself as allowed by the Lord God Almighty. (Rev. 13:5^b).

5. Moreover, it is impossible for Russia, or any other power, to interrupt the peace granted to the Beast to control the entire world and launch an invasion of the Holy Land during the midst of the Tribulation Period. So, it is essential for Russia to undertake its swift and deadly excursion into the Middle East sometime at the very beginning of the Tribulation Period. Of course, Russia does not have any suspicions about the occurrence of the Rapture of the Church at the very time that she prepares for an assault on Israel. The agnostic government of Russia could not even care about either religion or the fulfillment of the prophetic message of the Word of God. The Red Army's concern is about this European Supremacy and its achievements to gobble up many lands and territories of the world, especially the strategic land of Israel. It must do something to frustrate the success of the newly Revived Roman Empire.

II. A Swift March into the Holy Land

6. At the time of the Rapture of the Church, God prepares the way for this Russian Invasion to take place. He puts in the heart of Gog to expeditiously accomplish this deed; and he does. As the head of the confederated armies, Gog mounts an assault on the Holy Land that is swift and devastating. The Word of God says: "Thou shalt ascend and come like a storm, thou shalt be like a cloud to cover the land, thou, and all thy bands, and many people with thee" (Ez. 38:9). As the armies of this confederation occupy the Holy Land, God says, "that my fury shall come up in my face. . . . Surely in that day there shall be a great shaking in the land of Israel" (Ez. 38:18, 19). Yet, within this huge army, God will cause "every man's sword [to rise] against his brother" and companion in-arms (Ez. 38:21). God further says:

> I will plead against . . . [Gog] with pestilence and with blood; and I will rain upon him, and upon his bands, and upon the many people that are with him, an overflowing rain, and great hailstones, fire, and brimstone. Thus, will I magnify myself, and sanctify myself; and I will be known in the eyes of many nations, and they shall know that I am the Lord (Ez. 38:22, 23).

7. With these words, the Lord God of heaven declares his purpose in putting hooks into Gog's jaws, and bringing him up against the mountains of the Holy Land where he shall cause him to "fall upon the mountains of Israel" (Ez. 39:4^a). In this manner will the God of heaven make Himself "known in the eyes of many nations, and they shall know that I am the Lord. . . " (Ez. 38:23). And I will "make my holy name known in the midst of my people Israel. . . " Ez. 39:7^a). Through this action, God is able to accomplish two important things: Make Himself known in the eyes of many nations; magnify himself in the midst of His people.

8. Contrary to what some Bible scholars have provided as the timing of their interpretation; should this episode take place in the middle of the tribulation period, it would be hardly likely that any nation would be inclined to give recognition and ear to the Almighty God's calling. And yet, God says, I will make myself known "in the eyes of many nations, and they shall know that I am the Lord" (Ez. 38:23^b). Yet, it is well known, that by the middle of the Tribulation Period, all nations as nations are determined to steer away from God and to despise the Almighty. The Beast has promised them everything and has brought about much tranquillity and prosperity. The deception he will bring about to the people of the world is, undoubtedly, gladly accepted. For we read in Matthew:

> *For there shall rise false Christs, and false prophets, and shall shew great signs and wonders: inasmuch that, if it were possible, they shall deceive the very elect (Matt. 24:21, 24).*

9. Moreover, in the book of Revelation we are told that despite the plagues from heaven, men "blasphemed the name of God, which hath power over these plagues: and they repented not to give him glory" (Rev. 16:9). Again, "And [they] blasphemed the God of heaven because of their pains and their sores, and repented not of their deeds" (Rev. 16:11). Again, "And [they] said to the mountains and rocks, [f]all on us, and hide us from the face of him that sitteth on the throne, and from the wrath of the Lamb: For the great day of his wrath is come; and who shall be able to stand?" (Rev. 6:16, 17). Men's hearts are so hardened and removed from the God of mercy, the Almighty who has created them, that they will ask "the mountains and rocks" to fall on them and to hide them from the face of God rather than repent and give glory to the Almighty.

10. Undoubtedly, this "chief prince of Meshech and Tubal" will devise a strategy and will set his armies in motion and give orders to move forcefully and swiftly against the Holy Land. Interestingly, an ever-ready army of occupation, which, most probably, is primarily drawn from the ranks of his five allies: from Persia, Ethiopia/Sudan, Libya, Gomar and Tugarmah, is now ready to take action. While in Ezekiel, Chapter 38, Verse 5, the King James translation of the original Hebrew word, **kush**, is Ethiopia; according to Hindson, and this author fully agree with him, since the word covers also the land of Sudan, it would be more appropriate to translate it as, *Sudan*,[1] which today is an Arab country. Like most Arab countries, Sudan has its own resentment against Israel.

11. These huge armies will vigorously provide a devastating strike on Israel; these coalition forces, assisted with Gog's mighty air power, will swiftly enter the land of Israel and will occupy it. But before Gog attempts to devastate the land and its people, the Lord God from heaven will rain fire and brimstone on Gog and on his armies. He will send pestilence among the armies' ranks; God will set each man's sword to be drawn against his own brother-in-arm. He will leave only one sixth of its armies to hasten back home with the devastating news of their defeat and destruction in their confrontation with the enemy.

III. God's Punishment of Gog

12. There are three major punishments which God pours upon Gog and upon the armies of his allies. First, He will set each man's sword to be used against his own brother-in-arm, his own compatriot, his own ally. Secondly, God will devastate the huge armies with pestilence and with blood, and will rain upon them and upon their armies with great hailstone, fire, and brimstone. Thirdly, the Almighty God will send a fire on Magog; the very heart of his homeland shall be burned with fire, even before he is able to return safely to it in retreat. God will earmark Gog and his land with the burning fire for having devised this gross mischief.

13. Since it will take Israel seven years to burn the weaponry of this multi-nation excursion led by Russia (Ez. 39:9^{b}), it is inevitable that this invasion take place at the time of the rapture, at the very beginning of the seven years of the Tribulation Period, as some Bible scholars suggest. Had the invasion taken place in the middle of the Tribulation Period, the time it would take to burn the enemy's weapons alone could overlap the first three years of the beginning of the Millennial Age. But this could not be! The "red horse" of Revelation, Chapter 6, — which many Bible scholars equate with the assault Gog mounts against Israel — appears to have come about simultaneously with the dedication and presentation of the Beast or immediately thereafter. In the four seals of Revelation, Chapter 6, the first horse is white and is mounted by the impostor, the Beast; the second seal is red, and is mounted by a personage that takes away peace from the earth. We read in the book of Revelation the following:

> *And there went out another horse that was red: and power was given to him that sat thereon to take peace from the earth, and that they should kill one another: and there was given unto him a great sword (Rev. 6:4).*

14. It becomes very obvious, therefore, that several important events do take place immediately after the Rapture: First, the Beast is given the rule over the ten-nation European coalition, the Revived Roman Empire; secondly, he is also given power by the Dragon to establish a One-World Empire. Thirdly, the Northern Invasion takes place immediately before or after, or simultaneously with the Dragon's declaration of the Beast as the new Messiah of the world. The passage related to the "red horse," "that they should kill one another" (Rev. 6:4), is very similar in structure to the passage in which the Lord caused the armies of the Gog's configuration to fight one another, "every man's sword shall be against his brother" (Ez. 38:21^{b}).

15. Some prophecy interpreters suggest that the meaning of the word, **rosh**, signifies "Russia" (Ez. 38:2). Etymologically, this cannot be so! There are two grammatical reasons why *this* is impossible. The *first* reason is that the word has the letter *Alep* in it being weak is silent for its middle radical, as in **ro'sh**, which makes it commensurate with the other Semitic root for the same word. The second reason is that the word following the word **rosh** lacks the conjunctive particle, *Waw*, which has the meaning of *and*, used to link between itself and the immediately preceding word, **nasi'** *prince*. Accordingly, in the absence of this *Waw*, the phrase, **nasi' ro'sh meshekh vetuval**, could only be translated appositively (*Gram.*) as, *the chief, the prince of Meshech and Tubal*, or simply, *"the chief prince of Meshech and Tubal."*

16. Etymologically speaking, what is Gog, and what is Magog? It is very likely that the very root of the word, "Gog," is related to the now inactive Aramaic root **gug**, or its active colloquial form, **juj**, which has the meaning of, *to walk, to move*, and its transitive form, *to shake*, to *agitate*. Although, originally a biliteral root, it is treated as a weak verb of a triliteral root, as most such roots are dealt with in the Semitic languages and in Assyrian Aramaic. In Hebrew, there is a verb, **zuz**, which appears to be related somewhat to **gug**, which means, *to move, go away*. Nonetheless, the Hebrew verb **gug**, its derived noun **gog**, and its derivative noun of place, **Magog**, is the place where Gog lives and agitates against the Almighty God of heaven. The word is used eight times in Ezekiel, Chapters 38 and 39. The term is also used in the book of Revelation, Chapter 20, Verses 7 and 9, where this Gog is devoured by fire broadcast by the God of heaven.

IV. Countries Allied with Gog

17. Who are the countries that are allied with Gog? The first country mentioned is Persia. Many years ago, when the country of Iran, the old Persia, under the late king, Shah Riza Pahlavi's regime, was solidly allied with the United States of America, I used to point in my teaching of prophesy to this passage in the Scriptures. The question most often asked used to be: "Persia is our ally, how can this be?" Many Bible scholars of the time have interpreted Persia as other than modern Iran. The same question would be raised about Ethiopia/Sudan and Libya; again, each of these countries have often been interpreted or suggested to be some different country.

18. Today, this is not a difficult question to understand, especially when considering the enmity Persia, Sudan, and Libya have harbored against Israel. It is interesting to notice how Syria, Jordan, and Egypt — all three front-line, confrontational countries — are not mentioned in this alliance. If the Arabs were the most diehard enemies of Israel, surely, they should have joined Persia, Libya, Sudan, and the rest of the allied countries. Yet, these Arab countries are neither a part of the confederation, nor are they, directly or indirectly, involved in this wicked Northern Invasion. It is very possible that these neighboring countries had already been neutralized by the United States of America and thus have stayed out of this conflict. Indeed, two of these countries have already recognized Israel: Jordan and Egypt.

19. Who are the people covered by Gomar and by Tugarmah? It is believed that Gomar represents the Germanic people. How does Germany — assuming that the prophesy talks about today's Germans — figure in this alliance? At the present, it is not clear. But when the time comes for the invasion to be carried out, there will indeed be Germans in that army. Of course, there used to be a small Republic of Germans within the old Soviet Union, and which, I believe, now falls within the boundaries of the Russian Federation.

20. Tugarmah is yet another nation that will be united with Russia for the invasion of Israel. Most Bible scholars agree that Tugarmah represents the Turkic elements, which formerly exist within the Soviet Empire. But the Russian Federation itself has a number of large Turkic elements within its borders. Many of these elements are mountain dwellers, and are well suited for warfare in mountainous terrain. Israel is predominantly hilly and mountainous and requires such a variety of warriors to accomplish a swift occupation.

V. Invasion Limited to Israel

21. One item of great interest here is that this Russian excursion into the Holy Land will almost exclusively concentrate on the land of Israel. Gog's assault will deviate neither to the right nor to the left. It concentrates on the Holy Land, on the state of Israel alone. It is not clear whether Russia would have moved to any other land after its occupation of Israel had she been allowed to stay longer there. So swiftly and meticulously God punishes Russia and her five allies that they barely have enough time to retreat to their lands. So, we read in Ezekiel:

> *To take a spoil, and to take a prey; to turn thine hand upon the desolate places that are now inhabited, and upon the people that are gathered out of the nations, which have gotten cattle and goods, that dwell in the midst of the land. Sheba, and Dedan, and the merchants of Tarshish, with all the young lions thereof, shall say unto thee, Art thou come to take a spoil? Hast thou gathered they company to take prey? to carry away silver and gold, to take away cattle and goods, to take a great spoil? (Ez. 38:12, 13).*

22. The end of this invasion is calamitous, to say the least. God Almighty personally interferes and destroys the forces of this confederation almost completely. Three types of "strikes" God unleashes against Gog and against his numerous forces. In a short period of time, God brings this unholy alliance to a naught. The Bible says that only one sixth of its invading armies survived God's onslaught. It will take seven years to burn its weaponry with fire — both the shields and the bucklers, the bows and the arrows, and the hand staves, and the spears. And God will give a place of burial in Israel, in a place called "The valley of Hamon-gog. And seven months shall the house of Israel be burying of them, that they may cleanse the land" (Ez. 39:11^b, 12). As swiftly these coalition armies entered into the Holy Land, so expeditiously they exited it. Israel is once again, although for a very short period of time, free from foreign domination, especially as the Beast, immediately thereafter, it appears, negotiates with her what appeared to be a covenant of seven-year peace, which, nevertheless, he will repudiate in the middle of the Tribulation Period.

CHAPTER 12

THE DEMISE OF APOSTASY

And the ten horns which thou sawest upon the beast, these shall hate the whore, and shall make her desolate and naked, and shall eat her flesh, and burn her with fire. For God hath put in their hearts to fulfill his will, and to agree, and give their kingdom unto the beast, until the words of God shall be fulfilled (Rev. 17:16, 17).

I. The Demise of Religious Apostasy

1. IMITATING KING NEBUCHADNEZZAR of Babylon, the Beast demands a world-wide worship of his own image. Sinful and unfaithful as the Apostate Church will have become by this time, it resists the worship of the image. United possibly under the primacy of papacy, the Church as an institution, categorically refuses to worship the idol. Its refusal to do so is not because of its faithfulness to the Almighty. Would to God that were the case! Yet, it rejects the Beast's worship, because of its own pride and love for ultimate power. In his fury, the Beast directs the ten horns, the rulers of the General Council of the ten-state coalition, namely, the Revived Roman Empire, to destroy the whore.

2. Immediately after the destruction of the Apostate Church as an institution — and only as an institution — the False Prophet officially presents the Beast as the promised Messiah to his own coreligionists, the Jews. He now demands of them, too, to worship the Beast's image. However, the zealous Jews, who do not bow the knee to Baal, the false Messiah, refuse to worship him. Their flagrant refusal to worship the image will provoke the Beast and provide him with a long sought-after pretext to lay waste Israel, to utterly destroy its religious institutions, and to desecrate its newly built temple. Accordingly, large numbers of the Jews will realize that this "Idol Shepherd" (Zech. 11:16, 17), who only three and a half years ago had brought peace and tranquillity to their land through a covenant of peace (Dan. 9:27), is not indeed *their* Messiah. They remember what God had said to Moses:

> *I am the Lord thy God. . . . Thou shalt have no other gods before me. Thou shalt not make unto thee any graven image. . . . Thou shalt not bow down thyself to them, nor serve them: for I the Lord thy God am a jealous God. . . . (Ex. 20:2-5).*

3. At this very critical juncture, almost midway between the first and the second halves of the seven-year Tribulation Period (Rev. 12:6), the Beast, who is now in the very presence of the Dragon, who himself has recently been cast out of the air by the Archangel Michael (Rev. 12:9), seeks to subdue Israel, first through the breaking of his covenant with the Jewish nation. Secondly, he will feverishly amass huge numbers of armies in the Holy Land. Consequently, many believing Jews will flee into "the wilderness" for refuge. It appears that in Revelation, Chapter 12, there are at least "two Scriptural references" given of such an escape by the woman into the wilderness. Of this flight, John says:

> *And the woman fled into the wilderness, where she hath a place prepared of God, that they should feed her there a thousand two hundred and threescore days (Rev. 12:6).*

> *And to the woman were given wings of a great eagle, that she might fly into the wilderness, into her place, where she is nourished for a time, and [two] times, and half a time, from the face of the serpent, [the Lucifer]" (Rev. 12:14).*

4. Up to this moment, when the Beast has broken his covenant with Israel, he had enjoyed a glorious success almost on all fronts. With the destruction of the Apostate Christendom, he had reached, one might say, the zenith of his power. But now as he enters the Great Tribulation Period, the second half of the seven years of the Tribulation, not only natural calamities are multiplying on the earth (Matt. 24:8), but even the heaven itself, it appears, is contravening with human affairs. Accordingly, the refusal of the Jews to worship the Beast's image makes it necessary for this Dictator to strike hard at the Jewish people and, if possible, to exterminate that nation (Rev. 12:3-6), thereby repeating Hitler's folly and the atrocities of the Spanish Inquisition.

5. To achieve his sinister objective, the Beast assembles the armies of his far-flung Empire, along with the forces of his many allies, and deploys them in the Plain of Jezreel in Israel, which is spiritually called, the Valley of Jehoshaphat (Joel 3:2, 14), where God shall crush the might of the Gentile nations. Nevertheless, the Beast will have God-sanctioned power over Israel throughout the second half of the Tribulation Period (Dan. 7:25). Because this is "the time of Jacob's trouble" (Jer. 30:7), the day during which God shall refine His people through fire. (Zech. 13:9).

6. To the unbelieving masses of ordinary people on the earth, both Jews and Gentiles, the world is experiencing only an extraordinary armed conflict between and among countries, alliances, and diverse regions of the earth. The many occurrences of flood, earthquakes, pestilences and famines over the entire world (Matt. 24:7, 8) are either brushed aside, or deemed, particularly by the media of the day, as only unusual catastrophes and tragedies brought about by a displeased, *naughty, naughty* "Mother Nature." The *el-Nino* and the *la-Nina* are considered to be responsible for many of these calamities. Somehow, the two natural forces — the el-Nino and the la-Nina — which have existed since the foundation of the world, are the ones suddenly to be blamed.

7. But the hated and harassed new believers on the earth during this Tribulation Period know better. They know that, during the last three and a half years, there will occur extremely distressful events, both for the unbelieving Jews whom God is now refining through fire, and for the arrogant Gentiles whose might and disdain He aims to bring to naught, once and for all. Satan's strategy, on the other hand, is to subtly gather all the armies of the entire world in Israel and to prepare them for a final assault against the Lamb of God, the Lion of Judah, who is about to land at Mount Olives. And the sovereign God is behind all this gathering; "for the day of the Lord is near in the valley of decision" (Joel 3:9-14).

II. Judaism Scrutinized by God

8. After Jesus was rejected, during the days of his earthly ministry, by His own people from becoming their King, with a broken heart, He completely ignored them and left them to their own capriciousness. The Lord had prophesied that their house would be left in ruins for their rejection of Him: "Behold, your house is left unto you desolate" (Luke 13:35ᵃ). They rejected Him who had given His very life a ransom for their sins. It was not easy for the Lord to give up his people to the wiles of the Devil. On the one hand, the Jews could not understand Christ's offering of his body for a ransom for their sins; on the other, because their stony hearts were so adversely set in their wicked attitude towards God Almighty, He left them to their inclination. For we read in the book of John the following:

> *He that rejecteth me, and receiveth not my words, hath one that judgeth him: the word that I have spoken, the same shall judge him in the last day" (John 12:48).*

> *I am come in my Father's name, and ye receive me not: if another shall come in his own name, him ye will receive (John 5:43).*

9. Throughout His ministry on the earth, Jesus spoke of his death and resurrection for the backslidden people of God. His pronouncements were in anicdotes and allegories so that the average man in the street would not want to understand them. They were earthly (John 8:23); He was heavenly (John 6:38ᵃ). With such powerful and impeccable words, Jesus talked with them saying: I am the good shepherd (John 10:11ᵃ, 14ᵃ); I am the door (John 10:9ᵃ); I am from above (John 8:23); If ye believe not that I am he, ye shall die in your sins (John 8:24ᵇ); I tell you the truth, ye believe me not (John 8:45); Before Abraham was, I am (John 8:58ᵇ); My sheep hear my voice (John 10:27ᵃ); I and my Father are one (John 10:30); Search the scriptures, for in them ye think ye have eternal life (John 5:39); For I came down from heaven (John 6:38ᵃ); I am the bread of life (John 6:35ᵃ); I am the living bread: if any man eat of this bread, he shall live for ever (John 6:51); Ye shall know the truth, and the truth shall make you free (John 8:32^b); I am the light of the world (John 8:12^a). Realizing man's spiritual weakness and dilemma, Paul wrote to the Corinthians the following:

> *But the natural man receiveth not the things of the Spirit of God: for they are foolishness unto him: neither can he know them, because they are spiritually discerned (I Cor. 2:14).*

10. The unusual military escalation in the Middle East alarms the kings of the East. With an army of two hundred million strong, the Eastern nations move towards the Middle East and towards Israel to check the West's military reinforcements in the area and possibly to execute a total occupation of this strategic, oil-rich region. To facilitate their march to the Holy Land, God sends "the sixth angel [who] poured out his vial upon the great river Euphrates; and the water thereof was dried up, that the way of the kings of the east might be prepared" (Rev. 16:12).

11. In the fulfillment of "the time of Jacob's trouble," as we shall see in due course, God from heaven gathers all the nations — East and West — against Jerusalem (Zech. 14:2, 3) to destroy it and its unbelieving inhabitants. For Jerusalem, too, had succumbed and had gone the way of the Gentiles. Many are the innocent Christian believers nowadays who are constantly asked to "Pray for the peace of Jerusalem," according to the instructions given in the book of Psalms (Ps. 122:6). Yet, in the book of Revelation, Chapter 11, Verse 8, we are clearly cautioned that, during this dispensation of grace, Jerusalem has become "the great city, [which] spiritually . . . [is] called Sodom and Egypt, where also our Lord was crucified" (Rev. 11:8^b). We are indeed called upon to pray for the peace of the Middle East ceaselessly and fervently always, especially for the salvation and peace of the people of Israel.

12. It should be recalled here that since the time of the creation when the Dragon had been cast out from heaven to the ground, the Old Lucifer and his angels (Is. 14:12), "the rulers of darkness of this world," had turned the "high places" (Eph. 6:12) into his headquarters. And now in preparation for the descent of our Saviour with His saints from this region, from the high places, to Mount Olives to reclaim his rightful possession, Michael has now amply prepared the way. Despite the Old Serpent's thwarting, puffing and putting up a fight with the Archangel, yet the Dragon and his armies were defeated and were swiftly cast down to the earth.

13. Now God has brought all nations to battle against Israel, against the city of Jerusalem. For, God must first chasten His own people and deal with a sinful nation who has trampled His laws and the precepts of His Word under its feet. Israel has defied God and has gone after other gods; it has pursued wealth over righteousness, prosperity over holiness. It has become a nation that is satisfied in its own righteousness. God is sick of it; He will deal with the Jewish Apostasy as He has already dealt with the Christian Apostasy. But now the time of Jacob's trouble has to be fulfilled, and the "nation of God" has to be chastened. God seriously condemns His people's apostasy. We read in Jeremiah about this spiritual degeneration:

> *The children gather wood, and the fathers kindle the fire, and the women knead their dough, to make cakes to the queen of heaven, and to pour out drink-offerings unto other gods, that they may provoke me to anger [says God Almighty] (Jer. 7:18).*

> *But we will certainly do whatsoever thing goeth forth out of our own mouth, to burn incense unto the queen of heaven, and to pour out drink-offerings unto her, as we have done, we, and our fathers, our kings, and our princes, in the cities of Judah, and in the streets of Jerusalem. . . . And when we burned incense to the queen of heaven, and poured out drink-offerings unto her, did we make her cakes to worship her, and pour out drink-offerings unto her, without our men? (Jer. 44:17, 19).*

14. Despite the fact that the people of Judah had committed abominations before their God, their refusal to worship the Beast impels the Beast to strike harder at the inhabitants of Jerusalem and to exterminate them if possible (Rev. 12:3-6). To achieve this nefarious objective, he assembles his armies, along with the forces of his many allies and supporters, and deploys them in the Plain of Jezreel, which is spiritually called the Valley of Jehoshaphat (Joel 2:14), where God intends to judge harshly the Gentile nations.

15. On the surface, the huge gathering of the Beast's many armies on the pretext to fight the little state of Israel and to strengthen his control over it becomes tantamount to an intended slaughter. And while the average man in the street does not fathom the ramifications of these unusual, end-time events, the Satanic Trinity — the Beast, the False Prophet, and the Dragon — all are in cohort. They are preparing to fight not primarily Israel or the kings of the East, but the very heavenly armies of the Lord Jesus Christ who with his saints is about to descend from the air region to take over the earth. Of this affliction, the Lord said in the Gospel of Luke the following:

> *And when ye shall see Jerusalem compassed with armies, then know that the desolation thereof is nigh. Then let them which are in Judæa flee to the mountains; and let them which are in the midst of it depart out; and let not them that are in the countries enter thereinto (Luke. 21:20, 21).*

16. Encouraged by the presence of the Dragon on the earth and supported by the immeasurable number of demonic forces of Satan, the Beast immediately enters Jerusalem and utterly destroys it, desecrates the sanctuary, sets his image in the holy temple, and presents himself as the God of this world to be worshipped. Of this, Paul gives us a glimpse in his Epistle to the Thessalonians:

> *Who opposeth and exalteth himself above all that is called God, or that is worshipped; so that he as God sitteth in the temple of God, showing himself that he is God (II Thes. 1:4).*

17. Despite his swift occupation of Jerusalem, the Beast relentlessly continues his devastation of the Great City and the country side. Using

this Jewish rebellion as his new pretext, he also continues to expand and strengthen his military presence in the Holy Land. The Beast utterly destroys the nobility of Israel and its governmental institutions and supplants them with his own brand of administration, a most likely Jewish leadership that would be faithful to him and to his commanders. In an attempt to acquire a speedy peace in the state of Israel and, for that matter, in the entire Middle East, especially now that the "trouble making woman" has escaped to Edom, into the wilderness, he dictates that every political and governmental particular, no matter how insignificant, be brought to him directly to deal with it expeditiously and in person.

18. So, God is determined to bring all the Gentile nations of the world to the state of Israel, to the Holy Land, against the city of Jerusalem, to destroy it for its wickedness. The devastation of the city is unparalleled in the history of mankind. The Bible says, that not only the city will be taken, but its houses will be ransacked, its women will be assaulted, and half of its people will be taken captive. The Scriptures tell us the following about the capture and destruction of Israel:

And when ye shall see Jerusalem compassed with armies, then know that the desolation thereof is nigh. . . . Jerusalem shall be trodden down of the Gentiles, until the times of the Gentiles be fulfilled (Luke 21:20. 24^b).

For I [God] will gather all nations against Jerusalem to battle; and the city shall be taken, and the houses rifled, and the women ravished; and half of the city shall go forth into captivity, and the residue of the people shall not be cut off from the city (Zech. 14:2).

III. Faith Sustained by Obedience

19. As it was mentioned earlier, during the tribulation period, neither the Church, nor the Holy Spirit, not even God's grace has remained on the earth. Being the seventieth week of Daniel, the personal relationship of the believer, during this period, with the Lord Jesus Christ is identical to that which the Old Testament saints had in the Messiah who was to come. While the Tribulation Period is the fulfillment of the seventieth week of Daniel, God, through the mouth of His prophet, had determined upon His people to exercise faith in the Redeemer which is by far more difficult than it was during the years covering the first sixty-nine prophetic weeks. For, it is the time of Jacob's trouble. It is a "time" of calamity and dooms-day not only for the Gentile world, but primarily for the very people of God, the Jews.

20. In His sermon on the mount, speaking about this period, Christ clearly stated: "But he that shall endure unto the end, the same shall be saved" (Matt. 24:13). You must endure against the wiles of Satan and his cohorts; and, if it need be, you must die for the Saviour. It is no wonder then that heaven is full of millions of martyrs of this period. If God's grace was present on the earth during the Tribulation Period, then why were all the millions of souls of martyred believers present at the throne of God in heaven seeking God's vengeance upon their tormentors on the earth? Literally, millions upon millions of believing martyrs are present in heaven at and about the throne of God Almighty. For we read in the book of Revelation the following:

> And they [the martyrs] cried with a loud voice, saying, How long, O Lord, holy and true, dost thou not judge and avenge our blood on them that dwell on the earth?

21. Salvation, during this time of distress, is through faith in Jesus Christ; however, for this salvation to take effect in the life of the new believer, when the grace of God is absent from the earth, *endurance to the end* and *steadfast perseverance* are inevitable. You either must become a martyr for Jesus; or you are likely to follow the devil and take his sign, the mark of the Beast, to survive on the earth. Spiritually speaking, there is hardly any other avenue for the believer of this period to survive the Devil's onslaught.

22. Particularly in the second half of this Great Tribulation Period, every individual will be put to a severely scrutinizing test. The inquisition is very swift and dictatorially imposed. If caught, the believer either adheres to his faith in the Lord Jesus Christ and is forthwith put to death; or he may compromise his stand and accept the mark of the Beast on his hand, or over his head, if he is to survive physically. Likewise, teeming millions will survive the devastation brought about by the Beast and his collaborators during this great time of testing. Yet, many other millions of believers are ready and willing to be martyred and die for the testimony of our Lord Jesus Christ and for the testimony of His Word.

CHAPTER 13

THE GREAT TRIBULATION PERIOD

But as the days of [Noah] were, so shall also the coming of the Son of man be. For as in the days that were before the flood they were eating and drinking, marrying and giving in marriage, until the day that [Noah] entered into the ark. And knew not until the flood came, and took them all away; so shall also the coming of the Son of man be (Matt. 24:37-39).

I. God's Divine Judgment

1. AS THE SECOND HALF OF THE Tribulation Period begins, which is called now the Great Tribulation (Rev. 7:10), several major events transpire: (1) The Apostate Church is destroyed. (2) The Beast's covenant with Israel is broken. (3) The persecution of the Jews, particularly those who believe, begins. (4) God miraculously provides the means for the believing Jews to escape into the wilderness, where they are protected and sustained, by God Himself, for three and a half years (Rev. 12:6). (5) Multitudes of Gentile and Jewish believers are martyred for their testimony of Jesus, and are now resting at the altar of God in heaven (Rev. 6:9).

2. As a result of the witnessing by the one hundred forty-four thousand young Jewish men, and of the testimony of the two witnesses, and of the preaching of the everlasting Gospel by the angel, millions, both Jews and Gentiles, repent from their sins and come to Christ for salvation. Of these, John declares: "After this I beheld, and, lo, a great multitude, which no man could number, of all nations, and kindred, and people, and tongues, stood before the throne, and before the Lamb, clothed with white robes, and palms in their hands" (Rev. 7:9). And John was further told: "These are they which came out of the Great Tribulation, and have washed their robes, and made them white in the blood of the Lamb" (Rev. 7:10). It is sobering to observe that this "great multitude," which is now in heaven and which no man could number, have no sooner accepted Christ as their Saviour on the earth, they were martyred for the testimony of Jesus. Their souls are then caught up to stand before the very throne of God.

3. The first thing the Lord Jesus talks about in response to the questions the disciples had asked him about the things to come, was that they should take heed that no man should deceive them. Realizing that deception would be the norm of the future events, particularly during the Great Tribulation Period, Christ warns them of what could take place at the end time. He admonished them about there being many false "christs", and false prophets that would work many great signs and wonders even to the extent of deceiving the very elect. Repeating His advice, Christ warned the disciples, saying: "Behold, I have told you before [hand, ahead of time]" (Matt. 24:25).

4. Christ describes the circumstances upon the earth, at the time of the Great Tribulation Period, and tells His disciples that these conditions would be like unto the conditions that existed during the days of Noah. All of mankind will be busy doing its deeds; they will be marrying and giving in marriage, eating, drinking, and merrymaking. The Lord warned His followers of the end-time conditions that would be so deceptive, like unto Noah's time, but that they would not know exactly when the Son of Man would return. As in the days of Noah, the people did not know "until the flood came, and took them all away" (Matt. 24:39a).

5. The Lord Jesus Christ warns the disciples of being betrayed not only by the enemy, but by their friends and their kinfolk alike. "Then shall they deliver you up to be afflicted, and shall kill you: and ye shall be hated of all nations for my name's sake" (Matt. 24:9). But God will shake the very "powers of heaven" (Luke. 21:26) for the sake of His elect. Likewise, Peter admonishes the believers of the words spoken in past to the holy prophets and presently to the apostles of the Lord Jesus Christ, saying:

> *That ye may be mindful of the words which were spoken*
> *before by the holy prophets, and of the commandment of us*

*the apostles of the Lord and Saviour: Knowing this first, that
there shall come in the last days scoffers, walking after their
own lusts, [a]nd saying, where is the promise of his coming?
. . . The Lord is not slack concerning his promise, as some
men count slackness. . . . But the day of the Lord will come as
a thief in the night. . . . (II Pet. 3:2-4ª, 9, 10).*

6. As the Great Tribulation Period floods the earth and its inhabitants, many severe plagues take place all over the world. These secretly held blows, which God had prepared to unleash upon the earth, come in terms of *seals, trumpets, woes,* and *vials* or *bowls.* Each set is more severe than the other; they will hurt the entire surface of the earth and its dwellers. It is believed that all these tormenting plagues come upon the earth during the second half of the Tribulation Period after the Beast breaks his covenant with the Jews. Often these plagues overlap; but they are all as deadly as they could be. The power of the Almighty God is behind them all.

7. The first group of these plagues is the seals. In general, these seals produce a state of chaos and confusion. The application of the first seal announces the coming of the Beast; the second seal (Rev. 6:4) robs the earth of its peace; the third seal is over prices and all food commodities; the fourth seal produces an unprecedented type of death; the fifth seal puts forth the suffering of the souls of the "slain for the word of God"; the sixth seal generates anarchy which dominates the entire earth; the seventh seal brings about silence in heaven and reveals the seven angels with their trumpets. These seven seals are the seven plagues that God brings upon the entire earth to be tormented during the Great Tribulation Period.

8. As the blowing of the seven trumpets occurs, cataclysmic events take place on the entires urface of the globe. After the first four trumpets are blown, the fifth is sounded, and it enlists a star from heaven which will open the bottomless pit that will unleash more woes upon the earth, including locusts. The sixth trumpet looses "the four angels which are bound in the great river Euphrates" (Rev. 9:14). When the Euphrates River is unbound, an army of two hundred million men are unleashed upon the earth which kills a third part of mankind. The seventh trumpet, along with the first woe, is sounded which declares the assumption of power, namely, the earthly rule, from Satan by our Lord, who declares: "The kingdoms of this world are become the kingdoms of our Lord, and of his Christ, and he shall reign for ever and ever" (Rev. 11:15[b]).

9. The wrath of God, in terms of vials, continues to fall upon the earth and its dwellers. These are the last plagues to torment mankind upon the earth. The first vial produces a "grievous sore upon the men which had the mark of the Beast, and upon them which worshipped his image" (Rev. 16:2[b]). The second vial turned the sea water into the "blood of a dead man: and every living soul died in the sea" (Rev. 16:3[b]). The third vial was poured out upon the rivers and fountains of waters; and they became blood and men drank it and most assuredly died. (Rev. 16:4-6). The fourth vial was poured upon the sun to scorch with its great heat the men that blasphemed the name of God. (Rev. 16:8, 9). We read in the book of Revelation the following:

> And men were scorched with great heat, and blasphemed the name of God, which hath power over these plagues: and they repented not to give him glory (Rev. 16:9).

10. As the plagues of these vials continue, the fifth vial was poured upon the Beast and his throne; his kingdom became darkened, and men "blasphemed the God of heaven because of their pains and their sores, and repented not of their deeds" (Rev. 16:10, 11). The sixth vial was poured upon the great river Euphrates which dried its water thereby opening the way for the kings of the East. The seventh vial was poured "into the air; and there came a great voice out of the temple of heaven, from the throne, saying, It is done" (Rev. 16:17). Then, the Word of God continues, saying:

> And there were voices, and thunders, and lightening; and there was a great earthquake, such as was not since men were upon the earth, so mighty an earthquake, and so great. . . . And there fell upon men a great hail out of heaven, every

stone about the weight of a talent: and men blasphemed God
because of the plague of the hail; for the plague thereof was
exceedingly great (Rev. 16:18, 21).

II. The Destruction of the First Babylon

11. In the book of Revelation, Chapters 17 and 18, we have the
mention of not one but two symbolically employed Babylons: The first is
the Mystery Babylon, which one can identify as the Apostate Religious
System that existed during the first part of the Tribulation Period. This
Babylon represents a global church composed of practically all the churches
of today and of all the denominations and is possibly headed by the leadership of the Roman Catholic Church. The Bible calls this Apostate Religious System a *harlot* and a *whore.* It religiously and even politically
dominates practically all the Christian denominations of the Tribulation
Period. It is called a harlot and a whore, since, on the one hand, it claims
to be identified with the Son of God, particularly through the Church's
invocation of Christ's name in worship services: "in the name of the Father, the Son, and the Holy Spirit." On the other hand, it has become a
harlot and a whore, for deviating from the commandments of the Scriptures. This Apostate Religious System claims to be the Bride of Christ;
yet it has fallen from its position of purity for the Lord. So, the Lord says
unto her:

> *Behold, I will cast her into a bed, and them that commit*
> *adultery with her into great tribulation, except they repent of*
> *their deeds (Rev. 2:22).*

12. This harlot is seen in the book of Revelation, Chapter 17, to be
"drunken with the blood of the saints, and with the blood of the martyrs of
Jesus" (Rev. 17:6). In verse two of the same chapter, John is asked to
approach and hear about "the judgment of the great whore that sitteth
upon many waters [nations] [w]ith whom the kings of the earth have committed fornication" (Rev. 17:1[b], 2[a]). "Spiritual fornication in the Scripture
has reference to adherence to a false system," said Pentecost[1]. Yet, we
see this harlot "arrayed in purple and scarlet colour, and, decked with

gold and precious stones and pearls, having a golden cup in her hand full of abominations and filthiness of her fornication" (Rev. 17:4[b]).

13. One would think that this Apostate Church has made it, indeed; it has attained the loftiest pinnacle of success. From all the appearances, it has achieved a high position within the new ruling empire of the Beast. As a matter of fact, this "woman," which is called a "harlot" and a "whore," appears in the Scriptures to be sitting "upon a scarlet coloured Beast, full of names of blasphemy, having seven heads and ten horns" (Rev. 17:3[b]). And, of course, that the woman is sitting upon the Beast, who has seven heads and ten horns, is an indication that the woman has great influence upon the Beast and his realm.

14. Undoubtedly, during the first half of the Tribulation Period, the Apostate Church's authority over the Beast is almost overwhelming; once this Superman is established on his "throne," however, he will immediately attempt to finally get rid of this major obstacle. He will order the ten-nation coalition of the Revived Roman Empire to destroy the harlot. Through his destruction of her, he will have consolidated his power over not only the ten-nation coalition states of the United Europe, the Revived Roman Empire; he will have also dominion over many other countries and states of the world which enter into a direct or indirect union with this new World Leader for their own political, military and trade benefits.

III. The Destruction of the Second Babylon

15. There is yet another Babylon mentioned in the Bible in conjunction with the Babylon we have just discussed. In Revelation, Chapter 17, the Ecclesiastical Babylon is described and then is given to destruction; Revelation, Chapter 18, gives us yet another Babylon. This is the Political and Commercial Babylon headed by the Beast who has just caused the destruction of the Ecclesiastical Babylon. In Revelation, Chapter 13, Verse 4, we see the people worshipping the Dragon and the Beast. The wicked seeds of this second Babylon began to mushroom as of that moment when the Apostate Political and Commercial Babylon was destroyed. But its great fall is announced by an angel who came down from heaven for its destruction.

And after these things I saw another angel come down from heaven, having great power; and the earth was lightened with his glory. And he cried mightily with a strong voice, saying, Babylon the great is fallen, is fallen, and is become the habitation of devils, and the hold of every foul spirit, and a cage of every unclean and hateful bird. For all nations have drunk of the wine of the wrath of her fornication, and the kings of the earth have committed fornication with her, and the merchants of the earth are waxed rich through the abundance of her delicacies (Rev. 18:1-3).

16. The Word of God puts forth the description of the awful destruction that befalls this second Babylon. This great calamity was caused by God Almighty. John hears a voice from heaven telling the believing Christians on the earth to come out of her, of this spiritually empty and bankrupt Babylon, and to disassociate themselves with her. "Come out of her, my people. That ye be not partakers of her sins, and that ye receive not of her plague" (Rev. 18:4[b]). The merchants of the earth shall weep and mourn over her; they shall stand afar off saying:

Alas, Alas, that great city[2] [country], that was clothed in fine linen, and purple, and scarlet, and decked with gold, and precious stones, and pearls! For in one hour so great riches is come to naught. And every shipmaster, and all the company in ships, and sailors, and as many as trade by sea, stood afar off. And cried when they saw the smoke of her burning, saying, What city is like unto this great city (Rev. 18:16-18).

17. It is very important to observe that, earlier, the political empire, the ten-nation Union, had destroyed the Ecclesiastical System of worship, the religious Babylon; this destruction, in all reality, was basically limited to the Leadership of the system of worship only. But the people that participate in that worship, blindly and yet gladly accepted the worship of the image of the Beast and submitted to this humanistic system of adoration. Through the destruction of this Apostate Christendom, the religious worship of the Beast is now strengthened, particularly as it is promoted by the False Prophet. The Beast now considers himself to be God and sits in the temple of God. Just as Jesus Christ proclaims Himself to be God, so will the Beast, the earthly creature, attempt to accomplish.

IV. The Time of the Gentiles

18. The Gentile World Power begins with the Imperial Kingdom of the Great Monarch, King Nebuchadnezzar, sometime during the sixth century B. C. It is to this king of Babylon that God had given many warnings and signs that "the living may know that the most High ruleth in the kingdom of men, and giveth it to whomsoever he will" (Dan. 4:17[b]). Repeatedly, God gives this same message to the Great Monarch; but, in every instance, King Nebuchadnezzar gave only lip service to the Almighty God of heaven. So, God lets this Great Monarch do as he pleases; only warning him of the consequences of his folly.

19. Since the time of the Babylonian captivity of the Jews — when Jerusalem had fallen into the hands of the Gentile nation of Babylon — until now, and even until the end of the Tribulation Period — when the Gentile nations will be judged and Jerusalem shall be liberated — the Gentile World Power will dominate the scene in the Middle East, particularly in Jerusalem. Exercising control over Jerusalem, the capital of Israel, means having under control the entire Middle East. It is a well known fact that right now there is no other power in that region as powerful and as well armed -- including possibly having nuclear warheads -- as Israel is.

20. During the Tribulation Period, there will be a realignment of nations that will constitute the final form of the Four World Empires. This secular humanistic empire will be the one that is portrayed in the Word of God to be smitten by the "stone [which] was cut out of the mountain without hands" (Dan. 2:45). The head of this Gentile World Empire will be a blasphemer (Dan. 7:8, 25), a persecutor of the saints (Dan. 7:25), who will, during the second half of the Tribulation Period, continue for three and a half years (Dan. 7:25) as the special enemy of Israel and of God's program for His people.[3]

21. Some think that, after Nebuchadnezzar's humbling experience to live and eat grass among the oxen of the wilderness for seven years, the Great King had repented and had accepted the God of Daniel. And on three occasions, the Lord God of heaven calls Nebuchadnezzar "my servant" (Jer. 25:9; 27:6; 43:10). Despite his many confessions about God Almighty, it does not appear that the Great King had demonstrated a real change of heart. Had he had a change of heart and of attitude towards God, as a result of Daniel's witness, the King, in that event, would still have not possibly repented since he would have succumbed, most likely, to the objections of the aristocracy of his court. It appears that his own grandson, Belshazzar, took over the Empire soon thereafter and over the nobility of his day.[4] We read in Daniel the following:

> *And at the end of the days, [the end of the seven years he had lived as an oxen among the cattle of the earth], I Nebuchadnezzar lifted up mine eyes unto heaven, and mine understanding returned unto me, and I blessed the most High, and I praised and honoured him that liveth for ever, whose dominion is everlasting dominion, and his kingdom is from generation to generation: And all the inhabitants of the earth are reputed as nothing: and he doeth according to his will in the army of heaven, and among the inhabitants of the earth: and none can stay his hand, or say unto him, [w]hat doest thou? (Dan. 4:34, 35).*

22. It is interesting to observe, however, that King Nebuchadnezzar, just before what appeared to be a dethroning, or during the last moments of his life, made a most sincere confession of the God of heaven. While making such an admission of the Almighty God, his understanding suddenly returned to him, and he blessed and praised and extolled and honored the king of heaven. Reading Verses 34 through 37 of Daniel, Chapter 4, and many other such passages in Daniel, one may admit that this Great King, indeed, had repented and accepted the God of Daniel. Alas, however, this is the last thing we hear from this Monarch or we know about this Great Emperor.

23. Perhaps, under the rule of the Beast, the Gentile World Power has reached its pinnacle. The Beast not only rules the armies of the ten-nation coalition of the Revived Roman Empire, but also he rules a vast array of armed forces belonging to his Super-Alliance. The Beast, who is the "little [young]horn" of Daniel, the eighth king, is now, for all practical purposes, exercising power over the entire world. On account of his supremacy and his wickedness, especially as he hates and is at enmity with the very God of heaven, the Scriptures present the Beast with a number of names commensurate to his character. Each of these titles designates one aspect of his heinousness, his individuality, and his relationship to the Dragon. Some of his names are:

1. The Profane Wicked Prince of Israel (Ez. 21:25-27).
2. The Little Horn (Dan. 7:8).
3. The Prince that Shall Come (Dan. 9:26).
4. The Vile Person (Dan. 11:12).
5. The Willful King (Dan. 11:36).
6. The Man of Sin (2 Thes. 2:3).
7. The Son of Perdition (2 Thes. 2:3).
8. The Wicked/Lawless One (2 Thes. 2:8).
9. The Antichrist (1 John 2:22).
10. The Angel of the Bottomless Pit (Rev. 9:11).
11. The Beast (Rev. 11:7; 13:1).
12. The Desolator (Dan. 9:27).
13. The Destroyer (Job 15:21; Ps. 17:4)
14. The Number 666 (Rev. 13:18).
15. The Spoiler (Is. 16:4).
16. The Extortioner (Is. 16:4).

24. Humanly speaking, the Beast has some of the most unique characteristics observed among the children of men. He will be the head of a two-tier government, each branch having its own council, covering the vast reaches of the world: the ten-nation coalition and the seven heads/kings in a Presidium, also drawn from the ten-nation coalition, are federated under his authority as king number eight. His influence through alliances with other nations (Dan. 8:24) makes him a ruler over almost all nations of the earth (Rev. 13:8). Of course, Satan totally dominates him. Through their blindness, the people under his authority accept him as their God (2 Thes. 2:11). He primarily places himself in opposition to Israel and attempts to annihilate the people of that country. But God will intervene directly and bring severe judgment upon him. When he is slain, along with the False Prophet, he will be cast into the lake of fire where the Devil is cast (Rev. 19:20; Ez. 28:10). Thus the end of the ungodly trinity and of this wicked Superman of the European Union and of the Western Atlantic Alliance will likewise be consummated.

25. When the leader of this Gentile World Power is destroyed by our Lord Jesus Christ at His Second Coming to the earth; the redemption of Israel and its Holy City, Jerusalem, from the Gentile dominion (Dan. 7:18, 22, 27) will have taken place once and for all. We should not consider the form of the Gentile World Power as a single unit of limited time and location. This Gentile World Power began with the Empire of Nebuchadnezzar; it appeared during the Persian Empire, then during the Grecian Empire of Alexander the Great and his four generals, and finally during the Roman Empire. It died for a season, to give chance for the Spiritual Kingdom of our Lord to fill the earth with its grace. But then it is now once again revived and once again destroyed.

[A]nd the stone that smote the image become a great mountain, and filled the whole earth (Dan. 2:35b).

V. The Doom of the False Prophet

26 The False Prophet is another beast mentioned in the book of Revelation (Rev. 13:11; 19:20; 20:10). He is clearly associated with the first Beast, so that he is even called that "the Second Beast" (Rev. 13:11). As mentioned earlier, the origin of this beast is most likely Jewish, especially since he arises out of the earth, or the land, which is most certainly the Holy Land. He was given the authority and "the power of the first Beast" (Rev. 13:12). As he came out of the earth, he was seen having "two horns like a lamb", (Rev. 13:11b), signifying that he had mustered the support of the two Apostate Religious Systems of his day: the Apostate Christendom and the Apostate Judaism. "He speaks as a Dragon," Rev.13:11 signifies that he is closely associated with the Dragon and with this counterfeit Trinity, and enthusiastically he does their bidding. He works signs and miracles apparently in an attempt to prove to his coreligionists, the Jews, that he is the Prophet Elijah that was to come.

27. Furthermore, the Second beast, the False Prophet, promotes the worship of idolatry; he has the power of death to compel men to worship the Beast. He controls economy and all commerce; he plants a mark "in their right hand, or in their foreheads" (Rev. 13:16b), that will establish the Beast's identity for all those who live and do merchandising at the time. As the Idol Shepherd of Israel (Zech. 11:17), this latter-day Antichrist, is capable of committing atrocious deeds in order to compel the masses, particularly the Jews, to worship the image. In the book of Revelation, we read the following:

> *And he deceived them that dwell on the earth by the means of those miracles which he had power to do in the sight of the beast; saying to them that dwell on the earth, that they should make an image to the beast, which had the wound by a sword, and did live. And he had power to give life unto the image of the beast, that the image of the beast should both speak, and cause that as many as would not worship the image of the beast should be killed (Rev. 13:14, 15).*

> *And he causeth all, both small and great, rich and poor, free and bond, to receive a mark [of the Beast] in their right hand, or in their foreheads: And that no man might buy or sell, save he that had the mark, or the name of the beast, or the number of his name. Here is wisdom. Let him that hath understanding count the number of the beast: for it is the number of a man: and his number is Six hundred three score and six (Rev. 13:16-18).*

28. Consequently, the False Prophet of Israel, the Idol Shepherd, like his master the Beast, came finally to his end. God had promised to eradicate sin, unrighteousness and all who participated in them for ever and ever. The calamity that befell the world at the end of the Tribulation Period is hardly imaginable. The Beast, the False Prophet, the kings and the leaders of the earth, and their armies "gather[ed] together to make war against him that sat on the [white] horse, and against his army" (Rev. 19:19). These armies were, nevertheless, defeated mercilessly by "the sword of him that sat upon the [white] horse, which sword proceeded out of his mouth" (Rev. 19:21). So we read:

> *And the beast was taken, and with him the false prophet that wrought miracles before him, with which he deceived them that had received the mark of the beast, and them that worshipped his image. These both were cast alive into a lake of fire burning with brimstone (Rev. 19:20).*

> *And the Devil that deceived them was cast into the lake of fire and brimstone, where the beast and the false prophet are, and shall be tormented day and night for ever and ever (Rev. 20:10).*

29. In the Messianic prophecy of Psalm 2, the Psalmist describes this episode with great imagination and vividness. He attributes to the heathen, the Gentile World, epithets that are full of disdain and derision. The Word of God declares that "The earth is the Lord's, and the fullness thereof; the world, and they that dwell therein" (Ps. 24:1). Through Daniel, God said to King Nebuchadnezzar: "until thou know that the most High ruleth in the kingdom of men, and giveth it to whomsoever he will" (Dan. 4:32^b). Thus God unleashes upon the Gentile World Power the greatest of calamities. We read in the book of Psalms the following:

> *Why do the heathen rage, and the people imagine a vain thing? The kings of the earth set themselves, and the rulers take counsel together, against his anointed, saying, Let us break their bands asunder, and cast away their cords from us (Ps. 2:1-3).*

He that sitteth in the heavens shall laugh: the Lord shall have them in derision. Then shall he speak unto them in his wrath, and vex them in his sore displeasure. Yet have I set my king upon my holy hill of Zion. I will declare the decree: the Lord hath said unto me, Thou art my Son; this day have I begotten thee (Ps. 2:4-7).

Ask of me, and I shall give thee the heathen for thine inheritance, and the uttermost parts of the earth for thy possession. Thou shall break them with a rod of iron; thou shall dash them in pieces like a potter's vessel (Ps. 2:8-9).

CHAPTER 14

GOD'S FINAL SUMMONS

*And it shall come to pass, that whosoever shall call on
the name of the Lord shall be delivered: for in mount Zion
and in Jerusalem shall be deliverance, as the Lord hath said,
and in the remnant whom the Lord shall call (Joel 2:32).*

I. God's Call To Repentance

1. AS THE MOST DEVASTATING catastrophes continue to strike
the human race during the Great Tribulation Period, God, who is great in
His mercies, provides yet another triple opportunity for the inhabitants of
the earth to repent and turn unto Him. Both Jews and Gentiles are bid to
repent for the reconciliation with the Lamb. Out of His great love (John
3:16) for a lost humanity (Rom. 3:23), God prepares three unusual and
diverse measures to provide a last opportunity for the Gospel of salvation
to be heard throughout a devastated earth. Although different in application, in each instance the message is the same, the testimony of Jesus and
their witness for the Lord God of heaven. These three measures are: the
144,000 sealed servants of the Most High God for the witnesses of our
Lord; the two historic witnesses; and, finally, the Angel of the Everlasting
Gospel.

a. The 144,000 Evangelists

2. God commands an angel to seal "the servants of our God in their
foreheads. And I heard the number of them which were sealed: and there
were sealed an hundred and forty and four thousand [144,000] of all the
tribes of the children of Israel" (Rev. 7:3b-4). It should be pointed out
here that "sealing" during the Tribulation Period is tantamount to and a
substitute for anointing with oil which is a symbol of the Holy Spirit who is
now departed from the earth and is with the Church in heaven. It should

also be made clear here, parenthetically, that the phrase "one of the least of these my brethren" uttered by our Lord, in Matthew, Chapter 25, Verses 40 and 45, during the judgment of the nations, refers not to the Jews in general, or the Jews of the Tribulation Period, as many Bible scholars have erroneously concluded, but to the 144,000 sealed young Jews, and who, indeed, are his brethren both spiritually and humanly.

3. About these 144,000 sealed servants of our God, two passages are given in the book of Revelation: the first is in Chapter 7, Verses 3 through 8; the second is in Chapter 14, Verses 1 through 5. Except for the similarity in their number, 144,000, there is almost nothing else common between the two passages. Stipulation, however, rises that the two groups are one and the same. In each case, they are described somewhat differently; yet, the youths of each group are sealed as servants of our God in their foreheads. It appears that in the first instance, the reference is that those evangelists are just about to be ready to be sealed for the Lord's work; in the second instance, they appear to have just fulfilled that mission, and now they are up in heaven with Jesus. In the book of Revelation, we read that "These are they which follow the Lamb whithersoever he goeth" (Rev. 14:4). Accordingly, they were with Jesus when He was judging the living nations of the earth to whom he pointed as "these my brethren."

4. While preaching the Gospel of the kingdom in a hostile world during the Tribulation Period, these young evangelists needed the clandestine support and care of other believers on the earth, both Jews and Gentiles. Scripturally speaking, neither the Jews nor the Gentiles can be considered to be our Savior's brethren unless they are born from above (Mar. 3:35). It should also be made clear here that the people to whom Christ was speaking at this moment were the saved inhabitants of the earth after the rapture of the Church. The only "brethren" Christ was speaking about, who had need for the care and support of the believers on the earth at this time, were these 144,000 sealed, or anointed, for the propagation of the Gospel of salvation to a spiritually dying world. If there ever was a cause to understand Christ's message concerning His filial relationship with mankind, it is to be found in his message concerning

His mother and His brethren, when they had come looking for him, as illustrated in the following verse:

> *Then one said unto him, Behold, thy mother and thy brothren stand without, desiring to speak with thee. And he stretched forth his hands towards his disciples, and said, Behold my mother and my brethren! For whosoever shall do the will of my Father which is in heaven, the same is my brother, and sister, and mother (Matt. 12:47- 50)*

b. The Two Witnesses

5. God is aware of the callousness of the heart of the people of the earth, and the lack of a desire, which many of them have demonstrated, to accept the message of the 144,000 preaching evangelists. But yet there are many individuals from all nations, tribes, and people who are on the verge of accepting Christ, no matter what, as their personal Saviour; it is they who really need such a last chance for the salvation of their souls. Thus, the Almighty God prepares yet another means by which to awaken the world, both Jews and Gentiles, to His serious calling. He knows that the sinful inhabitants of this world will not listen to the simple message of the Cross. As is portrayed in the story of "the rich man and Lazarus" (Luke 16:19-31), they will ask for someone to come from the dead and preach to them the gospel of redemption. So now, God sends to them two men resurrected from the dead, as it were — apparently Moses and Elijah to do the job. The righteous man, Enoch, does not appear to be one of them as some Bible scholars have concluded for he had neither power to make rain nor power over water to become blood.

6. God sends to the world these two men who were resurrected from the Old Testament period. God gives these two witnesses power so that "they shall prophecy [preach] a thousand two hundred and threescore days [the last three and a half years of the Tribulation Period], clothed in sackcloth" (Rev. 11:3). There should be no problem identifying who these two witnesses are. Clear-cut allusions to them, with respect to their ministry on the earth, "in the days of their prophecy" (Rev. 11:6), are provided in the Scriptures. The first must be Elijah who, during the wicked reign of Ahab, the king of Israel (1 Kin. 17:1), had "power to shut heaven that it rained not in the days of their prophecy" (Rev. 11:6). The second must be Moses, who in Egypt (Ex. 7:19) had "power over water to turn it into blood" (Rev. 11:6). These two witnesses, who also appeared with Jesus on the Mount of Transfiguration (Matt. 17:3), testify of the Saviour and perform miracles to corroborate the heavenly origin of their message to the people of the earth, and their call for them to repent.

7. At the very end of the Tribulation Period, only after they had completed "their testimony," does the Beast, which "ascendeth out of the bottomless pit," wage a war against them, overcome them, and kill them. Only after having completed their mission, at the very end of the three and a half years, is the Beast able to kill them — they become true "martyrs" to the testimony of their Lord. But, after three days and a half, God miraculously resurrects them and gloriously vindicates them before their enemies.

> *And after three days and an half, the spirit of life from God entered into them, and thy stood upon their feet; and great fear fell upon them which saw them. And they heard a great voice from heaven saying unto them, Come up hither. And they ascended up to heaven in a cloud; and their enemies beheld them (Rev. 11:11, 12).*

8. That the spirit of God came upon them only after "three days and an half", signifies that they were already dead, having no chance for revival on their own. It would have to be more than three days to guarantee their death; and they did indeed remain dead for at least another half a day. Had they been resurrected before the three days, or at the very end of the third day, their resurrection would have been, in some way, given to all sorts of misinterpretations and speculations. This was the same reason why Jesus delayed going to Judæa, before the end of the three days, to the death of His friend, Lazarus, whom He resurrected from the dead (John 11:1-44).

c. The Angel of the Everlasting Gospel

9. The third and the very last mission God undertakes during this Tribulation Period is the ministry of the angel who preaches the Everlasting Gospel. Throughout the dispensation of grace, God has graciously committed the ministry of the Gospel, almost in its entirety to the believers, to sinners saved by grace. Nonetheless, almost in desperation, you might say, and for the first time, the Almighty God entrusts the ministry of the preaching of the Gospel of salvation finally to an angel. This angel could speedily fly from East to West, and from the North pole to the South pole, and let the entire world hear the message of the everlasting Gospel at once.

> *And I saw another angel fly in the midst of heaven, having the everlasting Gospel to preach unto them that dwell on the earth, and to every nation, and kindred, and tongue, and people, Saying with a loud voice, [f]ear God, and give glory to him; for the hour of his judgment is come: and worship him that made heaven, and earth, and the sea, and the fountains of waters (Rev. 14:6, 7).*

10. This first angel is now followed by yet a second angel — who was sent to warn the people of the earth about the fall of Babylon — who declares: "Babylon is fallen, is fallen, that great city, because she made all nations drink of the wine of the wrath of her fornication" (Rev. 14:8). The second angel did not preach the Gospel; he had just one warning: the fall of Babylon. And yet a third angel follows the first two, "saying with a loud voice, If any man worship the beast and his image, and receive his mark in his forehead, or in his hand, [t]he same shall drink of the wine of the wrath of God, which is poured out without mixture into the cup of his indignation; and he shall be tormented with fire and brimstone in the presence of the holy angels, and in the presence of the Lamb" (Rev. 14:9, 10). The third angel warned the inhabitants of the earth of a sore punishment that awaits them. Scofield notes notwithstanding,[1] the Gospel, in its essence, is but one: it is God's good news of salvation to a lost humanity. Through God's final call for repentance and salvation, Christ's promise to

His disciples is now being fulfilled. Never before this moment, has the Gospel of Christ been preached to the world in its entirety as is now preached by this mighty angel of God.

> *And this Gospel of the kingdom shall be preached in all the world for a witness unto all nations; and then shall the end [of the Old Testament dispensation for which this promise was made] come (Mat. 24:14).*

11. As a result of this triple and final effort on the part of the Almighty God — the witness of the 144,000 young men, the testimony of the two mighty witnesses, and the preaching of the Everlasting Gospel by an angel — undoubtedly, millions of both Jews and Gentiles repent from their folly and accept Christ as their personal Saviour, especially the second and the third angels warned the entire human race about the fall of Babylon and about not to worship the Beast's image (Rev. 14:8-10). Alas, however, a great number of these newly saved are forthwith slain. Yet, even the slain rejoice to have become martyrs for the testimony of Christ, their Lord. Of these, John declares:

> *After this I beheld, and, lo, a great multitude, which no man could number, of all nations, and kindred, and people, and tongues, stood before the throne, and before the Lamb, clothed with white robes, and palms in their hands (Rev. 7:9).*

> *And he said to me, [t]hese are they which came out of the great tribulation, and have washed their robes, and made them white in the blood of the Lamb . . . . For the Lamb which is in the midst of the throne shall feed them, and shall lead them unto living fountains of water: and God shall wipe away all tears from their eyes (Rev. 7:14).*

II. Salvation through Relations

12. It is very interesting to observe how many believing Christians are saved during the Tribulation Period through the sheer testimony and prayers of a loved one, or of a friend, or of an acquaintance who has now been caught up in the rapture. Some of the people of the earth could be saved through the good and exemplary life some of the raptured believers had lived and had demonstrated before them; the majority of those who got saved, most likely, were saved because someone had presented to them the Gospel message itself. For the message of the Gospel of God and of our Saviour is powerful and able to convict the most wicked of sinners unto salvation by faith in Jesus Christ our Lord. In the books of Hebrews and I Peter, we read:

> *For the word of God is quick, and powerful, and sharper than any twoedged sword, piercing even to the dividing asunder of soul and spirit, and of the joints and marrow, and is a discerner of the thoughts and intents of the heart" (Heb. 4:12).*

> *Searching what, or what manner of time the Spirt of Christ which was in them did signify, when it testified beforehand the suffering of Christ, and the glory that should follow. . . . which things the angels desire to look into (I Peter 1:11 &12^b).*

13. How many a father, or a mother, or both, have spent many hours of their daily life praying for their "prodigal" son, or the "renegade" daughter, to come to Christ and be saved. Yet, their prayers seamed always unanswered, or ignored by their children. They came into their parents home and went out; they ate, and drank, and slept, paying no heed to their parents supplication for their salvation. When the day of the rapture finally came, however, their parents were caught up into heaven, and were gone into glory. Unless these children now repent and be saved, they will never see their kinfolk again. Now the rapture has, indeed, taken place; their parents have, indeed, been taken up to glory. It is very likely that such children will repent despite the threat of martyrdom by the forces of the Evil One.

14. What about the person who has prayed day-in and day-out, regularly and fervently, for his brother or for his sister, to come to the saving knowledge of the Saviour. Year after year, he or she has prayed that such a loved one may come to Christ; yet, it appears that it was all in vain. But now the rapture has taken place; it has taken that praying brother, or that praying sister, into heaven to be with the Lord. Their siblings, who are still on the earth, in order for them to see their glorified brothers and sisters, must decide, with bitter tears of repentance, to accept Christ as their personal Saviour. The only way to see their precious ones is to turn to the Lord Jesus for the salvation of their souls even if martyrdom clearly awaits them.

15. Under their present circumstances, it is not easy to confess Christ as the personal Saviour of their lives. Once confession in the Living Saviour is made, death, especially through beheading, is very likely. Thank God, they confess Christ as their personal Saviour and anticipate the worst under the dictatorial rule of the Beast. Many an adult is saved through the testimony of one of their own relatives. While yet on the earth, no matter what was said to them, they ignored the witness; now they are ready to accept the Saviour even though He is no longer on the earth. Although the Holy Spirit of God is no longer on the earth for their guidance, they accept the Redeemer. They are willing to die for the testimony of Jesus and for the testimony of the Word of God.

16. It should not be a surprise that many will be saved as a result of the church they worshipped in. God can use everything possible to bring sinners to repentance; and they do come from all aspects of life. So now the Almighty God is using the church building as a reminder of their loved ones who had been saved in that house of worship. Many a brother and a sister, or a father and a mother, or an acquaintance, will finally realize that, come what may, they must be saved. Many will enter that church edifice stealthily, if need be, and will kneel down on their knees, and will ask God's forgiveness for the salvation of their souls. Of course, it is not the church building that saves these penitent sinners; it is their recognition of their need for salvation that counts. What a joy they will receive! We read in the books of Luke and of Daniel the following:

> *Likewise, I say unto you, there is joy in the presence of the angels of God over one sinner that repenteth (Luke 15:10).*

And they that be wise shall shine as the brightness of the firmament; and they that turn many to righteousness as the stars for ever and ever (Dan. 12:3).

17. It is not very clear to us whether or not the sinner's repentance and salvation bring joy to the relatives above in heaven. During this Tribulation Period, many activities are taking place in heaven and believers are fully engaged in most of these activities. There is, first, the Judgment Seat of Christ where all believers' works are tried by fire; there is, secondly, the preparation for and the involvement of believers in the Marriage of the Lamb; there is, thirdly, the Marriage Supper of the Lamb; and, finally, there is also the resurrection of the martyred Christians on the earth, who had been beheaded for the testimony of Christ and the Word of God, as we have mentioned earlier.

18. Nevertheless, all the activities which we have mentioned above, could provide a distraction for the believers in heaven to pay attention to what is now occurring on the earth. Yet, it is very possible that these redeemed and glorified believers in heaven are aware of their loved ones who are coming to Christ for salvation. In spite of the martyrdom that eventually awaits them, because of their testimony for Christ Jesus, they come to the Saviour without hesitation or remorsefulness. What a joy and what a satisfaction their newly obtained salvation will bring into the hearts and lives of the new converts on the earth. The greatest joy belongs to heaven. "Woe to the inhabiters of the earth and the sea! [F]or the devil is come down unto you, having great wrath, because he knoweth that he hath but a short time" (Rev. 12:12^b). We read in the Gospel of Luke the following:

I say unto you, that likewise joy shall be in heaven over one sinner that repenteth, more than over ninety and nine just persons, which need no repentance (Luke 15:7).

CHAPTER 15

THE DREADFUL EVENTS ON EARTH

Behold, the day of the Lord cometh, and thy spoil shall be divided in the midst of thee. For I will gather all nations against Jerusalem to battle; and the city shall be taken, and the houses rifled; and half of the city shall go forth into captivity, and the residue of the people shall not be cut off from the city (Zech. 14:1, 2).

I. The Time of Jacob's Trouble

1. THE BATTLE OF ARMAGEDDON is a battle fought "Not by might, nor by power," of human undertaking, "but by my spirit, saith the Lord of hosts" (Zech. 4:6). It is a one-sided battle. It is the Lord of hosts that is gathering all these nations -- unbeknown to them -- to Armageddon where he will settle with them through a final punishment. God has delivered Israel into the hands of the Gentile nations to exercise over her the God-appointed "time of Jacob's trouble" (Jer. 30:7). God says over and again that, because of their sins, he will deliver His people to the Gentiles for chastisement, and at the end He will bring all nations to Jerusalem to destroy it and for their condemnation.

2. The time of Jacob's trouble, in its real essence, will take place during the latter part of the Tribulation Period. It is a day instituted by God Almighty and it must come about. God must chastise the Jewish people for their wickedness, as much as He has already destroyed the Christian Apostasy. It should be clearly stated here that this chastening, as dark and gloomy as it may be, is in reality to bring Israel to its ultimate repentance and glory. ". . . it is even the time of Jacob's trouble, but he [Israel] shall be saved out of it" (Jer. 30:7^b). For we read in Isaiah the following:

*How is the faithful city [Jerusalem] become an harlot!
[I]t was full of judgment; righteousness lodged in it; but now
murderers. . . . Thy princes are rebellious, and companions of
thieves: every one loveth gifts, and followeth after rewards:
they judge not the fatherless, neither doth the cause of the
widow come unto them. . . . Ah, I will ease me of mine adver-
saries, and avenge me of mine enemies (Is. 1:21-24^b).*

3. The severity of this chastisement God heaps upon His people,
Israelites, is unparalleled in the entire history of the Jewish nation. It is not
a judgment brought about for revenge to satisfy His anger against His
people; but, it is the depth into which His people have allowed themselves
to sink that defines God's ultimate anger. God is holy, and His holiness
requires his people to be holy. They have drifted apart from God and
from His holy commandments. They have departed from the Law God
had given them to practice. He had warned them that they were not
better than all the nations of the earth (Deut. 7:6-8); but because of His
promise to their forefathers — Abraham, Isaac, and Jacob — He has
treated them uniquely. But they have failed Him miserably. Now, however, He must judge the people with a just condemnation. We read in the
book of Luke the following:

*O Jerusalem, Jerusalem, which killest the prophets, and
stonest them that are sent unto thee; how often would I have
gathered thy children together, as a hen doth gather her brood
under her wings, and ye would not! (Luke 13:34).*

*And when he was come near, he beheld the city, and wept
over it, [s]aying, If thou hadst known, even thou, at least in
this thy day, the things which belong unto thy peace! but now
they are hid from thine eyes. For the days shall come upon
thee, that thine enemies shall cast a trench about thee, and
compass thee round, and keep thee in on every side, And shall
lay thee even with the ground. . . and they shall not leave in
thee one stone upon another; because thou knewest not the
time of thy visitation (Luke 19:41-44).*

4. God condemns the children of Israel for their wicked condition; He rebukes them for having forsaken His ordinances. "Ye have said, It is vain to serve God, and what profit is it that we have kept his ordinances" (Mal. 3:14ᵇ). You have encouraged evil and said, "Every one that doeth evil is good in the sight of the Lord, and he delighteth in them" (Mal. 2:17). God's heart is wide open for those who repent and turn to him. The Almighty God begs His people to come back to His fold. "For I am the Lord" says Jehovah, "I change not; therefore ye sons of Jacob are not consumed" (Mal. 3:6). So, God says to His people:

> *Return unto me, and I will return unto you, saith the Lord of hosts (Mal. 3:7ᵇ).*

> *Then they that fear the Lord spake often one to another: and the Lord hearkened, and heard it, and a book of remembrance was written before him for them that fear the Lord, and that thought upon his name. And they shall be mine, saith the Lord of hosts, in that day when I make up my jewels (Mal. 3:16, 17ᵃ).*

> *Then shall ye return, and discern between the righteous and the wicked, between him that serveth God and him that serveth him not" (Mal. 3:18).*

II. Led by False Leadership

5. God's promises to Israel are eternal and sure; He will never abandon her nor will He ever forsake her. Yet, because of His people's sins, He will chastise Israel once again before her final redemption takes place. Accordingly, the Almighty says to the Jewish nation: "Behold, the day of the Lord cometh, cruel both with wrath and fierce anger, to lay the land desolate: and he shall destroy the sinners thereof out of it" (Isa. 13:9). The Lord God promises that He will cut Israel to pieces; He will cut off its head and its tail. God will bring judgment upon the disobedient leaders of His people. For we read in Isaiah the following:

*Therefore the Lord will cut off from Israel head and tail,
branch and rush, in one day. The ancient and the honourable,
he is the head; and the prophet that teacheth lies, he is the
tail. For the leaders of the people cause them to err; and
they that are led of them are destroyed. Therefore the Lord
shall have no joy in their young men, neither shall have mercy
on their fatherless and widows: for every one is an hypocrite
and an evildoer, and every mouth speaketh folly. For all this
his anger is not turned away, but his hand [of mercy] is
stretched out still" (Isa. 9:14-17).*

a. Following the Idol Shepherd

6. The people of Israel are punished for following unfaithful leaders.
In the last days, God has raised an "idol shepherd" (**ro'e ha-elil**) in the
land. There is absolutely no doubt that this Idol Shepherd is the False
Prophet of Revelation, Chapter 13, Verse 11. God speaks of this Idol
Shepherd and all the prophets in Israel that supported him and followed
him as the one who causes the breaking of His covenant with His people.
So, the Lord God of heaven promises that "I might break my covenant
which I [had] made with the people. And it was broken in that day"
(Zech. 11:10, 11). God tells the prophet Zechariah the following:

*For, lo, I will raise up a shepherd in the land, which shall
not visit those that be cut off, neither shall seek the young
one, nor heal that that is broken, nor feed that that standeth
still: but he shall eat the flesh of the fat, and tear their claws
in pieces. Woe to the idol shepherd that leaveth the flock! the
sword shall be upon his arm, and upon his right eye: his arm
shall be clean dried up, and his right eye shall be utterly darkened (Zech. 11:16, 17).*

b. Following the False Pastors

7. Then, God turns his attention to and condemns the false pastors
(**ha-ro'im**) and raises an indictment against them. God makes known his
wrath upon such false pastors and how they, through their folly and through

their greed, lead the people astray. Their leaders take the first thing that comes unto them as from God; yet, they know the difference. They know how to distinguish the good from the evil. They know Jehovah's precepts and kind judgments; yet they deceive the people of God for the positions and the wealth they are to receive. They will blabber utterly false promises to the people; they will say, this is the Messiah, our eternal King. In the book of the prophet Jeremiah, we read the following:

> Woe be unto the pastors that destroy and scatter the sheep of my pasture! saith the Lord. Therefore thus saith the Lord God of Israel against the pastors that feed my people; Ye have scattered my flock, and driven them away, and have not visited them: behold, I will visit upon you the evil of your doings, saith the Lord (Jer. 23:1, 2).

c. Following the False Prophets

8. Then, God will turn His anger against the false prophets (**ha-nvi'im**) of Israel; He will denounce them and will rebuke them for their false prophecy. Even the father and the mother of such a false prophet will rebuke the disobedient son who attempts to prophesy in the name of the Lord and will tell him: "Thou shalt not live; for thou speakest lies in the name of the Lord" (Zech. 13:3). Many of these prophets will realize that their prophecy was nothing but falsehood, and will desist from issuing the Lord's word through false prophecy. In Zechariah, we read:

> And it shall come to pass in that day, that the prophets shall be ashamed every one of his vision, when he hath prophesied; neither shall they wear a rough garment to deceive: But he shall say, I am no prophet, I am an husbandman [a farmer]; for man taught me to keep cattle from my youth (Zech. 13:4, 5).

d. Following the False Priests

9. Again, the Lord God of heaven will bring the time of Jacob's trouble upon his people, and will punish them for following the false priests (*ha*-kohanim) who do not have the knowledge of God's Law. The false priests, just like the Idol Shepherd, just like the false pastors, just like the false prophets, who all taught falsehood to their people, who should have discerned between the truth and the falsehood, between good and evil, between right and wrong; but they did not hearken nor were they attentive. So we read in Isaiah and in Hosea the following:

> *Woe unto them that call evil good, and good evil; that put darkness for light, and light for darkness; that put bitter for sweet, and sweet for bitter (Is. 5:20).*

> *My people are destroyed for lack of knowledge: because thou has rejected knowledge, I will also reject thee, that thou shalt be no priest to me: seeing thou hast forgotten the law of thy God, I will also forget thy children. As they were increased, so they sinned against me: therefore will I change their glory into shame (Hos. 4:6, 7).*

e. Following the Lying Princes

10. The Israelites followed the devices of lying princes; their nobility was wicked and corrupt; the people were directed by these mischief-working chieftains. Their lying princes (**ha-rashim**) had led the people to act mischievously and to receive wicked counsel from them. In just as much as "Ye have feared a sword; I will bring a sword upon you, saith the Lord God" (Ez. 11:8). God Almighty will judge His people with the sword of His mouth. "Ye shall fall by the sword; I will judge you in the border of Israel" (Ez. 11:10ª). Yes, the Lord God is angry with His people for they did not walk in His own statutes, nor did they execute His judgments.

III. The Great Day of Jezreel

11. As the time of Jacob's trouble befalls the Jewish nation, particularly during the Great Tribulation Period, God makes it clear that there is no escaping for anyone from the wrath of the Almighty. "Then shall the children of Judah and the children of Israel be gathered together, and appoint themselves one head, and they shall come up out of the land: for great shall be the day of Jezreel" (Hos. 1:11). The day of Jezreel is a day of infamy; for God "will break the bow of Israel in the valley of Jezreel" (Hos. 1:5). They have totally ignored the Almighty God of heaven.

12. God will bring distress upon the house of Jacob; He will pour out His wrath upon the entire land. This is exactly the condition in which Israel governs itself today. Israel has gathered itself together from all over the world and has appointed for herself a head, a president, instead of a king, or instead of letting God Almighty Himself rule over her. In the arm of flesh, Israel is now in her land. The people of Israel have, indeed, appointed themselves one head, and are, or should be, awaiting the time God "will break the bow of Israel in the valley of Jezreel" (Hos. 1:5). And the valley of Jezreel is, indeed, awaiting them. And the Almighty continues to say:

> *Neither their silver nor their gold shall be able to deliver them in the day of the Lord's wrath; but the whole land shall be devoured by fire of his jealousy: for he shall make even a speedy riddance of all them that dwell in the land [of Israel] (Zeph. 1:18).*

13. The Lord Jesus Christ told His disciples about the severity of the Tribulation Period, especially during the latter three years and a half. "Jerusalem," Christ said, "shall be trodden down of the Gentiles, until the times of the Gentiles be fulfilled" (Luke. 21:24^b). This period of distress that befalls the entire humanity is particularly severe as it affects the Jewish nation. The Jewish people will receive from the very hand of God their due chastisement. Paul emphasized this period of distress on the Jewish people by declaring to the Romans:

> *For I could wish that myself were accursed from Christ for my brethren, my kinsmen according to the flesh: Who are Israelites; to whom pertaineth the adoption, and the glory, and the covenants, and the giving of the law, and the service of God, and the promises; Whose are the fathers, and of whom as concerning the flesh Christ came, who is over all, God blessed for ever. Amen (Rom. 9:3-5).*

IV. A Remnant Shall Be Saved

14. This same covenant concerning the Jews is confirmed in the New Testament. Paul is raising an argument concerning Israel and is describing his feelings about that nation saying that though they be, for a season, despised and in blindness, they will be saved. God is true in his word to the Israelites that a *remnant* shall be saved. It is saved because it finally believes in the Son of God, their true Messiah, the one who died for them and for the sins of the entire world. We read in the book of Zechariah, the following:

> *And one shall say unto him, What are these wounds in thine hands? Then he shall answer, Those with which I was wounded in the house of my friends. Awake, O sword, against my shepherd, and against the man that is my fellow, saith the Lord of hosts: smite the [idol] shepherd, and the sheep shall be scattered: and I [the true shepherd] will turn mine hand upon the little ones [of Israel] (Zech. 13:6, 7).*

15. Thus, God will restore the house of Israel and will heal his nation forevermore. Throughout the Bible, the remnant is portrayed as approximately one-third of the total population of the state of Israel at the time.[1] Two out of three parts of Israel will disappear; one-third will remain. It is to this one-third of the redeemed Jews that God will restore all the promises and the blessings that he had promised the nation throughout the ages. God will restore the kingdom of David to His people; a kingdom of blessings and abundance. For God will listen to their cry as they implore Him for mercy, and as they beseech Him for kindness. In Zechariah and in Joel, we read:

> *And it shall come to pass, that in all the land, saith the Lord, two parts therein shall be cut off and die; but the third shall be left therein. And I will bring the third part through the fire, and will refine them as silver is refined, and will try them as gold is tried: they shall call on my name, and I will hear them: I will say, It is my people: and they shall say, The Lord is my God (Zech. 13: 8, 9).*

Let the priests, the ministers of the Lord, weep between the porch and the alter, and let them say, Spare thy people, O Lord, and give not thine heritage to reproach, that the heathen should rule over them: wherefore should they say among the people, Where is their God? (Joel 2:17).

16. God will restore the captivity of Israel; He will bring together its scattered sons and daughters. He will give a new vision to his people that they seek God and His Son as their redeeming ones. He will raise up the tabernacle of David and resurrect David to lead them in the way of the Lord God Almighty (Amos 9:11; Ez. 37:24ᵃ). And the Lord will fill the earth with the abundance of its yield. The valley, the hill, and the mountain will vie each other in their produce. God will multiply the fruits of the land. So, we read in Amos:

And I will bring again the captivity of my people of Israel, and they shall build the waste cities, and inhabit them; and they shall plant vineyards, and drink the vine thereof; they shall also make gardens, and eat the fruit of them. And I will plant them upon their land, and they shall no more be pulled up out of their land which I have given them, saith the Lord thy God (Amos 9:14, 15).

17. Israel shall be once more rejuvenated spiritually; she will be made perfect in the Lord her God. She will grow strong and be filled with the zeal of the Almighty for the testimony of Jesus. She will sing praises for Jehovah Shalom; for the land has made peace with the King of kings and the Lord of lords. Israel is now redeemed from her corruption and wickedness. She has become a new nation that neither sin nor unrighteousness will impair her walk before the Lord. Israel will sing with Habakkuk and Isaiah the following song:

Yet I will rejoice in the Lord, I will joy in the God of my salvation. The Lord God is my strength, and he will make my feet like hinds' feet, and he will make me to walk upon mine high places (Hab. 3:18, 19).

*Behold, God is my salvation; I will trust, and not be afraid:
for the Lord Jehovah is my strength and my song; he also is
become my salvation. Therefore with joy shall ye draw water
out of the wells of salvation. . . . Sing unto the Lord; for he
hath done excellent things: this is known in all the earth. Cry
out and shout, thou inhabitant of Zion: for great is the Holy
One of Israel in the midst of thee (Isa. 12:2-3, 5-6).*

18. God promises that in that day shall the Lord be filled with zeal for
His people; He will strike the heathen with His jealousy for the children of
Abraham. "And it shall come to pass in that day, that I will seek to destroy all the nations that come against Jerusalem" (Zech. 12:9). The spirit
of vengeance will go out of the Almighty and destroy the wicked for his
wickedness. The nations had rejoiced that they have been able to destroy
Israel. We read in Zechariah the following:

*And I will pour upon the house of David, and upon the
inhabitants of Jerusalem, the spirit of grace and of supplication: and they shall look upon me whom they have pierced,
and they shall mourn for him, as one mourneth for his only
son, and shall be in bitterness for him, as one that is in bitterness for his firstborn. In that day there shall be a fountain
opened to the house of David and to the inhabitants of Jerusalem for sin and for uncleanness. . . . (Zech. 12:10; 13:1).*

*And it shall be in that day, that living waters shall go out
from Jerusalem: half of them toward the former [east] sea,
and half of them toward the hinder sea: in summer and in
winter shall it be. And the Lord shall be king over all the
earth: in that day shall there be one Lord, and his name one
(Zech. 14:8, 9).*

19. The prophet Malachi announced in his day of how God has
proclaimed Israel — its inhabitants and its territory — to belong to Him.
God even had a book of remembrance set before Him to remember them
that were formerly forgotten. Jehovah calls these people "mine." I will

make up my jewels and I will spare my sons and daughters from the wickedness of the Gentile nations. My people shall return unto me; they shall repent and be saved from their sins; they shall "discern between the righteous and the wicked, between him that serveth God and him that serveth him not" (Mal. 3:18[b]). God Almighty will, likewise, "say to them which were not my people, Thou art my people; and they shall say, Thou art my God" (Hos. 2:23[b]). We also read in the books of Malachi, Hosea, and Romans the following:

And they that fear the Lord spake often one to another: and the Lord hearkened, and heard it, and a book of remembrance was written before him for them that feared the Lord, and that thought upon his name. And they shall be mine, saith the Lord of hosts, in that day when I make up my jewels: and I will spare them, as a man spareth his own son that serveth him. Then shall ye return, and discern between the righteous and the wicked, between him that serveth God and him that serveth him not (Mal. 3:16-18).

As he saith also in Osee [Hosea 2:23], I will call them my people, which were not my people; and her beloved, which was not beloved. And it shall come to pass, that in the place where it was said unto them, Ye are not my people; there shall they be called the children of the living God. Esaias [Isaiah] also crieth concerning Israel, Though the number of the children of Israel be as the sand of the sea, a remnant shall be saved (Rom. 9:25-27).

20. Parenthetically, it should be stated here that a possible semi-hidden prophetic message exists in the book of Hosea for the Church that prophesies about the atoning work of our Saviour and of His Millennial Kingdom. This is the message: "After two days will he revive us: in the third day he will raise us up, and we shall live in his sight" (Hos. 6:2). By way of interpretation we may conclude that during the first "two days" of the Church, which are equal to the first "two thousand years" of the blessed Church dispensation, He will give us life eternal in His Son, the Lord Jesus

Christ. At the beginning of the "third day," which is the beginning of the "third one thousand years" of the Millennial Kingdom, He will raise us up and rapture us to ever live with Him eternally. Should the rapture occur at around the end of the year 2000, the prophecy of this inconspicuous verse would be fulfilled.

V. The Battle of Armageddon

21. Armageddon is the name of the place where the greatest human conflict with God and His Son, the Lord Jesus Christ, will take place in the near future. Armageddon is the Greek equivalent of the two words in Hebrew tongue, **Har** and **Magiddo**, which mean *the Mount of Magiddon*. This mountain is located on the northwestern side of the valley of Jezreel and southeastern portion of Mt. Carmel. To be more precise, Armageddon falls on the southern border of the plain of Esdrael. Spiritually speaking, the valley of Jezreel is also referred to in Joel as the Valley of Jehoshaphat, in Hebrew **yehoshaphat** means: *The valley where God will judge* the Gentile nations. It is in this figurative valley of Jehoshaphat that the Almighty God will deal a mighty blow to the armies of the Gentile World Powewr led by the Beast. In Joel, God says:

> *I will also gather all nations, and will bring them down into the valley of Jehoshaphat, and will plead with them there for my people and for my heritage Israel, whom they have scattered among the nations, and [they]* **parted my land**. . . *. Multitudes, multitudes in the valley of decision: for the day of the Lord is near in the valley of decision (Joel 3:2, 14). (*Bold added*).

22. Where are these armies coming from? It should be recalled that the Beast with his huge armies had entered the Middle East some time earlier. The Beast, accompanied by the False Prophet, had come into the land of Israel, on the pretense of its protection, according to the requirements of the treaty he had earlier concluded with her; yet he demands from her the worship of his image. Practically speaking, he is come possibly to secure for himself and his allies, the Revived Roman Empire, their

SAVING THE TOUGHEST FOR LAST

Israelis and Palestinians have embarked on three years of negotiations to settle the final and thorniest issues of their peace process, begun nearly three years ago: the status of Jerusalem, Jewish settlements in Palestinian areas, the fate of 3 million Palestinian refugees and the drawing of final borders.

reliance upon the Middle East oil. The existence of such huge armies in the Holy Land alarms the kings of the East. An alliance is formed, their armies are gathered together, and along with the military leadership, they are heading West. On their way, they encounter the Euphrates River and are baffled with the abundance of its water. God, however, orders one of the angels to sound the trumpet, to dry the waters of the river, and to allow the armies of the East to go through. For we read in the book of Revelation the following:

> *And the sixth angel poured out his vial upon the great river Euphrates; and the water thereof was dried up, that the way of the kings of the east might be prepared. And the number of the army of the horsemen were two hundred thousand thousand. . . (Rev. 16:12; 9:16).*

23. At the battle of Armageddon, Satan will again gradually raise the level of warfare from an earthly one to a heavenly conflict.[2] Openly, the Dragon calls the Gentile World Power to fight against the kings of the East; underneath it all, he wants to fight the armies of the Almighty God of heaven, who is just about to appear from heaven. At this time, the Beast with his commanders and leaders are encamped in the Holy Land where he had just given the Israeli leadership a fatal blow. In pomp and circumstance, he is now seated in the Holy Temple of God, magnifying himself above God and everything else.

24. In God's prophetic message, hardly anything is mentioned about the Moslem world, or about the Indians, Chinese, Japanese, or about other such peoples as they have lived in other parts of the world. Nothing is mentioned about their religion or about their culture. This is understandable, because, according to our Old and New Testaments, God never instituted any religions for them. Not only this, but also they hardly figure in the prophetic message. Yet, here, God's Word tells us that the sixth angel poured his vial upon the great Euphrates River to dry it and prepare the way for the armies of the kings of the East. When the sixth trumpet sounds, four angels, which were bound in the great Euphrates River, unleash a mighty army:

> *And the number of the army of the horsemen were two hundred thousand thousand . . . and them that sat on them, having breastplates of fire, and of jacinth, and brimstone: and the heads of the horses were as the heads of lions: and out of their mouths issued fire and smoke and brimstone (Rev. 9:16, 17).*

> *For they are the spirits of devils, working miracles, which go forth unto the kings of the earth and of the whole world, to gather them to the battle of that great day of God Almighty. . . . And he gathered them together into a place called in the Hebrew tongue Armageddon (Rev. 16:14, 16).*

25. The Beast, having taken over the Holy Land, will exalt himself and will act presumptuously. He will do according to his own will. He will not only magnify himself above all gods, but he will set himself above every other leader there is in the world. The Beast will not care the least for his parents and any other kinfolk; he will neither take notice of women. As the Supreme Leader of the entire world, he will be too busy with the affairs of the state; he will not care for his human relations or the love of women. As an impersonation of the Son of God, the Beast is the best model mankind could provide for this ultimate service. And now, he will be too absorbed in attempting to imitate his counterfeit, the Lord Jesus Christ, thereby to fulfill his end-time mission. Daniel, the prophet, tells us about this world Dictator:

> And the king [the Antichrist] shall do according to his will; and he shall exalt himself, and magnify himself above every god, and shall speak marvelous things against the God of gods, and shall prosper till the indignation be accomplished: for that that is determined shall be done. Neither shall he regard the God of his fathers, nor the desire of women, nor regard any god: for he shall magnify himself above all. But in his estate shall he honour the God of forces [the Mother Nature]. . . . (Dan. 11:36-38ª).

26. It does not appear that the kings of the East had come to the West in support of the Beast; rather, they have come to challenge his armies who appear to have come to secure the rich oil fields of the Middle East. Such a claim will undoubtedly be challenged particularly by the head of the Eastern forces. The Dragon, of course, sees all these developments and is well-pleased about them. He is delighted about the two hundred million army which is armed with all sorts of modern weaponry and ready for the battle. The Dragon finally tells the kings of the East to join forces with his armies to fight against the common enemy, the enemy from heaven, who is just about to come down and take over the earth. You remember how once Christ entered Jerusalem on a donkey (Zech. 9:9; Matt. 21:1-11); He is ready now to reenter the same city, not a donkey, but on a "white horse," as the King of kings and the Lord of lords (Rev. 19:11-16).

27. God brings all the armies of the world to Israel for a triple-purpose: First, to punish the Gentile World for their condemnation and maltreatment of Israel; secondly, to denounce them for putting to death millions of new believers in Christ on the earth; and thirdly, to destroy their power for ignoring God in their daily affairs. Michael, the archangel, had earlier defeated the Dragon in the heavenlies and had cast him down into the earth; now, however, he must defeat him once more and cast him finally into the bottomless pit.

> *And I saw an angel [Michael] come down from heaven, having the key of the bottomless pit and a great chain in his hand. And he laid hold on the dragon, that old serpent, which is the Devil, and Satan, and bound him a thousand years. And cast him into the bottomless pit, and shut him up, and set a seal upon him, that he should deceive the nations no more. . . . (Rev. 20:1-3ª).*

28. For approximately seven and a half years, the Beast has dominated the whole world; he has ruled basically over the entire world system of government. The Beast has wrought havoc among and nauseated the believing Christians everywhere. He has attained the status of a Superman; and as a Superman, he has acted according to his own wishes, and he has accomplished his Master's predilections. He has destroyed the Apostate Christianity; he has devastated the Apostate Judaism. The entire armies of the West are in his embrace. With assistance from the Dragon, he has ruled *facile princeps* over the whole world. Now that all the legions of the world are behind him, his armies are ready and fully prepared for battle. But now, alas! He is about to be defeated and destroyed by the Lion of Judah. For we read in the Psalms the following:

> *The earth is the Lord's, and the fulness thereof; the world, and they that dwell therein. . . . Lift up your heads, O ye gates; and be ye lift up, ye everlasting doors; and the King of glory shall come in. Who is the King of glory? The Lord strong and mighty, the Lord mighty in battle. Who is this King of glory? The Lord of hosts, he is the King of glory (Ps. 24:1, 7, 8).*

29. In the end, it is the Lord Jesus Christ who shall remain supreme throughout the world. He shall rule the earth with an iron-fisted hand. He is coming down with His saints to capture the throne of David, which had been seized by the Beast. Christ is accompanied with a mighty force of His saints who are ready and prepared to give the enemy a deadly blow. But the Lord Jesus needs no encouragement or support. With the "sharp sword" of the Spirit (Rev. 19:15), with the word of His mouth, He will crush the millions of armed forces the Beast has and totally annihilate them. The Beast and the False Prophet will both be captured and be "cast alive into a lake of fire" (Rev. 19:20). For we read in the books of Daniel and of Revelation the following:

> *I beheld even till the beast was slain, and his body destroyed, and given to the burning flames (Dan. 7:11^b).*

> *And out of his mouth [Jesus Christ's] goeth a sharp sword, that with it he should smite the nations: and he shall rule them with a rod of iron: and he treadeth the winepress of the fierceness and wrath of Almighty God. And he hath on his vesture and on his thigh a name written, KING OF KINGS, AND LORD OF LORDS (Rev. 19:15, 16).*

> *And the beast was taken, and with him the false prophet that wrought miracles before him, with which he deceived them that had received the mark of the beast, and them that worshipped his image. These both were cast alive into a lake of fire burning with brimstone (Rev. 19:20).*

CHAPTER 16

WHO IS THE BEAST?

And the beast was taken, and with him the false prophet that wrought miracles before him, with which he deceived them that had received the mark of the beast, and them that worshipped his image. These both were cast alive into a lake of fire burning with brimstone. And the remnant were slain with the sword of him that sat upon the horse, which sword proceeded out of his mouth. . . (Rev. 19:20 and 21ª).

I. Identifying the Beast

1. THROUGHOUT THE STUDY of the Beast and the End-Time Evants, perhaps the most important question in our discussion has been: "Who is the Beast?" For centuries, this very question has also been raised throughout the Church history. And since the inquiry of prophecy has been with us for a very long time, the Beast has been discussed since the days of the Apostles in the early Church. Apostles Paul, Peter and John have frequently dealt with the same subject and have provided for us a clear-cut answer about this end-time Antichrist. The word "antichrist," to signify the Beast, is used by the Apostle John four times in his first and second Epistles. Although, John employs the word generically, he uses the word three times in Chapter 2 of his first epistle; and once in his second epistle. On one occasion, the word "Antichrist" is used to describe those who would deny "that Jesus is the Christ," thereby extending its denial to include "the Father and the Son" (I John 2:22). Twice the word "antichrist" has been used in conjunction with the repeated statement of warning that "it is the last time" (I John 2:18), or that it is the end time. "You had better be very careful," the Apostle warns them.

2. Many writers of prophecy have made every effort to identify this personage with some great man of history; normally, their efforts have gone in vain. Likewise, almost every great and calamitous catastrophe that has happened on this planet has been identified with the end-time events. In association with such an event, attempts have been made to identify the Beast, who supposedly will be behind these cataclysmic upheavals that befall the earth. Numerous attempts have been also made to identify him with his number which is given in the book of Revelation, Chapter 13, Verse 18[b], which is: "Six hundred three score and six." Up to now, history has proven that no one has succeeded to identify this "congenial" Superstar.

3. Many scholars of prophecy and even some amateurs have very often attempted to apply the Beast's number to the name of some famous personage to find out whether he would be the Beast. This author himself, as a young man, had made every attempt, in years past, to apply the number 666 to many great persons to affirm that such a person could be the Antichrist. The desire that rested within my heart to know who the real Beast was, was indeed phenomenal. As a youngster and for a long time, I had applied this number 666 to Hitler, to Mussolini, to Hirohito, to Stalin, and to a host of many other statesmen, politicians, and dignitaries of the world.

4. How do you apply this number to a person? Simply stated, by taking the number of the letters used in a name and adding them up to yield the number 666. Every letter of the twenty-two Semitic letters of the alphabet has a numerical value. This is true, particularly with Aramaic and Hebrew alphabets. The first nine letters of this alphabet have each the chronological number, 1 - 9; the next nine letters have each the chronological number in tens, 10 - 90; the following four letters have each the chronological number in hundreds, 100 - 400. Take the name "Stalin," for example, and apply the following numbers to it. Using the Aramaic letters to transcribe the name Stalin, we get for *Simkath* (S) 60; for *Taw* (T) 400; for *Lamadh* (L) 30; and for *Nun* (N) 50. Added together, they number 540, falling short by 126. Now, let us also add his first name, "Joseph." For, in its Aramaic/Hebrew form, we have "Yosip"; for *Yodh* (Y), we have 10: for *Waw* (W/O), we have 6; for *Simkath* (S), we have 60; and for *Pi* (P), we have 80. Adding them up, we have a total of 156, to which we add 540, and we obtain 696. It is apparent that Joseph Stalin could not have been the Beast!

5. A school of thought believes that the would-be Antichrist will, like Jesus, be brought back from the dead. The Bible tells us that he "was, and is not, even he is the eighth, and is of the seven, and goeth into perdition" (Rev. 18:11). In this connection, Judas Iscariot is often sited to be the one resurrected, at the end time, to become the Antichrist. On two accounts, this interpretation of prophecy is not plausible: First, Judas could not become the end-time Beast, since he is a Jew. The Tribulation Period is primarily concerning the Gentile World Power and its dominance. The Beast is a Gentile and exercises the Gentile World Power through and through. Accordingly, no person of the Jewish origin would fill that position. Secondly, the reference to his death and resurrection are primarily symbolic of the "death" of the Old Roman Empire and its rebirth and revival at the end time.

6. Some serious Bible scholars, who are also interested in prophecy, have toyed with the idea of presenting the Late John F. Kennedy, the former president of the United States of America, as a most suited candidate for the end-time Beast. Mr. Kennedy was shot in the head; he eventually died; he is buried at the National Cemetery; he shall be resurrected at the appropriate moment, and he will be healed and will recover to assume the position of the Beast. Some say that the flaming fire at the National Cemetery is a camouflage; Kennedy is buried in Greece, where his wife, Jacqueline Onasis lived until her death. While Mr. Kennedy was, indeed, street smart and some claimed that he was an intellectual, he hardly possessed any qualities that would make him become the Beast.

7. There are those who believe that the Beast will arise out of the Middle East, particularly someone who has knowledge about the area, an area which has been the center of contention throughout the ages. Such a notion is frivolous; since this Antichrist must be someone who comes out of the Roman legacy. The Scriptures tell us that he, the Beast, was dead and is resurrected at the end time. With the fall of the Old Roman Empire, the ruler of that empire, the Beast, is likewise dead. With the revival of this New Roman Empire, the new ruler of the ten-nation Union will, likewise, become the new Beast that will rule the end-time government.

8. Here below, we are presenting eight different views about the Beast expressed by eight writers, beginning with Ryrie and ending with Newell. It is not my desire to prove these writers right or wrong; I only want to present their individual views about the Antichrist as they have endeavored to describe this Man of Sin. I also believe that had I presented the contemplation of a much larger number of such authors, they all basically would have given the same limited description about the Beast. Nevertheless, these authors have made every effort to demonstrate, as best as they could, who the Beast is and who he shall be, at the end time.

II. Different Views About the Beast

9. How can we identify the Beast? It is a mystery for us to even make attempts to recognize who this dreadful Superman will be. Most Bible scholars and prophecy interpreters present to us an unusual personage whose description is somewhat peculiar and hard to understand. To some he is an antichrist; to others he is the Wicked Man; and still to many others he is a political ruler of the end-time united Europe. Where does he come from? Does he come from Europe? Does he come from the United States of America? Does he spring up from Russia? Does he represent the Gentile World Power? Many are the questions about him, and few are the answers. Here below are some answers provided by eight Bible believing, prophecy scholars chosen at random.

10. Charles C. Ryrie's View[1]

Though there have been many antichrists throughout the church history, this is the great and final Antichrist who is still to come (I John 2:18). In this vision he arose, 'out of the sea,' which many understand to be a symbol of the masses of people (Rev. 17:15). But perhaps his origin out of the sea simply distinguishes him in the vision from the second beast, who arises out of the land. . . .

The seven heads are also explained in [Rev.] 17:9 as the seven hills of the city (Rome) in which his power centers. They also stand for seven Roman rulers, of which he is the last.

11. Robert G. Gromacki's View[2]

Therefore, the 'prince that shall come' must be a *Roman prince*. This means that he will be a European or possibly an American (since the United States is basically an extension of European idea and peoples). . . . Since the beast of Revelation 13 has the same animal characteristics as they, he also must have a Gentile origin.

Many feel that in order to carry off the counterfeit, he must be a Jew, but this is not so. Since he is a fake, he will be *complete* fake. However, his right-hand man, the false prophet, will be a Jew. . . . (Rev. 13:11-18). He will combine the logic of a Churchill, the emotion of a Hitler and the wit [street-smart] of a Kennedy into a Hollywood-type image.

12. Bob Shelton's View[3]

It is obvious from the description that this horn represents a man. This man is often spoken about in the chapters and books that follow. He is called by different names, but in each case, he is the same man who is destined to play an important role in the prophetic drama. . . . The Antichrist will arise from among the nations of the revived Roman Empire. We are not told from which of the ten nations he will come, but as surely as God's Word can be trusted, he will make his appearance at just the right moment in the prophetic plan.

13. Herbert Vander Lugt's View[4]

Antichrist will also be a man of gross blasphemy. As soon as he feels secure in his position of leadership, he will boldly and arrogantly express his disdain for God. . . . Because he will need the support of the Jews as he rises to world power, however, he will make a seven-year treaty with Israel. . . . This man, however, will boldly reject every historical religious system. . . . A number of today's scholars believe he will show no regard for human affection and tenderness, virtues highly prized by women. The fact that this statement about his showing no regard for 'the desire of women' occurs in such a close relationship to his blasphemous activities makes me think in terms of an open promotion of homosexuality.

14. Sir Robert Anderson's View[5]

It is the KING OF MEN, the great head of the Hellenic race, the man whom a thousand galleys and a hundred thousand men submitted to on a simple recognition of his personal qualities, and obeyed for ten long years. . . .

It is no longer a confederacy of nations that is bound together by treaty, with a Napoleon rising up in the midst of them and struggling for supremacy; but a confederacy of kings who are the lieutenants of one great Kaiser, a man whose transcendent greatness has secured to him an undisputed pre-eminence.

And this is the man whom the Dragon will single out to administer his awful power on earth in days to come. And from the hour in which he sells himself to Satan he will be so energized by Satan, that 'ALL power and signs and lying wonders' shall characterize his after course.

15. J. Dwight Pentecost's View[6]

This world is headed toward a unified, political system and a unified, religious system that begs description and defies imagination. Satan brings his great masterpiece, the man of sin, the lawless one, the Beast, on the world scene as the head of a great confederation of nations.

This world ruler is going to show special antagonism against the Most High and against His saints, and he shall seek 'to change times and laws' This individual is to have this worldwide authority for the last three and a half years of the seven years of the Tribulation Period.

They [the Jews] will feel he has fulfilled the Abrahamic covenant. They will acknowledge him as God and Messiah. This man in his dictatorship so dominates and controls the circumstances in the world that if God did not bring an end to his corrupt government, he would destroy man off the face of the earth.

16. John Hagee's View[7]

The Antichrist will be a man who makes his debut upon the stage of world history with hypnotic charisma. He will probably come from the European Union or a country or confederation that was once part of the Roman Empire, which stretched from Ireland to Egypt and included Turkey, Iran, and Iraq. The Antichrist will be a man who has 'paid his dues' in the military and the political scene, and many will willingly follow him.

The Antichrist's three-point plan for world domination consists of a one-world economic system in which no one can buy nor sell without a mark sanctioned by the Antichrist's administration; a one-world government, now being called 'The New World Order'; and a one-world religion that will eventually focus its worship on the Antichrist himself.

17. William R. Newell's View[8]

The Beast, therefore, of Revelation 13 is a man who controls absolutely the royal authority of the ten kings at the time of the end, and this by their own united will. Satan, being the prince of this world and the god of this age, and being desperately set on *ruling* men and being *worshipped* by them, is now given his chance. Because men by trifling with the trust, and by utter impenitence have opened the way, God will now send them a strong delusion that they may believe the devil's lie.

Even the Beast himself will retreat one step from man, in the same way, when an 'image' is made of him by the *second* beast! Thus will lie in the deluded world's inner consciousness 'the likeness of an image' of *man*, a wonderful man, who has returned in a manner beyond their knowledge from the unseen realm of the dead. And all the while the *worship* of all men will really be retained by Satan himself; for it will be known by all that it is the *dragon himself* that has given 'his authority unto the Beast.'

III. How Does One Consider the Beast?

18. I see the Beast as the best example of humanity mankind could ever offer. He could be 6' 2" to 6' 5" or more tall; he could weigh 180-200 lbs.; and he is, most likely, in his mid-forties to mid-fifties. He is well educated and, especially, he is very street-smart individual. "... his mighty and versatile intellect, his unlimited acquirements, his superhuman wisdom, his powerful administrative and executive ability, his absolutely unyielding will, his never varying success, and the irresistible fascination of his personal attractions, will gain him applause and enthusiastic supporters wherever he turns."[9] His commitment to carry out his duties will prevent him from being preoccupied with the love of his parents or the affection of a woman. As is the case with the Lord Jesus Christ, whom he imitates, the Beast, who is a subtle imitator, will have no claim either for his parents or for women.

19. Since man, as we know him nowadays, is weak and belligerent, the Beast must become glorified and elevated, in the mind of men, far above the realm of heaven. This is the same sin Lucifer committed from the very beginning. His earthly standards must be improved considerably.

The religion of [his] future must include the salvation of humanity for this present time. It has to be a sincerity of life, in place of pretended belief; a religion of science, in place of superstition; of joy instead of sorrow; of man's ascent instead of his fall; a religion of fact in the present, and not of mere faith for the future; a religion of work rather than of worship; a reality instead of delusive idealism; and in place of the deathly creeds, with all their hungry parasites of prey, a religion of life actual, life here, life now, and no longer the mere promise of life hereafter.[10]

20. It is interesting to observe that, with respect to the "challenge" given to the reader of the book of Revelation this challenge is straightforward and lacking any subtleties of language. "And here is the mind which hath wisdom. The seven heads are seven mountains, on which the woman sitteth" (Rev. 17:9). After contemplating to some extent over this verse, its interpretation becomes somewhat indisputable (See Appendix B). Yet, there is another verse in the book of Revelation which gives us yet another such a "challenge" for which no one has as yet an answer. The challenge we are given there is: "Here is wisdom. Let him that hath understanding count the number of the beast: for it is the number of a man; and his number is *six hundred three score and six*" (Rev. 13:18). (*Italics added*).

21. Thus far no one has been able to interpret this "challenging" question. And, I believe, no one will ever be able to expound it. I am firmly convinced, the number is given for the people of the Tribulation Period; they will then solve the problem and make up their mind as to whether to accept the Beast as their ruler and go with him into perdition, or to reject him and accept Christ as their Saviour even at the cost of martyrdom. What a strong evidence for the recognition of the Beast during that time. No one who has the knowledge of the number 666 can justify living during this period which is controlled by the Beast and his cohorts. Unless a person is altogether wicked, or out of touch with Christ and His saved people, he cannot live under the Beast. This author's prayer is that men and women will repent and come to the saving knowledge of the Lord.

22. Whatever the outcome of this study, the fact is that neither in this book that we are providing, nor in any other such book, will we ever be able to determine who the Antichrist is. No matter how much studying we do, or how often we apply a number to the potential name, in my simple judgment, we will never accomplish anything positive with respect to the end-time Beast. Thus far, no one has ever been able to identify this "Monster"; at the same time, no one will ever be able to apply 666 accurately. This "Animal" becomes an enigma, through and through. But God's people will have no need to know the Beast, since they will all be raptured to glory. It is the people of the earth, after the rapture of the believers, who will gladly want to know who this Scoundrel is. His end is destruction; his abode will be in the lake of fire and brimstone.

CHAPTER 17

THE MILLENNIAL KINGDOM

I am Alpha and Omega, the beginning and the end, the first and the last. . . . I am the root and the offspring of David, and the bright and morning star. And the Spirit and the Bride say, Come. And let him that heareth say, Come (Rev. 22:13, 16[b], 17[a]).

I. The Judgment of Nations

1. THE DRAMATIC events of the coming of "the Son of Man" to the earth after the defeat of the armies of the Beast and of the Dragon, is presented in Matthew, Chapter 25, and Joel, Chapter 3. God is angry about his people and about the *parting of his land*.[1] He is displeased with the nations of the earth for their folly, and for their indifference towards his people. So, the Lord Jesus Christ will come down to Jerusalem to judge the nations. It is the Day of the Lord, the Day of Decision, in the Valley of Decision. It is here, in Jerusalem, that "the Lord will be the hope of his people, and the strength of the children of Israel" (Joel 3:16[b]).

2. In Matthew, Chapter 25, the Word of God gives us an almost proverbial description of what is likely to happen to the living people on the earth immediately after the Tribulation Period. Having declared himself to be "the Son of man," the King of kings and the Lord of lords will render justice with respect to His "brethren." The question that was raised earlier, in a former chapter, can be re-examined here once again: Who are "the least of these my brethren" mentioned in Matthew, Chapter 25, Verses 40 and 45. Scofield notes identify these brethren as "the Jewish Remnant" who will have preached the Gospel of the Kingdom to all nations during the Tribulation Period.[2] This, however, is not and cannot be the case; the Jewish Remnant, which could have preached the Gospel, has already been flown to the wilderness of Moab, to a place prepared for them by God Himself.

3. It is possible that, during the Tribulation Period, many Jews will be converted after a large segment of their coreligionists left for the wilderness; like the Gentiles of that time, however, they had no special distinction in the matter; if caught, they will be martyred. Hence, the brethren which Jesus referred to are none other than the 144,000 sealed servants of our God. It is to these sealed servants, chosen from the twelve tribes of the children of Israel, that the Lord referred to as "these my brethren." These, indeed, are His brethren both in the flesh and in the spirit. They were His emissaries who preached to the entire Gentile nations during the Tribulation Period. Many of them possibly suffered great persecution for the testimony of Jesus. But those who gave them food to eat and water to drink; those who provided for them a place to sleep, and gave to them clothes to put on; and when they were sick or imprisoned, they visited them; to these alone Christ calls "these my brethren," both spiritually and humanly.

4. The judgment of the nations on the earth is very simple, quick, and just. The Lord Jesus, through His angels, divides the remaining living nations of the earth into two simple groups: the sheep, those who are saved, He places on His right hand; the goats, those who are not saved, He places on His left hand. The King, the Great Shepherd, bids those on his right hand to come and "inherit the kingdom prepared for you from the foundation of the world" (Matt. 25:34^b). The Eternal King gives the ones on his right hand the reason why they should inherit the kingdom. Protesting their innocence from having done for Him the things He had just enumerated for them; the answer comes: "Inasmuch as ye have done it unto one of the least of these my brethren, ye have done it unto me" (Matt. 25:40^b).

5. The Lamb of God has now become the Lion of Judah. He turns to His left hand and says to the wicked: "Depart from me, ye cursed, into everlasting fire, prepared for the devil and his angels" (Matt. 25:41^b). You have done nothing for any of these 144,000 sealed servants of our God. When they were in great need for food, for water, for shelter, for clothes, you gave them nothing; in sickness and in prison, you visited them not. Alas, what an end for you! You ignored them and you have ignored their witness; you have spurned their testimony for Christ the Saviour.

6. Alas! What a punishment awaits these poor hypocrites. They are rejected by the Master and are sent to eternal damnation in the unquenchable fires of hell. This hell which was created for the Devil and his cohorts, is now, likewise, the eternal abode of the wicked ones, who were more eager to follow the easdy road, than to follow Satan and his emissaries. They preferred "to enjoy the pleasures of sin for a season," than to esteem "the reproach of Christ greater riches than the treasures in Egypt" (Heb. 11:25^b, 26^a). They preferred to follow the Beast and his "goodness," than to take up the cross and follow Jesus and enter into His eternal Kingdom.

II. Life in the Kingdom

7. It is interesting to notice how the Millennial Kingdom will begin with the judgment of the nations. Having condemned the wicked to "Depart from me, ye cursed, into everlasting fire, prepared for the devil and his angels" (Matt. 25:41^b); now Christ tells those on His right hand, "Come, ye blessed of my Father, inherit the kingdom prepared for you from the foundation of the world" (Matt. 25:34^b). For it is with these regenerates and righteous nations of the earth, the blessed residue of the Tribulation Period, that the Lord Jesus will begin anew His rule over the earth. It is again very interesting to observe that this Kingdom was prepared for them and has been waiting for them "since the foundation of the world." Teeming millions of living saints enter, at this time, into the blessed Kingdom of our Saviour.

8. The continued personal work of the 144,000 sealed servants of our God, the continued testimony of the two dedicated and resurrected witnesses, and the preaching of the Everlasting Gospel by none other than the angel of God, have evangelized and produced great results of soul winning for the Kingdom. Millions upon millions of peoples of all nations, tongues, and kindreds are converted and have been feverishly awaiting the appearing of the King of kings and Lord of lords from the heavenly places. While many millions of these believers are martyred for the testimony of our Saviour, many more are still alive and are awaiting their King to descend from heaven for their final deliverance.

9. It is very important to observe that a very large number of living children under the age of accountability, children who "cannot discern between their right hand and their left hand" (Jon. 4:11), who have escaped the Tribulation Period, are alive and ready to enter the Millennial Kingdom. It is possible, however, that most children under the age of six would fall into the category of the age of innocence. While the exact upper age of innocence is not known to us, nor is it possible for us humans to understand that age, especially as it varies from one child to another; God, however, does all things well. Nevertheless, children of this early age are usually very tender hearted and very innocent. This does not mean that they are sin-free; but that they have not knowingly, personally committed a sin to displease God. And, of course, there are millions of unborn, or especially still-born, or miscarried, or aborted children in heaven standing before their Almighty God and enjoying His presence.

10. While also men, women, and children from the living nations, which have entered the Millennial Kingdom, are saved, they cannot commit sin that should carry them unto a spiritual death. They are eternally secured in their salvation. But, it is their descendants, and the children of their children's descendants, that may, later on, rebel against the Lord Jesus Christ and His government. As time goes by, many of the new nations will begin to complain: they will once again clandestinely begin a rebellion against God and against the Lord Jesus Christ. By the time the Millennial Age comes to an end, there will be many disobedient, sinful and wicked people on the earth. Despite the fact that the rule of our Saviour will be dictatorial and iron-fisted, sin will gradually begin to abound once again. One thing needs to be emphasized here: Satan has no direct part in this new worldwide disobedience; he is still bound with chains and cast into the bottomless pit for the total of a thousand years.

11. Imagine a thousand years of blessed life of fellowship with the Saviour and with the born again kinfolk during the Millennial Kingdom.

Imagine that there is hardly a sickness, or a malady; a fight or a quarrel. Also imagine that the life's span for each individual person is prolonged to its maximum — several hundred years and more. Imagine, once again, how a new couple may have 10, 15, or more healthy babies during their married life. If the increase in the growth of population would reach 10 to 15 percent annually, before too long, the world's population could have grown dramatically to unprecedented limits. In a very short time, there would be millions upon millions of people, even billions, scattered all over the earth.

III. Christ's Rule in the Kingdom

12. Christ's rule on the earth will be such a blessed experience that one is hardly able to define it. The spread of knowledge becomes a reality throughout the world; many find it conducive to studying and to achieving great successes. The existence of peace on the earth, the existence of plenty of food and many other accommodations for the people, the support of one person to another, are all exercised daily. There is a general feeling of easiness and calmness among the people of the world that surpasses everything imaginable. This Millennial Kingdom of our Lord is so uniquely blessed and endowed with endless earthly goods, that nothing comes short of those dwelling in it.

13. Throughout the world, traveling from one place to another will become simple and affordable to all. Huge planes are developed and put to service everywhere. Trains and cars abound. Technology is so widespread that it provides every potential student a computer at home and in the classroom. "[A]nd knowledge shall be increased" everywhere (Dan. 12:4^b). Travel into space will, likewise, be intensified and man will become a frequent visitor to many a near and distant planet. Even the animal kingdom will learn to live together in peace and harmony. For we read in the book of Isaiah, saying:

> *The wolf also shall dwell with the lamb, and the leopard shall lie down with the kid [child]; and the calf and the young lion and the fatling together; and a little child shall lead them.*

And the cow and the bear shall feed; their young ones shall lie down together: and the lion shall eat straw like the ox. And the sucking child shall play on the hole of the asp, and the weaned child shall put his hand on the cockatrice' den" (Isa. 11:6-8).

14. No sooner the Millennial Kingdom begins its rule over the earth, the Lord will gather His people, the Israelites who are now saved, from all parts of the earth. He will bring his nation from every country and every land. He will bring them to their land, to the land of their forefathers. There would be no one in the entire world who would object to the Jewish people returning to their homeland. The Arabs have become their friends and the Russians their bosom buddies. "Behold, the former things are come to pass, and new things do I declare: before they spring forth I tell you of them" (Is. 42:9). God promises that His Word will not return to Him empty. "I am the Lord, your Holy One, the creator of Israel, your King" (Is. 43:15). Furthermore, Isaiah says:

Fear not: for I am with thee: I will bring thy seed from the east, and gather thee from the west; I will say to the north, give up; and to the south, Keep not back: bring my sons from far, and my daughters from the ends of the earth (Is. 43:5, 6).

He shall feed his flock like a shepherd: he shall gather the lambs with his arm, and carry them in his bosom, and shall gently lead those that are with young (Is. 40:11).

15. During the Millennial Kingdom, Christ's rule will primarily focus on the people of Israel. A Triumvirate Union will be set up in that day composed of Assyria, Egypt, and Israel. The Lord Jesus Christ will perform miracles the likes of which there has never been before, nor will ever be thereafter. First, God will chastise the Egyptians in order to bring them down to their knees in repentance and supplication (Isa. 19:20, 22); and so the Egyptians will turn unto the Lord and beseech God for their salvation and conversion. Once Egypt is converted, it is also healed from its wickedness and its false religion. Thirdly, the Lord will assemble "the remnants of his people [the Assyrians], which shall be left from Assyria," and establish them in their land to be ready for the new coalition. The Lord will then bring together in one union three nations — Assyria, Egypt, and Israel (Isa. 19:23-25); it will be a union of prosperity and blessings from God the Father. And, thirdly, the Lord will extend His blessings upon this Tripartite Empire of the three nations, saying:

> *In that day shall there be a highway out of Egypt to Assyria, and the Assyrian shall come into Egypt, and the Egyptian into Assyria, and the Egyptians shall serve with the Assyrian. In that day shall Israel be the third with Egypt and with[3] Assyria, even a blessing in the midst of the land: Whom the Lord of hosts shall bless, saying, Blessed be Egypt my people, and Assyria the work of my hands, and Israel mine inheritance (Is. 19:23-25).*

IV. Believers' Rule with Christ

16. Christ had promised His disciples that they would govern with Him in the Millennial Kingdom. Not only the disciples, but also all those who are eager to serve the Master during their lives on the earth. The Christian believer who has a high position in the affairs of this world, who has remained faithful and true to the witness of the Saviour, and who has demonstrated his willingness to testify of the Lord Jesus Christ, will most likely become a ruler in the Millennial Kingdom. Not only such people will become rulers in the Dominion of our God, but anyone who is found faithful and true to the testimony of Jesus and to the Word of God. We read in Matthew the following:

> *And Jesus said unto them, Verily I say unto you, [t]hat ye which have followed me, in the regeneration when the Son of man shall sit in the throne of his glory, ye also shall sit upon twelve thrones, judging the twelve tribes of Israel. And every one that hath forsaken houses, or brethren, or sisters, or father, or mother, or wife, or children, or lands, for my name's sake, shall receive an hundredfold, and shall inherit everlasting life (Matt. 19:28, 29).*

17. It is very interesting to observe how, in the Olivet discourse, the returning landlord tested his servants; those who brought to him the gains they had faithfully produced were rewarded in accordance to the goodness of their heart and the resilience of their faithfulness. Their master had given each "man according to his several ability" (Matt. 25:15). The first two men went into the market and right away doubled their talents; but the third man, because he was fearful, he went and hid the talent in the earth. Also notice that despite the difference in the profits the first two had made, they had received the same reward. The lackadaisical man, however, received nothing but the worst punishment. We read in Matthew about this:

> *His lord said unto him, [w]ell done, thou good and faith-*
> *ful servant: thou hast been faithful over a few things, I will*
> *make thee ruler over many things: enter thou into the joy of*
> *thy lord (Matt. 25:21, 23).*

> *His lord answered and said unto him, Thou wicked and*
> *slothful servant, thou knewest that I reap where I sowed not,*
> *and gather where I have not strawed: Thou oughtest there-*
> *fore to have put my money to the exchangers, and then at my*
> *coming I should have received mine own with usury. Take*
> *therefore the talent from him, and give it unto him which hath*
> *ten talents. . . . And cast ye the unprofitable servant into outer*
> *darkness: there shall be weeping and gnashing of teeth (Matt.*
> *25:26-28, 30).*

18. The Millennial Kingdom is not only a time of blessing and fellowship of the believers with each other, as the redeemed ones by the precious blood of the Saviour, but also a time during which there will be merrymaking with each other and even with the Lord. He has promised his disciples that He would drink of the fruit of the vine with them during His blessed reign in the Kingdom. While it is not known how much interaction the Lord Jesus will have with the common believers during the Kingdom Age, one thing is clear: His life on the earth demonstrates the way He will treat all believers. What a blessed fellowship that will be!

For we read in the Gospel of Luke the following:

> *Verily I say unto you, I will drink no more of the fruit of the vine, until that day that I drink it [a]new in the kingdom of God (Mar. 14:25).*

V. Worship in the Kingdom

19. In his book, Prophet Ezekiel provides for us the description of a specific form of temple used for the worship during the Millennial Age. The description of and the dimensions for this new temple are all given in Ezekiel, Chapters 40 through 48. The blue-print for the construction of this temple, its varied dimensions, and its use by the living believers on the earth, are all faithfully described by this prophet. While there is much debate over the system of "sacrifices" described in Ezekiel, this temple does not appear to be an attempt to restore the old Mosaic system of Law and worship at Jerusalem. While the Mosaic Law was specifically carved and fashioned for the people of God, the temple worship is, likewise, specifically designed for all the people of the Millennial Kingdom. In every age and in every dispensation, the system of worship and its requirements, which God has instituted, vary considerably.

20. Salvation is eternal in all of its ramifications: the source of it, the application of it, the objects (persons) saved by it, its eternality, whether it be during the grace period or during the Millennial Kingdom, are all possible by a much "higher grace" of God, the source of which is the Lord Jesus Christ. However, in order to demonstrate their faithfulness to the Saviour, the living believers of the Millennial Kingdom are instructed to make sacrifices as an act of obedience to the Master. This is the only way the believer can prove himself openly faithful and obedient to the Lord Jesus Christ during the Millennial Kingdom. In so doing, the earthly believers will prove their continued commitment to the Almighty God of heaven. Of course, all worship and sacrifices are normally rendered under the direct supervision of "the Prince." This is what Pentecost says about this prince: "In all probability this personage will be an earthly representative of the king-priest ministry of Christ after the order of

Melchizedek, perhaps the resurrected David, as previously suggested."[4]

21. We must not forget that one of the three major functions of Christ our Saviour is his priestly ministry. He is not only the King of kings and the Lord of lords; He is not only the Redeemer of mankind, the blessed Saviour; but He is also our High Priest who is seated at the right hand of the Majesty interceding for us. "(. . . The Lord sware and will not repent, Thou art a priest for ever after the order of Melchisedec:) By so much was Jesus made a surety of a better testament. For such an high priest became us, who is holy, harmless, undefiled, separate from sinners, and made higher then the heavens. . ." (Heb. 7:21, 22, 26). But in the Millennial Kingdom, the Saviour will be present and will expect from the living believers their obedience. And so, many shall come from the uttermost parts of the globe to render such peace offerings to demonstrate their obedience to the Lord. Those who refuse to do so, shall be scourged with various natural calamities, such as lack of rain, or pestilences, or calamities of some sort (Zech. 14:16-18). As the priest of a new covenant, Christ Jesus must be obeyed and sacrifices must be rendered unto Him regularly according to the instructions given in the book of Ezekiel (Ez. 43:19-27).

22. It is this "mountain kingdom" of the Lord that will be established above all other "mountain kingdoms" in the land; it will be the people of God, the saved Jews, being supported and assisted, in that day, by the Assyrians and the Egyptians, the members of the blessed Tripartite Union, that will be ruling the entire world. Many nations from many parts of the world will come to Jerusalem for worship and to receive blessings from the Almighty God. In Jerusalem, they will learn the ways of the Lord and how they shall walk in His path. For Zion issues the Law; the Word of God comes from Jerusalem. We read in Isaiah the following:

> And it shall come to pass in the last days, that the mountain of the Lord's house shall be established in the top of the mountains, and shall be exalted above the hills; and all nations shall flow unto it. And many people shall go and say, Come ye, and let us go up to the mountain of the Lord, to the

house of the God of Jacob; and he will teach us of his ways,
and we will walk in his path: for out of Zion shall go forth the
law, and the word of the Lord from Jerusalem (Is. 2:2, 3).

23. It is interesting to observe that during the Millennial Age there will be no more war in any place on the earth. Instead of producing a sword, the people will produce plowshares; instead of making a spear, they will make pruninghooks. The concern of the people of the earth will be from henceforth the tilling of the earth to produce enough food and the development of technology and industry. Agriculture and agricultural products will be the main preoccupation of man throughout the Millennial Age. Warfare for supremacy will become a past reminiscence and even forgotten; battles and wars for the occupation of more territory will be the thing of the past. Again we read in Isaiah the following:

[T]hey shall beat their swords into plowshares, and their
spears into pruninghooks: nation shall not lift up sword
against nation, neither shall they learn war any more. O house
of Jacob, come ye, and let us walk in the light of the Lord (Is.
2:4, 5).

And many nations shall come, and say, Come, and let us
go up to the mountain of the Lord, and to the house of the
God of Jacob; and he will teach us of his ways, and will walk
in his paths: for the law shall go forth of Zion, and the word
of the Lord from Jerusalem. . . . But they shall sit every man
under his vine and under his fig tree; and none shall make
them afraid: for the mouth of the Lord of hosts hath spoken it
(Mic. 4:2, 4).

CHAPTER 18

THE GREAT WHITE THRONE AND BEYOND

And I saw a great white throne, and him that sat on it, from whose face the earth and the heaven fled away; and there was found no place for them. And I saw the dead, small and great, stand before God; and the books were opened: and another book was opened, which is the book of life: and the dead were judged out of those things which were written in the books, according to their works. . . . And whosoever was not found written in the book of life was cast into the lake of fire. (Rev. 20:11, 12 and 15).

I. The Great White Throne

1. At the end of the Millennial Kingdom, Satan will be once again "loosed out of his prison (Rev. 20:7b)," out of the bottomless pit. As the magnet draws all ferrous objects to itself; likewise, Satan will draw all the sinners, who have clandestinely thus far exercised hypocrisy in their hearts against the Lord and have become a problem of disobedience to the authority and the rule of the Lord Jesus Christ and to the heavenly Father. They will unite themselves to each other and rally themselves to the Devil for the sole purpose of once again to fight God Almighty. These unsaved people will be so displeased with the Saviour that they will once again arise and fight against the hosts of God. The now emancipated Satan will go out to deceive the nations of the earth, especially the territory of Gog and Magog, and bids them once again to be ready for battle. For we read in the book of Revelation the following:

And when the thousand years are expired, Satan shall be loosed out of his prison, [a]nd shall go out to deceive the nations which are in the four quarters of the earth, Gog and Magog, to gather them together to battle: the number of whom is as the sand of the sea. And they went up on the breadth of

the earth, and compassed the camp of the saints about, and
the beloved city: and fire came down from God out of heaven,
and devoured them (Rev. 20:7-9).

2. Isn't it astonishing that the Almighty God would never punish a strayed believer, or an unrighteous or wicked human being, without first justifying Himself before His own elect? Read the Scriptures, my friend, and examine them very carefully; you will find how, time and again, God, before meting out a punishment to someone, elected or condemned, or to a nation or a people, must first of all make His children aware of what He is about to do. The intercession of Abraham about Sodom and Gomorrah is just one such an example. "And Abraham drew near [to God], and said, Wilt thou also destroy the righteous with the wicked?" (Gen. 18:23). God harkened to the intermediary prayer of Abraham and, from the fifty righteous men, according to Abraham, that could have been in the two cityies, God went down to even ten men; but there were none. And the two cities were forthwith destroyed.

3. As the book of Revelation describes the punishment measured out to the resurrected sinners of the "second death" in a very unusual fashion, it is very interesting that each sinner's name is *individually* called, and brought before the Great White Throne, and dealt with. The name thus called is matched with the names existing in "the book of life" (Rev. 20:15). These "were judged every man according to their works" (Rev. 20:13[b]). Those whose names were not found in the book of life (Rev. 5), were cast into the lake of fire (Rev. 20:14[b]). With them also were "death and hell" (Rev. 20:14) cast into the lake of fire. Likewise, the Dragon, that Old Serpent, Lucifer, "was cast into the lake of fire and brimstone, where the Beast and theFalse Prophet are, and shall be tormented day and night for ever and ever" (Rev. 20:10).

And I saw a Great White Throne, and him that sat on it,
from whose face the earth and the heaven fled away; and
there was found no place for them. And I saw the dead, small
and great, stand before God; and the books were opened:
and another book was opened, which is the book of life: and

the dead were judged out of those things which were written in the books, according to their works. And the sea gave up the dead which were in it; and death and hell delivered up the dead which were in them: and they were judged every man according to their works. And death and hell were cast into the lake of fire. This is the second death. And whosoever was not found written in the book of life was cast into the lake of fire (Rev. 20:11-15).

4. Lucifer, that great and "anointed cherub that covereth," was perfect in his creation, "till iniquity was found in [him]" (Ez. 28:15^b). Lucifer, the Devil, Satan, whose beginning is marked with his disobedience and transgression against God Almighty. "Thine heart was lifted up because of thy beauty, thou hast corrupted thy wisdom by reason of thy brightness" (Ez. 28:17^a). God finally has caught up with Lucifer. His lies, his deceit, his corrupt ways, his iniquity, his violence, and his pride, all are now sited before him and brought to judgment. "Lucifer, thou hast been sentenced and condemned to the lake of fire"! The prophecy of Isaiah the prophet is now being fulfilled about him. For we read in the book of Isaiah the following:

Yet, thou shall be brought down to hell [sheol or Hades], to the sides of the pit [abyss] (Is. 14:15).

Hell from beneath is moved for thee to meet thee at thy coming. . . (Is. 14:9^a).

Thy pomp, with the noise of thy viols, is brought down to the grave. . . (Is. 14:11^a).

How art thou fallen from heaven, O Lucifer, son of the morning! (Is. 14:12).

How art thou cut down to the ground, which didst weaken the nations! (Is. 14:12).

[How was thou, Lucifer,] cast into the lake of fire and brimstone. . . (Rev. 20:10^a).

5. Perhaps of the seven mysteries of heaven presented in the Gospel of Matthew, the last mystery is the most directly related to the kingdom of heaven. The Lord tells us that the drag-net was cast into the sea to gather everything. When it was full, the Bible mentions, that it was drawn to the shore and from it men gathered the good into the vessel, but cast the bad away. (Matt. 13:47-48). The Lord Jesus continues His statement as follows:

> *So shall it be at the end of the world: the angels shall come forth, and sever the wicked from among the just, [a]nd shall cast them into the furnace of fire: there shall be wailing and gnashing of teeth (Matt. 13:49-50).*

6. Before the creation of a new heaven and a new earth, namely, a *third world,* for the people of God to live on in bliss and in tranquillity, Jesus Christ will finally submit all things to the Father, seeing that His assignment is now complete. The Lord Jesus has now accomplished everything for which He had come to the earth. According to the promise, the Father has put under the Son's feet all things; having thus received all things under His feet, the Saviour "delivers up the kingdom to God, even the Father" (I Cor. 15:24). For we read in Paul's first epistle to the Corinthians the following:

> *Then cometh the end, when he [Christ] shall have delivered up the kingdom to God, even the Father; when he shall have put down all rule and all authority and power. For he must reign, till he hath put all enemies under his feet. The last enemy that shall be destroyed is death. (I Cor. 15:24-26).*

> *And when all things shall be subdued unto him, then shall the Son also himself be[come] subject unto him that put all things under him, that God may be[come] all in all" (I Cor. 15:28).*

II. A New Heaven and A New Earth

7. It is not easy for our finite mind to fully understand the program that our God Almighty and our Saviour, the Lord Jesus Christ, has for mankind. Man with respect to God appears to be the ultimate in the creation of the Almighty; he is the beginning and the continuous fulfillment of the institutions of God. Despite man's sins, righteousness was made available for him; the believing Christian is the ultimate aspiration of the Father in His Son. Speaking of higher dispensations, two "worlds" have passed away; and, behold, a third "world" is now newly created for the man who is the crowning glory of the Creator. But this man is now free at last; he is free from sin and from iniquity. This man, though earthly, is now sinless and spotless from the quagmire of transgression and bloodthirstiness. This man deserves the best "earth" to live on, and the best "heaven" to live under. God will create for the redeemed ones "a new heaven and a new earth" (Rev. 21:1ª).

8. And so, the Apostle John says, "I saw a new heaven and a new earth: for the first heaven and the first earth were passed away; and there was no more sea" (Rev. 21:1). Out of heaven, I saw, says John, "the holy city, new Jerusalem, coming down from God out of heaven, prepared as a bride adorned for her husband" (Rev. 21:2). The sequel of the new things continues, as John, the beloved disciple, maintains their description.

> *Behold, the tabernacle of God is with men, and he will dwell with them, and they shall be his people, and God himself shall be with them, and be their God. And God shall wipe away all tears from their eyes; and there shall be no more death, neither sorrow, nor crying, neither shall there be any more pain: for the former things are passed away. And he that sat upon the throne said, Behold, I make all things new. And he said unto me, Write: for these words are true and faithful. And he said unto me, It is done. I am Alpha and Omega, the beginning and the end. I will give unto him that is athirst of the fountain of the water of life freely. He that overcometh shall inherit all things; and I will be his God, and he shall be my son (Rev. 21:3-7).*

9. The new city of Jerusalem has no temple in it; "for the glory of God did lighten it, and the Lamb is the light thereof" (Rev. 21:23ᵇ). While the city is occupied by the redeemed ones, "the kings of the earthly dwellers bring their glory and honour into it" (Rev. 21:24^b). The city has twelve gates; each gate is guarded by one angel. Each gate has the name of one tribe of the twelve tribes of Israel written on it. The city appears to be a square on its bottom and an equal square on its side; and on each side of it there are three gates: "On the east three gates; on the north three gates; on the south three gates; and on the west three gates" (Rev. 21:13). The city is cubic where only the saved will dwell; only those who love the Saviour and sing praises to Him will become its citizens.

10. It should be the desire of every believer, this author included, that the Lord Jesus will reign in his life, that the Saviour is coming soon to establish His Kingdom, that the heavenly vision will become a confirmed reality, and that those of us who have believed in Him, who is the source of every blessing, will cause us to reign with Him in the eternal Kingdom. The world is full of sin and iniquity and profits none of those of us who have put our faith on the Crucified One. Together we should shout with joy: "Come quickly, Lord Jesus." Amen.

III. We Should Be Ready for the Kingdom!

11. John opens his book of Revelation with these words: "The Revelation of Jesus Christ, which God gave unto him, to shew unto his servants things which must shortly come to pass. . . . Blessed is he that readeth, and they that hear the words of this prophecy, and keep those things which are written therein: for the time is at hand" (Rev. 1:1 and 3). John was imprisoned in the island of Patmos, "for the word of God, and for the testimony of Jesus Christ" (Rev. 1:9). Here, John was commanded to write to seven Churches about "the things which thou hast seen, and the things which are, and the things which shall be hereafter. John writes the following.

12. And to the angel of the church of Ephesus, John writes:

> *I know thy works, and thy labour, and thy patience, and how thou canst not bear them which are evil: and thou hast tried them which say they are apostles, and are not, and hast*

found them liars: And hast borne, and hast patience, and for my name's sake hast laboured, and hast not fainted. Nevertheless I have somewhat against thee, because thou hast left thy first love. . . . To him that overcometh will I give to eat of the tree of life, which is in the midst of the paradise of God. (Rev. 2:2-3).

13. And to the angel of the church of Smyrna, John writes:

I know thy works, and tribulation, and poverty, (but thou art rich) and I know the blasphemy of them which say they are Jews, and are not, but are the synagogue of Satan. Fear none of those things which thou shall suffer. . . . [B]e thou faithful unto death, and I will give thee a crown of life. . . . He that overcometh shall not be hurt of the second death. (Rev. 2:8-11).

14. And to the angel of the church in Pergamos, John wrtites:

I know thy works, and where thou dwellest, even where Satan's seat is: and thou holdest fast my name, and has not denied my faith, even in those days wherein Antipas was my faithful martyr, who was slain among you, where Satan dwelleth. But I have a few things against thee, because thou hast there them that hold the doctrine of Balaam. . . . Repent; or else I will come unto thee quickly, and will fight against them with the sword of my mouth. . . . To him that overcometh will I give to eat of the hidden manna. . . . (Rev. 2:12-17).

15. And unto the angel of the church of Thyatira, John writes:

I know thy works, and charity, and service, and faith, and thy patience, and thy works; and the last to be more than the first. Notwithstanding I have a few things against thee, because thou suffers that woman Jezebel. . . . But that which ye have already hold fast till I come. And he that overcometh, and keepeth my works unto the end, to him will I give power

over the nations. . . . And I will give him the morning star.
(Rev. 3:18-28).

16. And unto the angel of the church in Sardis, John writes:

*I know thy works, that thou hast a name that thou livest,
and art dead. Be watchful, and strengthen the things which
remain, that are ready to die: for I have not found thy works
to be perfect before God. Remember therefore how thou hast
received and heard, and hold fast, and repent. . . . Thou hast
a few names even in Sardis which have not defiled their garments; and they shall walk with me in white: for they are
worthy. He that overcometh, the same shall be clothed in
white raiment; and I will not blot out his name out of the
book of life, but I will confess his name before my Father, and
before his angels. (Rev. 3:1-5).*

17. And to the angel of the church in Philadelphia, John writes:

*I know thy works: behold, I have set before thee an open
door, and no man can shut it: for thou hast a little strength,
and hast kept my word, and hast not denied my name. Behold, I will make them of the synagogue of Satan, which say
they are Jews, and are not, but do lie; behold, I will make
them to come and worship before thy feet, and to know that I
have loved thee. Because thou hast kept the word of my patience, I also will keep thee from the hour of temptation, which
shall come upon all the world, to try them that dwell upon the
earth. Him that overcometh will I make a pillar in the temple
of my God, and he shall go no more out: and I will write upon
him the name of my God, and the name of the city of my God,
which is new Jerusalem, which cometh down out of heaven
from my God: and I will write upon him my new name. (Rev.
3:8-10, 12).*

18. And unto the angel of the church of the Laodiceans, John
writes:

I know thy works, that thou art neither cold nor hot: I would thou wert cold or hot. So then because thou art luke-warm, and neither cold nor hot, I will spue thee out of my mouth. Because thou sayest, I am rich, and increased with goods, and have need of nothing; and knowest not that thou art wretched, and miserable, and poor, and naked. . . . (Rev. 3:15-16)

I counsel thee to buy of me gold tried in the fire, that thou mayest be rich; and white raiment, that thou mayest be clothed, and the shame of thy nakedness do not appear; and anoint thine eyes with eyesalve, that thou mayest see. As many as I love, I rebuke and chasten: be zealous therefore, and repent. (Rev. 3:18-19).

19. John concludes his message to the seven church of Asia by saying:

Behold, I stand at the door, and knock: if any man hear my voice, and open the door, I will come into him, and will sup with him, and he with me. To him that overcometh will I grant to sit with me in my throne, even as I also overcame, and am set down with my Father in his throne. He that hath an ear, let him hear what the Spirit saith unto the churches. (Rev. 3:20-22).

I Jesus have sent mine angel to testify unto you these things in the churches. I am the root and the offspring of David, and the bright and morning star. And the Spirit and the bride say, Come. And let him that heareth say, Come. . . He which testifieth these things saith, Surely I come quickly. Amen. Even so, come, Lord Jesus (Rev. 22:16-17ᵃ, 20-21).

APPENDIX A

But there is a God in heaven that revealeth secrets, and maketh known to the king Nebuchadnezzar what shall be in the latter days. . . . But as for me, this secret is not revealed to me for any wisdom that I have more than any living, but for their sakes that shall make known the interpretation to the king, and that thou mightest know the thoughts of thy heart" (Dan. 2:28ᵃ, 30).

METHOD OF INTERPRETATION

THE METHOD OF AND CONSISTENCY in the interpretation of prophecy are as important as the content of the prophetic message itself. Cross-referencing of Scriptures, when possible, is the only recommended and sound approach. The principal points of interpretation adhered to in this book are: (1) A sound interpretation must be in harmony with the general content and intent of the entire biblical message. (2) When the Bible provides its own answer on a prophetic passage, or on a parable, no other interpretation is necessary, let alone valid. (3) Opinionated interpretations should be identified through such cliches as: *in my opinion, I believe, it would appear, I am convinced, possibly, apparently,* etc. (4) Procedurally, a sound interpretation of prophecy considers the historical-grammatical aspects of the prophetic passage as well. (5) Any interpretation based upon mythology of any type is a disservice to the Word of God. Interpretation of hidden things belongs to God, points out Daniel: "But there is a God in heaven that revealeth secrets, and maketh [them] known. . . " (Dan. 2:28). Again, "He [God] revealeth the deep [difficult] and secret things. . . " (Dan. 2:22).

APPENDIX B

SYMBOLIC TERMS INTERPRETED

1. THE BOOK OF REVELATION, Chapter 17, Verse 9, presents a challenge to *"the mind that hath wisdom."* The challenge is: "The seven heads are seven mountains, on which the woman sitteth" (Rev. 17:9). This statement provides the key to the interpretation of a number of relevant terms which are symbolically used in prophecy.

a. The first clue

2. The interpretation of the first of these terms is found in the following statement: "The seven heads are seven mountains." The proposition being a *nominal* or *equational sentence*, it implies that a "head" is equal to a "mountain," and vice-versa. Since the term "mountain" is not employed here geographically, it symbolizes a "kingdom" (Dan. 2:35; Isa. 2:2). Hence, the seven heads are seven kingdoms, or seven major powers, or the leaders of the seven major powers, or a combination of them.

b. The second clue

3. The interpretation of the second clue is found in the clause, "on which [i.e., on seven mountains] the woman sitteth." If these seven "mountains" are seven "kingdoms," the woman then sits on them, viz., she welds a great deal of religious influence over the heads of these seven kingdoms. In Revelation, Chapter 17, Verse 3, the woman sitting upon "a scarlet coloured beast. . . having seven heads and ten horns" signifies her initial influence and control over the blood-thirsty Beast and over his supporters which are the seven leaders, or heads, or kings, and the ten horns, or kings (Rev. 17:11). This is a two-tier governmental institution over which the Beast rules.

c. Who is the Beast?

4. Daniel, Chapter 7, Verse 8, mentions that "another little horn" came up and joined the remaining seven heads, or kings, of the original ten horns. John continues, "And the beast. . . is the eighth [king], and is of the seven [kings]" (Rev. 17:11). In Revelation 17, Verse 12, the ten horns, who unanimously give their power to the Beast, are also identified as ten kings. Hence, a horn is a king; the Beast himself is a king, the king number eighth (Rev. 17:11). The Beast is also the "little horn" of Daniel, Chapter 7, Verses 7 and 8. This "little horn" is not one of the ten horns of the revived Roman Empire, as a large number of interpreters of prophesy concludes; he joins the ten horns as an outsider, as king number eleven.

d. What does a horn signify?

5. In Hebrew, the word **qeren** means *horn.* This term is often used also to signify "power," "defense," "refuge," "support," etc. Just as a ram, or a bull, has horns on its head for its defense, so also the Beast appears as having the support of the seven heads and the ten horns. You must have observed how the seven heads overlap with the ten horns to represent basically the same states in a two-tier government.

e. Who is the woman?

6. The three women mentioned in Revelation, Chapter 17: (1) the "woman" sitting upon "a scarlet coloured beast" (Rev. 17:3); (2) the "woman" sitting upon the "seven mountains" (Rev. 17:9); and (3) the great whore [or harlot] that sitteth upon many waters [gentiles]" (Rev. 17:1 and 15) — are all one and the same woman which represents the end-time Apostate Church. John is also told to write: "And the woman which thou sawest is that great city [Rome], which reigneth over the kings of the earth" (Rev. 17:18).

f. Which city is referred to here?

7. Undoubtedly, the city spoken of here is the city of Rome. This city, however, is *not* described as the one sitting upon the seven mountains, but as one "which reigneth over the kings of the earth" (Rev. 17:18^b). Until its destruction, as described in Rev. 17:16, the city of Rome will indeed serve as the headquarters for the end-time church and its leader, which will be the leader of this One-World Apostate Christendom.

8. Immediately after the desolation of the Apostate Christendom, a one-world secular, possibly humanistic religion, will be instituted with the Beast as its leader and its object of worship. In addition to the adherents of the Apostate Christendom, this new system of worship will also incorporate the Apostate Judaism and many other cults and faiths.

g. What does the term "waters" signify?

9. The term "**waters**" given in Revelation 17, Verse 15, symbolizes "peoples, and multitudes, and nations, and tongues" (Rev. 17:16), over which Rome, before its destruction (Rev. 17:16), will exercise religious influence and consequently over the Beast and his Empire. Moreover, since the word "sea," or "seas," generally symbolizes the Gentile peoples and nations, the Beast rising out of the sea then will most likely be a Gentile. On the other hand, since the Hebrew word **ha-Arets** means *earth*, or *land*, or simply *Israel*, the Second Beast will most likely be a Jew. (Rev. 13:11).

10. That the Beast has, "seven heads" and "ten horns" simultaneously, indicates that his support is composed of an overlapping, two-tier representation, namely, two Parliaments: a Higher and a Lower Houses. This two-tier government would be composed of a local European Council, with a parliament representing the ten-nation coalition (of the ten horns of Dan. 7:8) of the European Union (EU), which would deal with the internal matters of the Revived Roman Empire. The Upper House, the Presidium, on the other hand, would be composed of the above mentioned European Council, along with a Supreme Council. The Supreme Council would be composed of the seven heads (Rev. 13:1) chosen from among the original ten-nation kings, the coalition of the European Union . It appears that, at least initially, the Presidium, like the European Council, would be governed by a rotating, or by a "one hour" presidency, — a presidency where each ruler presides over the coalition for a specific moment (Rev. 17:10, 12). This two-tier government would most likely operate ultimately under the chairmanship of the Beast, who becomes king number eight.

h. What do the "two horns" mean?

11. The **"two horns like a lamb"** of the Second Beast (Rev. 13:11), symbolize the religious support this False Prophet will receive from the two Unorthodox Religious Systems of the end-times: Apostate Christendom and Apostate Judaism. Christendom and Judaism — which were the only two religious institutions directly instituted by God and which subsequently went astray — could only figure in the prophetic message of the Bible, and only they could become apostate. The other religions do not count at all in the prophetic plan of God Almighty; they are man-made and are not instituted by God. The meaning of the term "lamb," here indicates that the second beast is a Jew having no power of his own; he receives his power from the Dragon, just as the first Beast did. In this, the

Second Beast imitates the Holy Spirit who likewise receives His power and authority from God the Father.

i. What does "plucked by the roots," mean?

12. What does the **three plucked up by the roots** (Dan. 7:8), or **he shall subdue three kings** (Dan. 7:24) mean? Since all ten horns of Daniel, Chapter 7, Verses 7 and 8, were still mentioned in Rev. 13:1 and Rev. 17:12 and 16, more than two millennia later, it means that none of the ten horns was either "subdued," "plucked up by the roots," or destroyed," as some have suggested. They were only excluded from membership in the Supreme Council, the Presidium of the end time. In order to compose a two-tier ruling body, the Presidium will have only seven heads, or kings, drawn out from seven major states of the ten-nation coalition. Accordingly, three of the ten kings have to be left out. The three, however, will still keep their representative position in the ten-nation European Council, or the Lower Parliament.

j. What does "five are fallen," "one is," and "the other one is not yet come" mean? (Rev. 17:10)?

13. As used in Revelation, Chapter 17, Verse 10, the statement signifies: (1) that **five** of the seven kings have already served their (one-hour) term of presidency each and are now out; (2) that, **one**, the sixth king, *is* now serving his (one-hour) term of presidency; and (3) that **the other**, the seventh king, has as yet to assume his (one-hour) term of presidency. No sooner does he become president, however, he expeditiously surrenders his governing power to the Beast, who is the eighth king of Revelation, Chapter 17, Verse 11, possibly under unusual political and military upheavals.

14. Now, that the Bible itself has provided the interpretation of the several symbolic terms which it uses — "woman," "head," "mountain," "horn," "king," "waters," etc. — we should no longer worry about where the "seven hills," are located, or whether Rome is situated upon seven hills or seventy hills, where it is more than seven; or how a "multi-headed, multi-horned" monster would supposedly represent the Beast. The Beast himself is a highly polished, highly educated, very eloquent individual; there is none like him among the children of men.

15. Daniel's prophecy covers the events that began in his days and will last through the Tribulation Period. John's prophecy deals with "the things which shall be hereafter" (Rev. 1:19). Since the Beast of the end-time appears to the world during the events of the Tribulation Period (Rev. 13:1-5), no justification exists to associate the "three of the first [ten] horns plucked up by the roots," or "he shall subdue three kings" (Dan. 7:8, 24), or the "five [kings] are fallen" (Rev. 17:10), with the fate of any former rulers of the Grecian or the Roman Empires, as most interpreters of the Bible prophecy have erroneously proposed.

APPENDIX C

NEW INTERPRETATIONS

The uniqueness of this book is in its attempt to present the Beast and the end-time events with new meanings and new interpretations in view. Some of these interpretations are provided here, in this Appendix, for the benefit of the reader.

1. Nimrod was a mighty hunter *before* the Lord and not *against* the Lord. There is absolutely no mention in the entire Bible that Nimrod was an evil man.

2. The Gentile World Power started with the Late Babylonian Empire which superseded the Assyrian Empire.

3. In the plan of God, Assyria has yet a spiritual role to play at the end time (Isa. 11:16; 19:23-25). As wicked and evil as this Assyrian Empire was, God will forgive and gather her (Is.11:16) as He has forgiven Israel and forgiven Egypt. A blessed future triumvirate awaits that nation with Egypt and Israel.

4. This author believes that America figures strongly in the end-time prophecy. It will provide to the ten-nation coalition the Beast as a Superman for the end-time events.

5. Those Jews who were exiled to Assyria and later to Babylon were free to do anything they wanted once there. They were not slaves to anyone.

6. Historically, Syria has no enmity with the Jews. In the ancient past, the Greek who ruled over Syria were anti-Israel; as a colony under the Greek rule, the native Syrians, like the Jews, fought the Saleucid Empire. Syria's animosity towards Israel today — right or wrong — is over Arab territory held by the Israelis.

7. The interpretation of "the ten kings," the seven kings," "the eight kings" "five are fallen," etc., etc. (Rev. 17:10-12), belong to the future, to the end-time events. See the Appendix B for their interpretation.

8. Extreme exaggeration exists with respect to the KJV translation of the three kings/horns "plucked up by the roots" of Daniel. They were only removed from the higher governing body, the Presidium.

9. It is exciting to find out that God's throne, at the end time, will be transferred from upper heaven to the lower heaven, to the heavenly places. God wants to be located close to His people. In this work, a whole chapter is dedicated to this topic.

10. As a nation, Israel, during the Millennial Kingdom, will be directly ruled by King David who will be resurrected for the purpose. Jesus, who is the King of kings and the Lord of lords, will rule the whole world.

11. Lucifer, Satan, was the first and the highest archangel God had ever created. It appears that his future mission would have been to take care of or to cover the affairs of man whom God was about to create.

12. The resurrection of Israel (the Jewish nation) will take place at the rapture, along with the Church, and not separately, after Jesus arrives on the earth, as some interpreters of the Bible prophecy have advocated.

13. At the Marriage Supper of the Lord, Israel will have no special place of honor. The martyrs of the Tribulation Period, who presently are about the throne of God, could be the guests of honor. Like all the believers of all the dispensations, the believing Jews of both Testaments will be included in the wedding, but not as special guests.

14. According to Paul, the Church of Jesus Christ incorporates the saints of both Testaments, the Old and the New. This includes the Old Testament Jews.

15. If the presence of the friends of the Bridegroom is essential at the Marriage of the Lamb and at the Marriage Supper of the Lamb, the martyrs of the Tribulation Period would be entitled to fill up that slot.

16. The Russian invasion of Israel will take place either immediately after or concurrently with the rapture of the Church. Any other time, during the Tribulation Period, would clash with and contradict the Scriptures.

17. The False Prophet, the second beast (Rev. 13:11), who "had two horns like a lamb," implies that he has tentatively the support of the two end-time apostate systems of religion: the Apostate Christendom and the Apostate Judaism.

18. The Hebrew term **rosh**, means "head, leader." It cannot be translated as "Russia"; because it contains *Alep* for its middle radical. Grammatically, the word is not followed by the conjunction *Waw*, "and," to properly connect it with the following word.

19. **Gog** is possibly related to the inactive Aramaic word **gug**, and its active colloquial root **juj**, both meaning *to move, to go around*, etc. The derivative, **majwij** (originally **magwig**), means *to shake, to agitate*. **Gog** and **Magog** would imply, the **agitator** and the place where he **agitates**.

20. During the Judgment of Nations (Matt. 25:40, 45), the Lord used the phrase, "these my brethren," to refer not to the Jews of Tribulation Period in general, as Scofield notes indicate, but to the 144,000 sealed young Jews who preached the Gospel under harsh circumstances during the same period. It was these sealed young Jews who needed to be taken care of during this time of persecution; it was these 144,000 Jews whom the Lord calls "my brethren."

APPENDIX D

(The following took place as this book
was readied for printing.)

TERRORISM STRIKES AMERICA

1. America will never forget what happened on September 11, 2001. Shortly before nine o'clock in the morning, an American passenger jet plane was highjacked, and with its passengers was rammed into one of the two World Trade Center Towers. Moments later, as the reporter and the monitor of the TV News Program were guessing whether the act was an accedent or a sabotage, another American passenger jet plane slammed into the second of the twin highrise buildings. This happened while we were watching with horror and tears over such calamity.

2. Within another two hours, the two highrise buildings collapsed taking with them thousands of lives of all nationalities. Moments later, another such plane hit the Pantagon, resulting in several hundred persons killed and a great damage. A few moments later, yet another passenger jet plane, with its passengers, fell into their detriment in a field south of Pittisburgh, Pennsylvannia. Fortunately, with respect to this last passenger jet plane, a man had just contacted his wife who had told him what was happening, he told her that he and a few other men were determined to hassle with the highjackers.

3. Today, they are stil digging the debris and trying to find clues of the burned and disintegrated bodies of the dead. More than five thousand persons perished in these four attacks. This tragedy has made the december 7, 1940, Japanese military kamikaze attack over Pearl Harbor, which had killed more than 2,000 soldiers and civilians, pale in comparison. As a result, today this country has come out of this tragedy far more united, the two parties much more committed to bipartisanship, and politically more determined to strike back at this terrorist evil until finish. President George W. Bush has acted courageously. He has amassed together a coalition of almost the entire world.

4. After two weeks of uninterrupted air strikes on Afghani territory, our Special Forces are now fighting on the soil of that country. While the war may drag; the local government will, of necessity, collapse, and another friendly coalition government will take over. Sooner or later, Osama Bin Laden will either be killed, handed over to the American authorities, or will be captured by American and British forces. In its history, the American people have suffered greatly from this most devastating strike on its own territory than any other calamity.

5. It is believed that the perpetrators of these heneous crimes are related to Osama Bin Laden, a Saudi wealthy man, believed to be in exile in Afghanistan. From that country, Ben Ladin leads his al-Qaeda terrorist organization, which is scattered all over the world, and is supported by the Taliban rulers of Afghanistan. Today, there is one billion dollar placed on his head for his capture -- dead or alive. Countries who are deemed suspicious of supporting such acts will, in their turn,face the same consequences. The United States of America, supported by its alies, will not stop its war against terrorism until that whole ugly system of terror comes to an end, as they had done to piracy of the past century.

ENDNOTES

INTRODUCTION

[1] On China and India, see the following two books. *The Lost Churches of China*. Leonard M. Outerbridge. Philadelphia, The Westminister Press. 1952. And *Eastern Christianity in India*. Cardinal Eugene Tisserant. Orient Longmans. Bombay, 1957.
[2] Wilkinson, *Nineveh*. 4th Quarter. Vol. 21, No. 4, Berkeley, California 94702, USA.
[3] Wilkinson, *Nineveh*. 4th Quarter. Vol. 21, No. 4, p. 12, Berkeley, California 94702, USA.
[4] Gromacki, *Are These the Last Days?* p. 82, 1970.
[5] Kautzsch, *Gesenius' Hebrew Grammar*, p. 24, 1956.

CHAPTER 1: The Beast's Beginnings

[1] Larkin, *The Book of Revelation*. p. 104, 1919.
[2] Greece was divided into four parts: Greece and Macedonia, Asia Minor, Syria, which was ruled by Seleucus Nicator, and Egypt, which was ruled by Ptolemy I.

CHAPTER 2: Daniel's "Little Horn"

[1] See Scofield, Note 1, on Daniel, Chapter 8, Verse 9.
[2] The Aramaic word, **qárna**, or its Hebrew counterpart, **qéren**, means primarily, *horn*. The word has many connotative meanings, such as, *beam, ray; strength, power, glory; fund, reserve, stock*, etc.
[3] The Aramaic compound verb, **mistakkal hweyt**, provides a tense having a continuous-durational action that should be translated as, *while I was considering* the horns.
[4] While both Old Testaments: The Urmia, Persia, Peshitta Version of 1852, and Biblia Sacra Peshitta version of Mosul, Iraq, 1950, say, *And a small horn went up from among them.* The Hebrew Bible, Biblia Hebraica, Kittel, Stuttgart, 1954, says: Another horn went up among them.
[5] *Matthew Henry's Commentary*; p. 1446, 1992.

6 Walvoord, *Daniel*, p. 162, 1971.

7 Feinberg, *Revelation: A Grand Finale.* p. 124; classical writers spoke of "the city of seven hills."

8 Feinberg, *Revelation: A Grand Finale.* p. 124; quoting, cf. R. H. Charles, op. cit., II, p. 69; Barclay, op. cit., p. 181 *et al.*

9 The complexity of the original verse led the author to provide a spontaneous translation based upon both the *Peshitta* version of Syriac Aramaic and the Babylonian Aramaic employed by Daniel.

CHAPTER 3: Present Developments

1 Catholic Girl's Manual and Sunday Missal. Edited by Rev. William A. Carroll. Catholic Book Publishing Co. New York. August 15, 1952.

2 Quoted from the book entitled, *Their Blood Cries Out*, which in turn it was quoted from "Vietnam: *Free Market, Captive Conscience*, pp. 40f."

CHAPTER 4: The Transfer of God's Throne

1 The word "heavens" usually implies "the heavenly places," or "the air" region which is closer to the earth, to mankind. In general, "heaven" means the upper reaches of the universe; in a less general way, "heaven" usually signifies the uppermost parts of the universe, the seventh heaven.

2 Newell, *Revelation: Chapter-by-Chapter.* p. 91, 1994.

3 Contrary to Scofield's footnote explanation, regeneration here, almost as in Tit. 3:5, implies, with respect to the disciples, the time of their glorification when the real regeneration becomes truly complete. Salvation without resurrection and glorification remains partial.

CHAPTER 5: The Lord's Returning

1 Lockyer. *All the Messianic Prophecies of the Bible.* 1973.

2 Permission has been granted to the author by Dr. Joseph Brown, Pastor of the Manna Bible Baptist Church, Baltimore, Maryland, to quote him on this "verbal" statement he had made on radio.

3 Consult Scofield's introductory remarks about II Thessalonians, under
   Theme.
4 The following references are just a very few such cases where a cloud,
   or clouds, are used by God to fulfill his will: Gen. 9:13-16; Ex. 13:21,
   19:9; Lev. 16:2; Num. 9:15; I Kin. 8:10; Job. 37:15; Luke 9:34, 35; Ps.
   36:5; 104:3; 108:4; etc.
5 The hymn, "Jesus Is Coming Again" was authored by Mabel Johnston
   Camp. 1871-1937 and was copyrighted 1913.

CHAPTER 6: Satan: The Beginning and the End

1 The term, *time, occasion,* in Greek, *kairón*; in Hebrew, *mo'éd,* or
   pà'am, used as a prophetic word, signifies, a year; hence, a time, (two)
   times, and half a time, equals a year, (two) years, and half a year.

CHAPTER 7: The Rapture of the Church

1 Pentecost, *Things to Come.* p. 214.
2 Jones, Sr., Dr. Bob. *Three Sermons*: "The Second Coming of Christ,"
   pp. 45, cleveland, Tennessee, 1934 [?].
3 The hymn, "To Meet the Lord in the Air," was written by the author of
   this book in 1997.

CHAPTER 8: The Indivisible Church

1 "[T]hou art Peter [petros — literally, 'a little rock']; upon this rock
   [Petra — the generic word for stone] I will build my Church" (See
   Scofield, Note 1, on Matthew, Chapter 16, Verse 18). In Aramaic
   (Syriac) *Peshitta* Bible, distinction is maintained through the gender of
   the demonstrative adjective qualifying the word "petros."
2 Newell, *Revelation: Chapter-by-Chapter.* p. 323, 1994.
3 The late Dr. Bob Jones Jr., the former President of Bob Jones University (1911-1997), authored this deeply moving hymn, "The shame He
   suffered left its brand."
4 Ryrie, *Are These the Last Days?* p. 44, 1996. He declares that Israel's
   resurrection will take place on the earth seven years after the rapture of
   the Church.

[5] Mabel Johnston Camp, who lived 1871-1937, authored the hymn: "He Is Coming Again."

CHAPTER 9: Glorious Events in Heaven

[1] The Greek word, *bema*, used in the New Testament, means the "judgment seat of Christ."
[2] Pinch, pp. 19-20, 1948.
[3] Only this group of believing martyrs has as yet not been resurrected. These are those, who prior to their resurrection, sat at the Supper of the Lamb, most likely, as the friends of the Bridegroom.

CHAPTER 10: The Rise of the Beast

[1] Reader's Digest, pp. 61-62, January 1996.
[2] January 5, 1996, reported in *The Washington Times*.

CHAPTER 11: The Northern Invasion

[1] Hindson, Final Signs: Amazing Prophecies of the End Times. p. 132, 1996.

CHAPTER 13: The Great Tribulation Period

[1] Pentecost, *Things to Come.* p. 364, 1958.
[2] The word **medina** "city" in some Semitic languages is often translated as "country." In the construct state of Hebrew grammar, the word is translated, especially in Israeli Hebrew, as "a state."
[3] Pentecost, *Things to Come.* pp. 317-318., 1958.
[4] In the Persian Verse Account, as quoted from *The New Unger's Bible Handbook*, it states that in his third year Nabonidus, son of King Nebuchadnezzar, entrusted the kingdom to his son, Belshazzar, and he himself took up residence at Tima (in Arabia).

CHAPTER 14: God's Final Summons

[1] See Scofield note 1, Revelation, Chapter 14, Verse 6.

CHAPTER 15: The Dreadful Events

[1] It should be understood that when God deals with a nation in prophecy, particularly the nation of Israel, He primarily means the people that are living in their internationally recognized land by the countries of the world.

[2] See "Michael's Victory," in Chapter 6.

CHAPTER 16: Who Is the Beast?

[1] Ryrie, pp. 95, 1996.

[2] Gromacki, pp. 82-83, 1993.

[3] Shelton, pp. 36-37, 1995.

[4] Lugt, pp. 24-26, 1983.

[5] Anderson, pp. 190, 215-216, 1954.

[6] Pentecost, pp. 80-86, 1961.

[7] Hagee, pp. 117-118, 1984.

[8] Newell, pp. 184-186, 1994.

[9] Pember, p. 33, 1988.

[10] Pember, pp. 42-43, 1988.

CHAPTER 17: The Millennium Kingdom

[1] Even as we are writing about this subject of dividing the land, the American President is pressuring the Israeli Prime Minister, Benjamin Netanyahu, to accept the final plan for the delivery of an additional 13% of the West Bank territory to Yasser Arafat, the Palestinian President.

[2] See Matthew, Chapter 25, Verse 32, Scofield Note 1.

[3] The expression in the original, **ve-'avdu Mis'rayim et-Ashshur**, has also the significance of *The Egyptians served the Assyrians*. Although, the objective particle **et** may also have the meaning of *with*.

[4] Pentecost. *Things to Come.* p. 524, 1958.

BIBLIOGRAPHY

Anderson, Sir Robert. *The Coming Prince*. (The Marvelous Prophecy Of Daniel's Seventy Weeks Concerning The Antichrist). Kregel Publications. Grand Rapids, Michigan, 1954.

Andrews, Samuel J. *Christianity and Anti-Christianity*: In their Final Conflict. Copyright, 1898, (Unusual Reprints) Bob Jones University Press. Green vile, S. C., year (?).

Brooke, Tal. *When the World Will Be as One*: The Coming New World Order. Harvest House Publishers, Inc. Oregon, 1989.

Chafer, Lewis Sperry. *The Kingdom in History and Prophecy.* 2nd. printing. Dunham Publishing Company. Grand Rapids, Michigan, 1967.

Davies, J. M. *Israel in Prophecy.* Good News Publishers. Westchester, Illinois, 1967.

Feinberg, Charles Lee. *A Commentary on Revelation: The Grand Finale.* BMH Books. Winona Lake, Indiana, 1985.

Gaebelein, Arno Clemens, DD.. *The Conflict of the Ages* (The Mystery of Lawlessness: Its Origin, Historic Development and Coming Defeat). Unknown Press. 1968.

Goetz, William R. *Apocalypse Next* (and the New World Order). Horizon House Publishers. Camp Hill, Pennsylvania, 1991.

Greene, Oliver B. *Russia, Israel and the End.* The Gospel Hour, Inc. Greenville, S. C.

Greene, Oliver B. *The Last World Ruler.* The Gospel Hour, Inc. Greenville, S. C., 1963.

Gromacki, Robert Glenn. *Are These the Last Days?* 4th printing. Regular Baptist Press. Schaumburg, Illinois, 1993.

Hagee, John. *Beginning of the End.* (The Assassination of Yitzhak Rabin and the Coming Antichrist). Thomas Nelson Publishers. Nashville, 1996.

Hartman, Fred H. Zechariah: *Israel's Messenger of the Messiah's Triumph.* The Friends of Israel Gospel Ministry, Inc. Bellmawr, NJ 1994.

Hawkins, O. S. *Jonah* (Meeting the God of the Second Chance). Loixeaux Brothers. NJ, 1990.

Hindson, Ed. *Final Signs.* (Amazing Prophecies of the End Times). Harvest House Publishers. Oregon, 1996.

Ice, Thomas & Timothy Demy. *The Truth About The Rapture.* Copyright 1996. (Pocket Prophecy Series) Harvest House Publishers. Eugene, Oregon, 1996.

Ice, Thomas & Timothy Demy. *The Truth About The Tribulation.* Copyright 1996. (Pocket Prophecy Series) Harvest House Publishers. Eugene, Oregon, 1996.

Larkin, Rev. Clarence. *The Book of Daniel.* Published by: Rev. Clarence Larkin Estate. Philadelphia, 1929.

Larkin, Rev. Clarence. *The Book of Revelation: Illustrated.* Published by: Rev. Clarence Larkin Estate. Philadelphia, 1919.

Levy, David M. *Joel: The Day of the Lord.* 4th printing. The Friends of Israel Gospel Ministry, Inc. Bellmawr, NJ, 1993.

Lindberg, Milton B. *Gog and Magog.* Chicago Hebrew Mission. 9th Edition. Chicago, Illinois, 1953.

Lindberg, Milton B. *Is Ours The Closing Generation of the Ages?* 7th Edition. Chicago Hebrew Mission. Chicago, Illinois, 1953.

Lindberg, Milton B. *The Jews and Armageddon.* 7th Edition. Faithful Word Publishing Company. St. Louis, 1940.

Lindsey, Hal. *Satan Is Alive And Well On Planet Earth.* 5th Printing. Zondervan Publishing House. Grand Rapids, Michigan, 1972.

Lockyer, Herbert. *All the Messiaic Prophecies of the Bible.* Zondervan Publishing House. Grand Rapids, Michigan, 1973.

Logsdon, S. Franklin. *Is the U. S. A. in Prophecy?* Zondervan Publishing House. Grand Rapids, Michigan, 1968.

Marshall, Paul with Lela Gilbert. *Their Blood Cries Out.* Word Publishing. Dallas, Texas. 1997.

McGee, J. Vernon. *Daniel.* Thomas Nelson Publishers. Nashville, 1991.

McGee, J. Vernon. *Revelation.* Chapters 6-13. Thomas Nelson Publishers. Nashville, 1991.

McGee, J. Vernon. *Revelation.* Chapters 14-22. Thomas Nelson Publishers. Nashville, 1991.

Newell, William R. *Revelation: Chapter by Chapter.* Kregel Classics. Grand Rapids, Michigan, 1994.

Nineveh, Assyrian Foundation of America. Vol. 21, No. 4. P. O. Box 2620. Berkeley, CA 94702.

Orr, William W. *The 1000 Year Reign of Jesus Christ!* (The Story of the Millennium). Golden Belt Printing, Inc. Great Bend, Kansas, 1989.

Pinch, E. Buckhurst. *The Return of the Lord Jesus Christ.* (a concise scriptural survey). The Marshal Press Limited. London, 1948.

Prince, Drake. *Prophetic Destinies:* Who is Israel? Who is the Church? Creation House. Lake Mary, Florida. Copyrighted 1992.

Rice, John R. *The Coming Kingdom of Christ.* Sword of the Lord Publishers. Wheaton, Illinois, 1948.

Rost, Leonhard. *Judaism Outside the Hebrew Canon.* (An Introduction to the Documents). Abingdon, Nashville, 1971.

Ryrie, Charles C. *Revelation: Everyman's Bible Commentary.* (New Edition). The Lockman Foundation. La Habra, California, 1977.

Shelton, Dr. Bob. *God's Prophetic Blueprint..* (Dr. Bob Shelton, P. O. Box 4499), Greenville, SC 29608. 1985.

Spurgeon, Charles H. *Satan: A Defeated Foe?* Whitaker House. Springdale, Pennsylvania, 1993.

Unger, Merrill F. *The New Unger's Bible Handbook.* Revised by Gary N. Larson. Moody Press. Chicago, Illinois, 1984.

Vander Lught, Herbert. *There's A New Day Coming!* (A Survey of endtime events). By Permission of Zondervan Bible Publishers. Copyrighted 1983.

Walvoord, John F. *Daniel: The Key to Prophetic Revelation.* 12th Printing. Moody Press. Chicago, 1981.

Walvoord, John F. *Revelation* — Chapters 6-13. Thomas Nelson Publishers. Nashville, 1991.

Walvoord, John F. *Revelation* — Chapters 14-22. Thomas Nelson Publishers. Nashville, 1991.

Walvoord, John F. *The Rapture Question.* (A Comprehensive Biblical Study of the Translation of the Church). 3rd printing. Dunham Publishing Company. Grand Rapids, Michigan, 1968.

Webber, David. *The Image of the Ages*: Bible Prophecy, Iraq/Babylon . . . Armageddon. Huntington House Publishers. P. O. Box 53788, Lafayette, LA 70505. USA. 1991.

Whitcomb, John C. *Daniel: Everyman's Bible Commentary.* Moody Press. Chicago, Illinois, 1985.

Wilson, Don. *Eschatologically Speaking.* Bible Truth Revivals, Inc. Greer, SC., 1996.

AUTOBIOGRAPHY

Dr. Zomaya S. Solomon was born of Assyrian parents and reared in the Middle East. In 1953, he arrived in the United States of America in pursuit of his advanced studies. He received BA and MA in the School of Religion from Bob Jones University, Greenville, SC.

At the Johns Hopkins University, Baltimore, MD., he completed credit work for Ph.D. in the interdepartmental fields of Semitic Languages, Ancient History and Archeology of the Near East. From the same University, later on, Dr. Solomon also received, another MA in Arabic and Islamic Studies. On May 3, 1997, Bob Jones University conferred on him the honorary degree of Doctor of Letters, making him the first Assyrian to ever receive such an honorary degree.

At the invitation of the late Rev. Peter Bisset, the Pastor of the Arlington Baptist Church, Baltimore, Maryland, Dr. Solomon founded in 1969 the Arlington Bible Institute. He founded the Arlington Bible College in 1972; in 1984, he began the Arlington Bible Seminary and was their president for twenty years. The Institute and the College are still continuing.

In 1983 and in 1994, Dr. Solomon was twice invited to Israel by the World Congress of Jewish Studies to deliver lectures on Assyrian Aramaic the proceedings of which were published in that Organization's proceedings.

From 1958 through 1992, Dr. Solomon worked for the US Department of Defense, as a senior linguist, researcher, and publisher. He has developed and published more than two dozen textbooks and dictionaries on all levels and in different languages. In recognition of his work, he has received many awards and commendations from civilian leadership and high-ranking generals, including the Linguist of the Year and the highly prized Meritorious Civilian Service Award.

Dr. Solomon and his wife, Nancy Jane, have two sons: Nathan Zomaya and Thomas Wayne. The two young men are married; the older has two children, the younger has one.

Zomaya S. Solomon

258